The YIN and YANG of Short Film Storytelling

The YIN and YANG of Short Film Storytelling

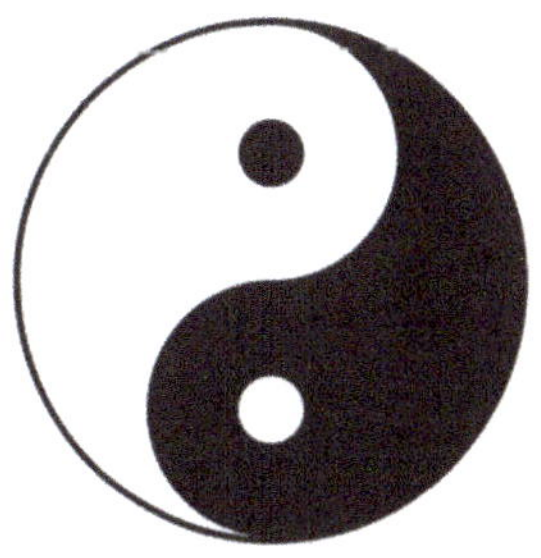

with focused studies and shot-by-shot breakdowns of ten modern classics

Richard Raskin

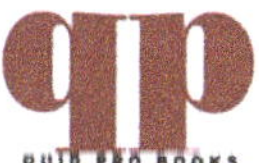

QUID PRO BOOKS
New Orleans, Louisiana

Published in 2022 by Quid Pro Books.

ISBN 978-1-61027-461-6 (trade paperback)
ISBN 978-1-61027-459-3 (ePUB)
ISBN 978-1-61027-460-9 (mass market pbk.)

QUID PRO BOOKS
5860 Citrus Blvd., Suite D
New Orleans, Louisiana, USA 70123
www.quidprobooks.com

On the front cover: colour-enhanced excerpt of Emperor Huizon's "Finches and Bamboo." Early 12th century China. Handscroll. Ink and colour on silk. Metropolitan Museum of Art. Public domain with the museum's permission.

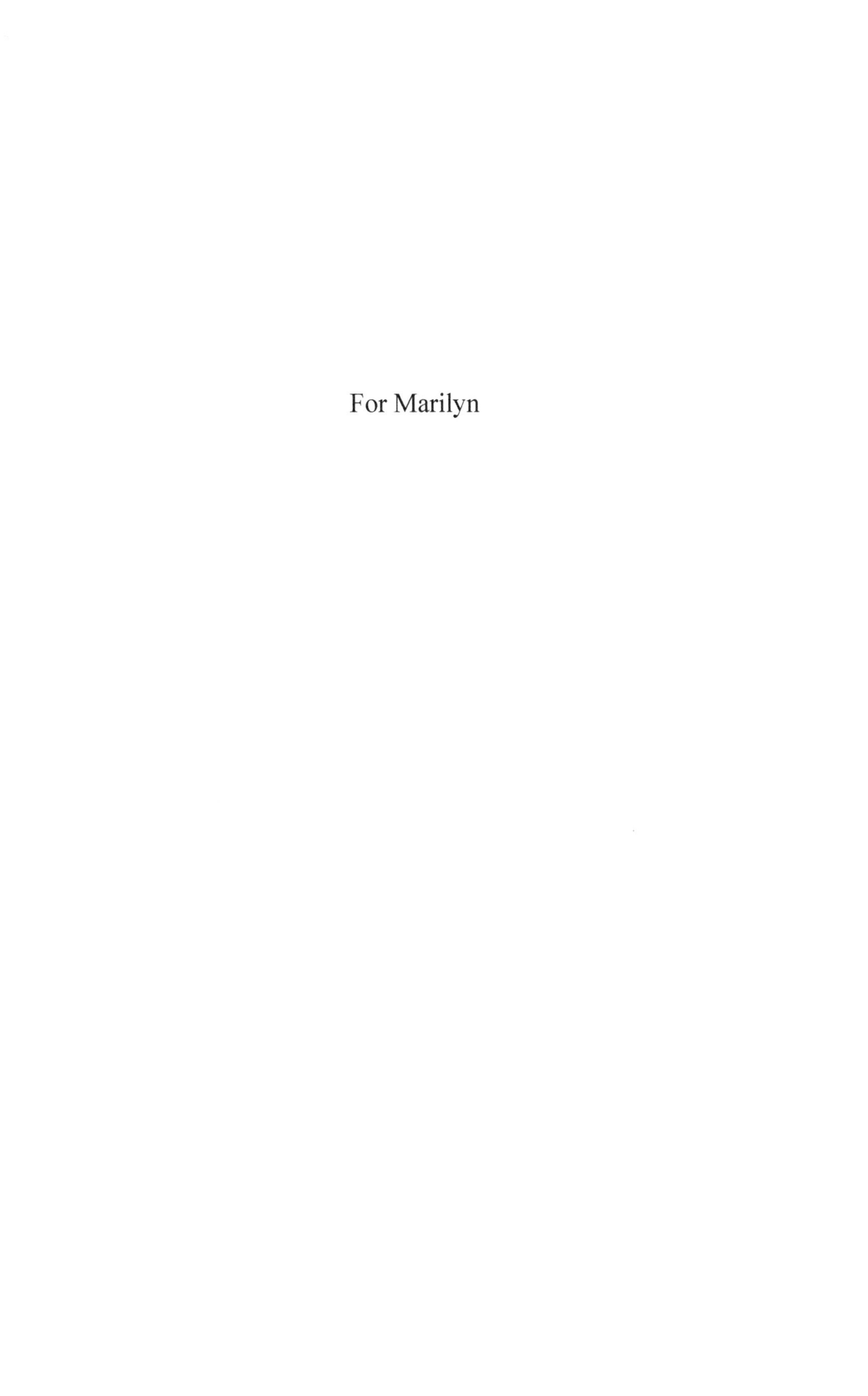

For Marilyn

Table of Contents

Preface

My overriding concern is with shining a light on aspects of the short film that have until now remained in the shadows. If any storytelling properties that might otherwise have gone unnoticed become visible in the perspective proposed here, then this book will have served its purpose.

I hope to be forgiven for liberties taken in adapting the concepts of *yin* and *yang* to short film production. Although every effort was made to keep a new paradigm in sync with Daoist principles – except for matters of gender which I perceive as biased – I gave priority to two goals: 1) enabling filmmakers to tell better stories; and 2) enabling students to understand more fully the subtleties of short film storytelling.

Whatever expertise I bring to this project is in the area of the short film. With respect to Daoism, I am merely an enamored novice doing my best on the basis of extensive readings and five years of untutored reflection.

Readers interested in learning more about the short film may find what they are looking for in this book, while readers wishing to know more about *yin* and *yang* would do well to look to Robin R. Wang's *Yinyang: The Way of Heaven and Earth in Chinese Thought and Culture* (2012), by far the most seriously researched book on the subject, or to Antony Cummins' *The Ultimate Guide to Yin Yang* (2021).

As the reader will soon see, every trace of an offensive sexist bias has been eliminated systematically from the *yin yang* complementarity as defined, ungendered, in this study.

Of the two systems of romanization of the Chinese, I am using the newer and more phonetically correct Pinyin system, rather than the older, more familiar Wade-Giles. I refer therefore to Daoism and the *Daodejing*, rather than to Taoism and the *Tao Te Ching*. And I understand that *yang,* if pronounced correctly, should rhyme with bong rather than with sang.

RICHARD RASKIN

The YIN and YANG of Short Film Storytelling

Introduction

Twenty years ago, I proposed a conceptual model for short film storytelling which is widely used in the teaching of film production and film analysis in Denmark today (Raskin 2001). Unlike sequential models, which focus on a series of steps a story is presumed to pass through as it unfolds, with a mounting level of conflict that is eventually resolved, my approach was based on the view that short film storytelling can best be described in terms of divergent properties that balance and complete one another in a dynamic interplay. Here is a brief outline of that 'parametric' model, with the seven forms of interplay couched here as guidelines for the filmmaker.

1. character-focus ⇄ character-interaction

Character-focus means clarity as to whose story is being told. The sooner viewers know whose story it is, the sooner they have a home base within the fiction. Make it clear whose story you are telling but keep that character interacting with others; it's interaction between characters that gives a short film the vitality needed to capture and hold the viewer's interest.

2. causality ⇄ choice

Have causality flow from the main character's choices; characters who make things happen are more interesting than characters things happen to. A common beginner mistake is to have too little causality at the heart of the film, in which case there are merely temporal and not causal relations between the beats of the story.

3. consistency ⇄ surprise

Characters in short films remain consistent with their initial definitions and do not change. There is no character arc. Instead there are character moments, moments when characters make choices that change their situation. Though characters remain consistent, their behavior should never be predictable, should constantly take the viewer by surprise.

4. image ⇄ sound

Make the action as interesting to the ear as to the eye. Devise situations in which characters produce sounds and react to sounds. Let sounds trigger events or in themselves be the events. Sound should be part of the action, not just an auditory backdrop for the action. Beginners often discover too late that the sound track for their film is uninteresting.

5. character ⇄ object and décor

Bring the viewer into the character's thoughts and feelings by connecting the inner with the outer. Let characters touch meaningful objects or their physical setting. Let them touch each other. Avoid theatricality. Have your actors underplay with relatively neutral expressions on their faces. Let the viewer work out how the characters must be experiencing these moments.

6. simplicity ⇄ depth

Keep the story simple. That can enable the viewer to enter and inhabit the film's inner space, to explore the story from within and construct meanings. Only a simple story will be experienced by the viewer as being deep. Clever twists are likely to keep the story superficial and hold the viewer at a distance.

7. economy ⇄ wholeness

Cut to the bone, kill all darlings and practice less-is-more. But also place a meaningful symbolic event just before your film ends. This will give viewers something to interpret and to replay in their minds as the credits roll. This will help leave the viewer feeling that the film is whole and rich, even if you have ruthlessly cut to the bone.

This model treats the short film as an art form in its own right, with its own storytelling properties which differ radically from those of longer narratives, including the 20–40 min. productions made as graduation films at film schools and which are really miniature feature films, often mislabeled as short films. I have argued (Raskin 2014 and 2016a) that short films

- run typically under ten minutes, max. 15;
- are not necessarily conflict-driven;
- have no character arc but rather character moments, moments when characters make choices that change their situations;
- and have wordless storytelling as a real option.

I agree that short films generally include conflict in their stories. But to those who claim that it is conflict that engages the viewer's interest, and that conflict is therefore a necessity, I would ask: if that were the case, then how can a short film in which the conflict first arises five minutes into the film, manage to capture and hold the viewer's interest during the film's crucial opening minutes? For my full argument that short films are performance-driven, not conflict-driven, please see Raskin 2016a (a link to the essay is provided in the bibliography).

In the present study, I propose that *in addition to* – not instead of – the basic model outlined above, an extra perspective or level of concerns be taken into account. And this additional level is inspired by the concepts of *yin* and *yang*. The new perspective proposed here is intended: a) for filmmakers who have already mastered the basics of short film storytelling and are ready for new challenges at a higher level; and b) for teachers and students who study short films and would welcome a new analytical resource that can reach beyond the scope of the basic model.

The first chapter in this book is simply a fact sheet on the *Daodejing*, the *yin yang* complementarity, the concepts of non-doing and non-being, and finally the connection of those concepts to *yin*. This material is presented concisely, at times in the form of reference points.

In Chapter Two, a paradigm is proposed, outlining forms of *yin* and *yang* both for filmmakers and for characters in short films.

In Chapter Three, ten modern short film classics will be studied in relation to the paradigm, one at a time and in chronological order. Each is an outstanding example of quality storytelling, whether or not it has won international awards. As a corpus, these ten films represent a broad spectrum of storytelling types and strategies. Each film will be presented along with a complete synopsis, a shot-by-shot breakdown and a link to the film. In sharply focused studies, selected forms of *yin* and *yang* in play in the film will then be described as concisely as possible.

Chapter Four will provide supplementary examples from other art forms, including painting, literature and feature films.

A nutshell summary, followed by a brief afterword, will then conclude this study.

With the exception of a preliminary article of my own (Raskin 2021b), this is the first comprehensive attempt to view short film storytelling with respect to the *yin yang* complementarity. The seed from which this study grew is a section called "Zen and the art of the short film" in *Cinematic Diamonds. Narrative Storytelling Strategies in Short Fiction Film* – the

2012 doctoral thesis of Saara Cantell who has since become one of the most productive film directors and screenwriters in Finland today. Cantell was the first to suggest that narrative properties valued in Asian esthetics coincide with such properties of short film storytelling as condensation, restraint, omission, allusiveness, irregularity, and simplicity (107). She noted that Iványi's short film *Wind*,

> in which for much of the time we see a near empty landscape and sky [...] is very much in the spirit of Zen. Its way of telling its story through incompleteness and allusiveness gives the spectator the opportunity to fill the available space with his/her own associations and emotions (170).

With regard to paintings that leave empty space, she writes that the "expression of emptiness is also associated with the concepts yin-yang" which like "Raskin's parameters are similarly concerned with a balancing of two (partially conflicting) poles: consistency vs. surprise, simplicity vs. depth, economy vs. wholeness" (109). Though while writing this book, I was not aware that I was further developing ideas proposed by Saara Cantell in her thesis, which I had the honour of directing, it is clear to me now in retrospect that I am deeply indebted to her ideas.

In *The Way of the Screenwriter* (2005), Amnon Buch–binder proposes a Daoist-inspired approach to the script-writing of the kind found in such feature films as *Galaxy Quest*, *The Fisher King* and *The Piano*. And although one of the precepts he evokes is from the eleventh chapter of the *Daodejing,* which I draw on extensively in my work, the fact that Buchbinder doesn't even mention the concepts of *yin* and *yang* should make it clear that my approach differs radically from his, not only regarding the art forms chosen for study – feature vs. short films – but also in the ways in which we each draw on Daoism.

Finally, in a book on writing short film screenplays, Claudia Hunter Johnson likens – in passing – a film's connection with the viewer to *yin* and the conflict driving its storytelling to *yang*. But intriguing parallels are not developed beyond the one paragraph she devotes to the issue (2000: 6).

So much for precursors, of whom only Saara Cantell has played an important role for me.

The less-is-more principle, so central to short film storytelling, has been followed in the writing of this book, all sections of which were kept as brief and to the point as possible. I am a fervent believer in Antoine de Saint-Exupéry's view: "It seems that perfection is achieved, not when there is nothing more to add but when there is nothing left to take away" (1939: 65).

Teachers on the lookout for meaningful short films for use in their courses may wish to consider one or more of the ten short films presented here with links, perfectly suited for classroom use and with shot-by-shot breakdowns that make it easier to keep track of specific details when discussing the films.

Finally, I would like to thank Marilyn Raskin for her radiant smiles and inspiration, without which I would have given up the ghost ages ago, and for her deft guidance of my writing. And I am grateful to the publisher, Alan Childress, for giving this book a life.

RICHARD RASKIN
Aarhus, Denmark
12 June 2022

Chapter One

REFERENCE POINTS IN DAOIST THOUGHT

1. On the *Daodejing*

- The *Daodejing* is the principal founding scripture of Daoism and said to be the second most widely translated book in the world, after the Bible.
- Literal meaning of the title:

  dao = way;
  de = virtue, integrity, power, nature;
  jing = canon, classic book, scripture.
- Some translations of the title:

  Classic of the Way and Power (Fung Yu Lan, Alan Watts)
  The Classic of the Way and Its Virtue (Wing-tsit Chan)
  The Classic Book of Integrity and the Way (Victor H. Mair)
  The Canon of Reason and Virtue (D. T. Suzuki and Paul Carus)
  The Book of the Good and Natural Way (Brian Brown Walker).
- The authorship of the *Daodejing* is nominally ascribed to a legendary Chinese sage called Laozi [Lao Tzu], – an appellation meaning "old master" or "old wise one." He may have lived as early as the 6th or as late as the 4th century BCE. Whether the *Daodejing* was written by "an actual lone man is doubtful […] What is more likely is that the body of teachings now known as the *Tao Te Ching* was developed over a period of two or three hundred years by five or six different sages. Some were almost assuredly women" (Walker 1995: n.p.).
- Originally called the *Laozi* [*Lao Tzu*], the book was first called the *Daodejing* by early Daoist scholar and philosopher Wang Pi, who died in 249 CE (Wong 1997: 25).
- First circulated as a book in the 3rd century BCE.
- Composition: The book is organized into 81 brief sections, usually called "chapters," though in most translations, they resemble poems in both layout and style. The book's division into chapters may have

originated in the Sui (581-618) or T'ang (618-907) dynasty (Chan 1963: 75). Although the book is said to be divided into two parts, with Part One consisting of Chapters 1-37, Part Two of Chapters 38 to 81, I see no differences between the two sets of chapters.

- A second major classic of Daoism is the *Zhuangzi* [*Chuang Tzu*], which probably dates from the 4th century BCE and deals in the form of anecdotes with many of the principles evoked more poetically and elliptically in the *Daodejing.* The two works have been described as conveying "a celebration of whimsy, spontaneity, and contradiction, and a metaphysic that often disdains Confucian duty and politics" (Barnstone and Ping 1996: ix-x).

2. On the *yin yang* complementarity

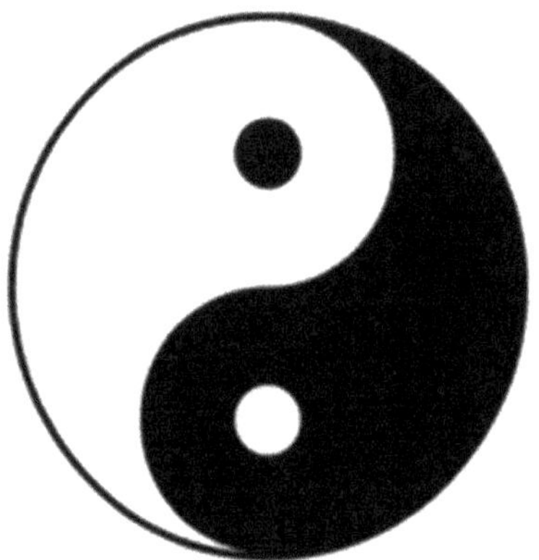

Emblems for *yin* and *yang* consisting of two interlocking spirals date from the 16th century, when they were given the name "taijitu" by Zhang Huang (Wang 2012: 205). Earlier representations they replaced were far more complex, such as Zhou Dunyi's five-part diagram of the "Great Ultimate," dating from the 11th century (Wang 2012: 75, 218-9). And since they are mentioned in Chapter 42 of the *Daodejing*, we know that the concepts of *yin* and *yang* have to date back at least as far as the 3rd century BCE, when the *Daodejing* was first circulated as a book.

The ideograms for *yin* and *yang* refer to the shady and sunny sides of a hill, respectively (Watts 2018: 21, Cummins 2021: 325).

In the current emblem, the white area, representing the *yang*, contains a black circle indicating that it has the seeds of *yin* within itself, while the black area of *yin* contains a white circle of *yang*. The presence of *yin* within *yang* and of *yang* within *yin* is an important part of this dialectical model, allowing for the dynamic interplay of opposites within any entity.

What follows now concerns my reasons for redefining *yin* and *yang* in ways that differ radically from their usual meanings.

In general reference works, the clusters of properties ascribed to *yin* and *yang* invariably connect the feminine to passivity and the masculine to activity. For example, in the *Encyclopedia Britannica*, "Yin is a symbol of earth, femaleness, darkness, passivity, and absorption. […] Yang is conceived of as heaven, maleness, light, activity, and penetration." And according to the *Oxford Companion to World Mythology* (2006), *yin* is "feminine, passive and accommodating," while *yang* is "male, active and firm."

In other more specifically Daoist sources, *yin* is feminine and weak and *yang* is masculine and strong (Slingerland 2014: 94; Watts 2018 [1975]: 21; Cummins 2021: 53).

Characterizing the masculine as active and strong and the feminine as passive and weak is offensive and sexist. Sociological studies have shown that bias against women in Chinese academia and Chinese society in general "is often justified with the Daoist concept of *yin-yang* […] with elements categorized into two sets: *yin* (female, dark, cold, negative) and *yang* (male, light, hot, positive)" (Leung 2014: 162, 175).

Arguments abound for overlooking or excusing the sexism, such as the "yin and yang are principles, not men and women" (Watts 2018; 22); or the female and male are "equal but different" (Cummins 2021: 82); or

> ...while most men are predominantly yang – male, fiery, active – they also contain a feminine aspect of yin. In some men, this yin aspect may be as great or even greater than the yang. Likewise, while women are predominantly yin, they also contain the masculine yang. Again, this can be as great or greater than their yin. Former British Prime Minister Margaret Thatcher is in fact worshipped in China today as such a woman of yang (Palmer 1997: 13-14).

Occasionally a commentator acknowledges possible misuses of a simplistic interpretation, and a need to remain vigilant, writing for example:

> All yinyang thought requires some differentiation between male and female, however it does not necessarily entail or demand an evaluative standard of good and bad. Heaven [yang] and earth [yin] are different, however this difference does not justify the normative claim that heaven is good and earth is bad. At this point we can see the importance of gaining a better awareness of yinyang interplay to prevent its misuses in social, political and cultural situations (Wang 2012: 109).

But in my view, as long as *yin* and *yang* are defined as gendered, a patriarchal bias is intrinsic to the framework. And the only real solution is to start from scratch in defining *yin* and *yang* with no reference whatsoever to the female or male.

This is why I will attempt to derive new definitions of the two concepts from relevant passages of the *Daodejing,* dealing especially with non-doing and non-being.

However, while dropping all reference to femininity and masculinity, I will retain from the standard definitions the opposition of weak vs. strong, which I will take the liberty of designating situationally as the *yin of vulnerability* and the *yang of being in charge*, both conceived as perfectly gender-neutral.

3. On non-doing (*wu-wei*)

The concept of non-doing, or *wu-wei,* is evoked in a number of verses in the *Daodejing*, including these, this time in the Walker translation (1995):

Chapter 3	Do by not-doing Act with non-action Allow order to arise of itself.
Chapter 48	Less and less is done, until one arrives at nonaction. The world is won by letting things take their own course.
Chapter 63	Act by not acting accomplish by not straining

There are several ways in which non-doing has been interpreted. For some, it means acting effortlessly. Arguing that the term should not be understood in a literal way, Slingerland suggests:

> ...it's not at all about dull inaction. In fact, it refers to the dynamic, effortless, and unselfconscious state of mind of a person who is optimally active and effective. People in *wu-wei* feel as if they are doing nothing, while at the same time they might be creating a brilliant work of art, smoothly negotiating a complex social situation, or even bringing the entire world into harmonious order (2014: 7).

In the same spirit, Watts defined *wu-wei* as "a form of intelligence – that is, of knowing the principles, structures and trends of human and natural affaires so well that one uses the least amount of energy in dealing with them." (2018: 76). Thinking of *wu-wei* in these terms can be illustrated by the story called "The Nurturing of Life" in the 4th century BCE *Zhuangzi.* When carving an ox, the butcher – Cook Ding [Ting] – has learned with his spirit how to see "the natural lines" in the flesh and his "knife slides through the great hollows, follows the great cavities, using that which is already there to [his] advantage." In this way, his knife never grows dull or needs sharpening (Palmer 2006: 23). Similarly, Watts wrote in another essay that when sawing wood, it is essential to go with the grain. "Let the saw do the work, let the teeth do the cutting." He added: "As our own proverb says, 'Easy does it.' And *wu-wei* means easy does it. Look out for the grain of things, for the way of things. Move in accord with it and work is thereby made simple" (2000: 45-46).

Essentially the same view was proposed by Hoff who wrote:

> Literally, *Wu Wei* means "without doing, causing, or making." But practically speaking, it means without meddlesome, combative or egotistical effort. [...]
>
> When we learn to work with our own Inner Nature, and with the natural laws operating around us, we reach the level of *Wu Wei*. Then we work with the natural order of things and operate on the principle of minimal effort. Since the natural world follows that principle, it does not make mistakes. Mistakes are made or imagined – by man, the creature with the overloaded Brain who separates himself from the supporting network of natural laws by interfering and trying too hard (1996: 76-77).

And Chan wrote that taking no action means "taking no artificial action, non-interference or letting things take their own course" (1963: 8).

In his history of Chinese philosophy, Fung described what he called the "general theory of reversal" at the heart of Daoism, by which he meant that overdoing involves the risk of "getting the opposite of what one wants" (1976: 20). He added:

> The well-known Taoist theory of *wu-wei* is also deducible from this general theory. *Wu-wei* can be translated literally as "having-no-activity" or "non-action." But using this translation, one should remember that the term does not actually mean complete absence of activity, or doing nothing. What it does mean is lesser activity or doing less.... The term "doing nothing" here really means "not over-doing" (100).

That would be consistent with such verses in the *Daodejing* (in the Walker translation) as:

Chapter 9	Filling to fullness is not as good as stopping at the right moment.
Chapter 32	To know when to stop is to be free from danger.

In the present study, instead of embracing one of the views mentioned above and dismissing the others, we will leave room for three interpretations of non-doing:

1. Non-doing in the sense of holding back, doing less, not overdoing, knowing when to stop, acting effortlessly;

2. Non-doing in the sense of letting things take their own course;
3. Non-doing in the sense of refraining from performing a specific behaviour that would normally be expected in the given situation.

4. On non-being (*wu*)

The 11th chapter of the *Daodejing* is the one most often quoted, and for good reason in that it tells something fundamental in a compelling and easily visualized manner. It describes an inner absence or emptiness as the basis for the concept of non-being. Here is that remarkable chapter in the Mitchell translation (1988):

> We join spokes together in a wheel,
> but it is the center hole
> that makes the wagon move.
>
> We shape clay into a pot,
> But it is the emptiness inside
> That holds whatever we want.
>
> We hammer wood for a house,
> but it is the inner space
> that makes it livable.
>
> We work with being,
> But non-being is what we use.

In a passage referring to the butcher story discussed on p. 13 above, Robin R. Wang (2012: 57) points out that:

> In its origin, *wu* (nothing) is not emptiness, loss or absence but rather the unseen, hidden and invisible. It is not a mere nothing but is the undifferentiated source of potency and growth that lets things function, such as the empty spaces between joints and muscles are what allows Cook Ding to cut with such ease in the famous story from the *Zhuangzi*.

5. From non-being and non-doing to *yin*

As already mentioned, *yin* and *yang* appear only once in the *Daodejing*, in Chapter 42, and in a way that leaves them completely undefined, at least for our purposes: "Therefore everything in existence carries within both yin and yang" (Walker translation). And although the *yin yang* complementarity is not explicitly mentioned in Chapter 11, it is generally understood that the non-being evoked in the three images – the emptiness within the wheel hub, the clay pot or the house – is *yin,* while the being – the outer or material shell, as structure – is *yang*.

For example, in his recent book on *yin* and *yang*, Antony Cummins explains what he calls an "old Chinese lesson" this way, in a passage under the heading SPACE AND STRUCTURE:

> Which part of a jug is more important: the clay structure (yang) or the space within it (yin)? The answer is that the empty space is the truly important part of the jug, because this is where the liquid is held. Without the space, the jug would not function (2021: 66).

Similarly, another commentator (Einzelgänger 2019) writes:

> Being is considered yang, while non-being is considered yin [...]. Now, while the functionality of yang seems obvious, the value of yin is often overlooked, yet it contains great power. A good example to show this power is the functionality of a mug.
>
> The yang-aspects of the mug are the material that it's made of, which is most likely hard and dry material. So, what makes the mug really useful? The answer is its *emptiness*. Without emptiness, a mug can't hold any liquids.

This commentator then goes on to identify the holding back of non-doing with *yin*.

From this point on, I will consider non-doing and non-being – or holding back and absence – to be forms of *yin*, and doing as well as being, presence or structure as *yang*.

Chapter Two

A PARADIGM

Schematic Overview

	YIN	YANG
for film-maker	1 YIN OF OMISSION 2 YIN OF INNER SPACE 3 YIN OF INTERPRETABILITY 4 YIN OF WELCOMING THE GIFTS OF CHANCE 5 YIN AS LOCUS	1 YANG OF STRUCTURE 2 YANG OF CAUSALITY 3 YANG OF MECHANIZED POWER 4 YANG OF CRAFTING THE PRODUCTION 5 YANG AS LOCUS
for char-acters	1 YIN OF NON-DOING 2 YIN OF DOUBT 3 YIN OF VULNERABILITY 4 YIN OF NOT BEING THERE	1 YANG OF DOING 2 YANG OF SEIZED OPPORTUNITY 3 YANG OF BEING IN CHARGE 4 YANG OF BEING THERE

Forms of Filmmaker Yin

1. YIN OF OMISSION

(no pun intended regarding a sin of omission)

Non-being for the filmmaker's work can also concern leaving things out, which can take many forms in a short film and might involve for example omitting dialogue and colour (*Two Men and a Wardrobe, Derailment, With Raised Hands, Wind*); omitting transitional shots (*Derailment*); omitting shots of love-making (*Derailment*); or even omitting the faces of the actors from our view (*Below the Belt*).

The *yin of omission* and the *yin of non-doing* might easily be confused with one another since they both involve not doing something. The distinction between the two depends on *who* is holding back. If it's a filmmaker who deliberately leaves something out of the film, it's *omission*. If it's a character who refrains from doing something, it's *non-doing*.

2. YIN OF INNER SPACE

In Chapter 11 of the *Daodejing*, there are references to non-being in the form of empty space at the hub of a wheel, in a clay pot and within the walls of a house. As we will see at a later point (p. 131), Paul Auster leaves a habitable space inside his stories by holding back on detail, keeping things simple. Holding back on pacing is another important factor. Concerning both simplicity and pacing, Marcell Iványi, whose film *Wind* will be studied here, stated in an interview:

> ...the short that makes a strong impression is one that is simple enough to give time to the viewer... when there's time and space for a viewer just to be there, and be settled about the whole theme - just be able to look at everything the way a child looks at things for the first time... (Raskin 1998: 20).

3. YIN OF INTERPRETABILITY

This form of *yin* involves the filmmaker's holding back on clarifying the meaning of a given scene or of an entire film, leaving it open for the viewer to make sense of it. For Buchbinder: "Subtext is the empty space at the center of the wheel" (2005: 186). Whether it be called subtext or interpretability, this openness results in the same active role for viewers, who are called upon to use their interpretive skills

Short films which are open to the viewer's interpretation, either as a whole or concerning specific scenes, include: *Two Men and a Wardrobe*, *The Office*, *Derailment*, *Wind*, and *The War Is Over*, in ways that will be discussed when each of the films is studied.

Experiencing a film's openness to interpretation can be pleasurable in itself, even if prospects of resolving uncertainties are poor. That uncertainties can in themselves be pleasurable may come as a surprise and require some getting used to.

However if uncertainties persist (*yin*) as a film's ending approaches, the viewer's experience of closure can be enhanced if *structural regularities* (*yang*) such as *symmetry* or *seriality* serve as counterweights to *interpretability*. This is the case for example with *Two Men and a Wardrobe*, when the ending *symmetrically* mirrors the film's opening shots. It also applies to *Wind*, when the camera's 360 degree panning brings us back to our point of departure and additional closural strategies fulfill their purpose, though uncertainties remain unresolved.

4. YIN OF WELCOMING THE GIFTS OF CHANCE

In the case of two of the films studied here, unexpected events which occurred during the shoot resulted in final productions that differed in important ways from the film as had been planned in the script. As we will see, in the case of *Andy Warhol Eating a Hamburger*, it was a misunderstanding on the part of the celebrity actor that resulted in the most interesting 45 seconds of the film. And with respect to *The War Is Over*, a dream Nina Mimica had the night before the shoot was over, resulted in a new opening sequence that makes little sense in purely logical terms but perhaps perfect sense in other ways. In both cases, the director welcomed the unplanned changes.

While maintaining a skillful control of the production process, planning every step as carefully as possible, the filmmaker should be prepared to let go of that control momentarily and to give up his or her original concept for a given shot, if for example an unexpected event during the shoot results in a take that differs interestingly from the scripted one. The unscripted take might just bring more life or meaning to the film than the originally intended one and might be used even if it creates inconsistencies in the storytelling.

The letting go is the *yin of welcoming the gifts of chance*, while the otherwise remaining in complete control is the *yang of crafting the production.*

5. YIN AS LOCUS

If in a film, there is a domain of the hidden, such as the storage room in *The Office,* and under the table for *Below the Belt,* that domain might be considered *yin as locus*. This will invariably be accompanied by the *yang* counterpart, designating a domain of appearances such as the public part of the office in *The Office* and over the table in *Below the Belt*.

Forms of Filmmaker YANG

1. YANG OF STRUCTURE

If a short film's beginning and end mirror each other symmetrically, as is the case with *Two Men and a Wardrobe,* or if the filmmaker creates a seriality by having the same phrase spoken six times in a row as at the end of *The Office*, those structural properties of the film are *yang* in the sense that they are heightened forms of presence – presence doubled or quadrupled – and presence is *yang* just as absence is *yin.*

2. YANG OF CAUSALITY

Causality means that one event makes another event occur, which in turn means that power is in play, and power is *yang* by nature. Sometimes a long causal chain can be found in a short film, as in Shots 50 to 75 of *Two Men and a Wardrobe,* where there are nine interlocking links of cause-and-effect, driving the story forward.

3. YANG OF MECHANIZED POWER

When machines of various kinds appear or are implicitly present in short films, they are sometimes embodiments of power. This applies for example to the subway trains in *Derailment*, whose hissing and metallic noises constantly remind us of their power; to the escalator in *Witness*, feared by the elderly woman and which proves to be fatal; to the mechanical control box for the hanging device in *On Suffocation*; to the camera used by the SS in *With Raised Hands* to produce trophy images of their victims; and to the unseen device used to enable the camera's 360 degree panning movement in *Wind*.

4. YANG OF CRAFTING THE PRODUCTION

Skillful choice-making in the planning and execution of a short film is a *yang* process, involving the disciplined power of creation. While the director is in charge of this process, it involves the coordination of work performed by the actors, the director of photography, the sound recordist, make-up, hair and costume people, and many more.

5. YANG AS LOCUS

In spatial terms, *yang* would be the domain of appearances, such as the public part of the office in *The Office*, and over the table in *Below the Belt.* This is only relevant when contrasted with the hidden domain of a *yin as locus*.

YIN FOR CHARACTERS

1. YIN OF NON-DOING

As mentioned above, we will leave room in this study for three different forms of non-doing: holding back and doing less; letting things take their own course; refraining from performing an expected behavior.

The third form just mentioned can be seen, for example, in the final scene of *Witness*, when mother and daughter are driving away from the shopping mall where the mother had just unintentionally caused the death of an elderly woman by badgering her into using an escalator she feared, with the daughter witnessing the accident. The viewer naturally expects the mother to defend herself. But neither mother nor daughter speak about the fatal accident, as they sit beside one another in their car, making a getaway from the 'crime scene,' in awkward silence. And it could be argued that if in her encounter with the elderly woman who was afraid to use the escalator, the mother had followed either of the other forms of non-doing – by knowing when to stop, or by letting things take their own course – the fatal accident would have been avoided.

Finally, at the end of *Two Men and a Wardrobe*, when the two men, having been repeatedly defeated, are heading back to the sea from which they had emerged, they have to cross a beach covered with mud pies made by a child. Despite the hardships they have endured, the two men carefully avoid disturbing any of the mud pies (*yin of non-doing*) while making their way to the sea (*yang of doing*).

2. YIN OF DOUBT

In *On Suffocation*, the young member of the execution team whose job it is to operate the hanging device with the aid of a control box, is visibly uneasy about the killing of the two young homosexuals condemned to death. The viewer can clearly read this character's doubts in his facial expression, as he fulfills his duty. And in this case, the viewer would naturally have preferred that those doubts result in the character's refusal to continue. In other imaginable cases, the viewer might hope that the doubts not interfere with the performance of the tasks at hand.

3. YIN OF VULNERABILITY

This is the status of characters who are defenseless and generally subject to domination by those in charge. In *Two Men and a Wardrobe*, the two men who have emerged from the sea are repeatedly rejected or even beaten, and clearly embody the *yin of vulnerability*. The same is true of the clients in *The Office*, who are bullied by the clerks, and more dramatically of the prisoners in *With Raised Hands* and in *On Suffocation*. As a rule, viewers are on the side of vulnerable characters who are bullied by characters enjoying the *yang of being in charge*.

4. YIN OF NOT BEING THERE

When the absence of a character or of an object from a designated spot is the focus of attention, as is the case for the boy and his cap in *With Raised Hands*, the *yin of not being there* is in play. In Shot 3 of that film, an SS man makes a point of planting a cap on the boy's head, and much of the film is about the cap's not being there. The same is true of the boy's presence or absence at his designated spot during the trophy photographing of the victims.

If a character is in some sense both there and not there, both present and absent, either at the same time or successively, the *yin of not being there* is in play along with the *yang of being there,* as is the case with examples drawn from two feature films, *Wings of Desire* (Wim Wenders 1986) and *Pimpernel Smith* (Leslie Howard 1941).

YANG FOR CHARACTERS

1. YANG OF DOING

In keeping with the less-is-more principle, characters in short films generally do small, subtle things when living out their stories. Yet when appropriate, they are capable of extravagant behavior, as when the woman in *Derailment* makes room for her legs by inserting her knees between those of the sleeping man seated across from her. In such cases, her *yang of doing* is heightened in power.

The *yang of doing* naturally includes *interaction between characters*, which is necessary for a short film to have any vitality. Since *character interacti*on will be present in any successful short film, it will not be singled out for attention in this study, despite its importance.

2. YANG OF SEIZED OPPORTUNITY

This refers to moments when a character in a state of vulnerability seizes an opportunity to gain at least momentary control of his or her own story. This occurs for example in *With Raised Hands*, when gusts of wind provide opportunities for the boy to distance himself from the scene of the filming and ultimately to escape from the Warsaw Ghetto.

3. YANG OF BEING IN CHARGE

This can be a positive property if for example a worthy character like Marco in *The War Is Over* is in charge of his own story, or a negative one when held for example by the bullying clerks in *The Office* or the threatening SS in *With Raised Hands*.

4. YANG OF BEING THERE

Typically serves as a foil to the *yin of not being there*, as when the cap or boy is missing in *With Raised Hands.*

Chapter Three

STUDIES OF SHORT FILMS

SHORT FILM 1

Two Men and a Wardrobe / Dwaj ludzie z szafa

Roman Polanski, Poland, 1958, 15 minutes, B/W

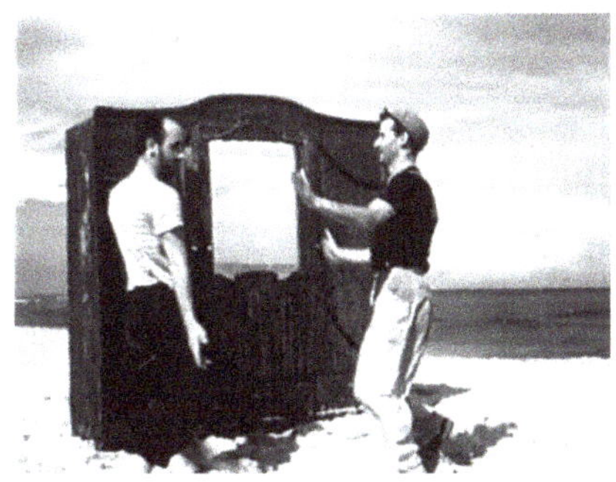

Screenplay and direction: Roman Polanski
Photography: Maciej Kijowski
Assistant directors: Andrzej Kostensko, Ryszard Barski
Camera assistant: Jakub Dreyer
Music composed by: Krzysztof T. Komeda
Music performed by: Sekstet Komedy
Production: Polish Film Academy, Lodz
Principal players: Jakub Goldberg, Henryk Kluba

Link to the film:
https://archive.org/details/twoMenAndAWardrobedwajLudzieZSzafa1958

Bronze Medal at the International Competition of Experimental Films, Brussels (World's Fair), 1958

Golden Gate Award, San Francisco Film Festival, 1958.

Synopsis [*NB. I am calling the two main characters Jakub and Henryk, using the given names of the actors.*]

Seascape. In the distance, a wardrobe bobs up to the surface of the sea and is carried by two men to the shore, where they joyfully celebrate their arrival on the beach. In the city they attempt to board a tram with their wardrobe but are kept off by irate passengers. The two men see a girl looking at a bird in a cage and show her their wardrobe but she walks away. As they carry the wardrobe along an embankment, we see two other men from behind, seated on a bench and laughing as one furtively steals the other's wallet. The two men with the wardrobe enter a restaurant and are forced to leave by the manager. A fish appears to be flying in the sky but is lying on the wardrobe mirror reflecting the clouds. The two men share the fish. When they bring a hotel manager out to see their wardrobe, his gestures of refusal leave them dejected. They carry their wardrobe past empty benches toward a deserted bandstand. A kitten that is licking its paws, is a target for four young thugs throwing apples at it. One thug then kills the kitten with a rock. One of the thugs shoves the dead kitten into the faces of his comrades as a joke. A young woman is waiting at a deserted spot on the sidewalk and sees in the wardrobe mirror that the leader of the thugs is walking toward her and brandishing the dead kitten. She makes her getaway and the frustrated thug leader throws the kitten in Jakub's face. Jakub makes boxing movements and is shoved into the wardrobe mirror which breaks. Henryk then begins boxing maneuvers and the thug leader sends him flying into a wall with a punch. The shortest thug (played by Polanski) is then allowed by the leader to hit the helpless Henryk in the face repeatedly. On a pier, Jakub washes Henryk's wounds. As the two men cross a bridge carrying their wardrobe, a drunk with a briefcase gets half way up an outdoor wooden staircase, then spins around and walks down again. The two men carry the wardrobe into a barrel storage depot and rest, leaning up against each other. A guard approaches, orders them off the property and when they refuse, beats them with a stave as they lie on the ground trying to fend off the blows. As the two men walk away with their wardrobe, we see one man killing another with blows to the head with a heavy rock, and then hurrying away. The two men carry the wardrobe down a sand-covered slope on their way to the sea. A little boy playing in the sand has covered the beach with mud pies. The two men carefully avoid disturbing any mud pies as they walk toward the water. They carry the wardrobe into the water and disappear as waves continue washing up on the beach.

Shot-by-shot breakdown of *Two Men and a Wardrobe*

What follows is merely a schematic overview of the film, making it possible to refer to specific shots by number.

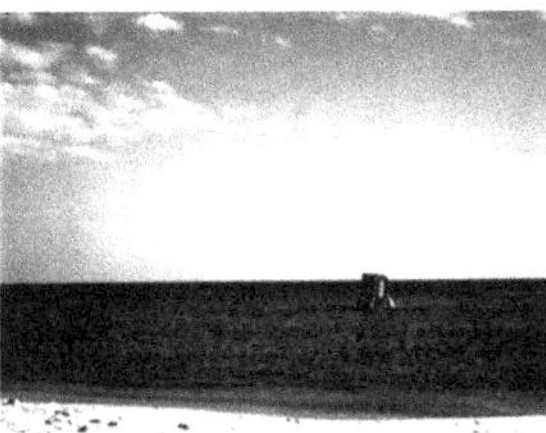

Shot 1 In the distance, a wardrobe bobs up to the surface of the sea, carried by two men who make their way toward the shore. (Dissolve.)

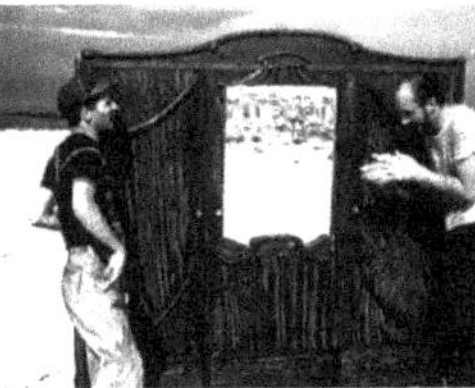

Shot 2 They set their heavy burden down on the beach.

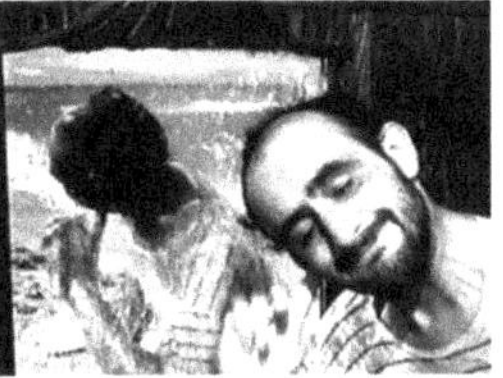

Shot 3 Henryk shakes water from his ears.

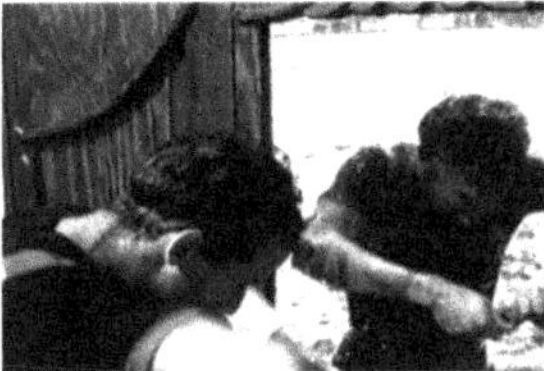

Shot 4 Jakub wrings his cap. The two men begin to dance.

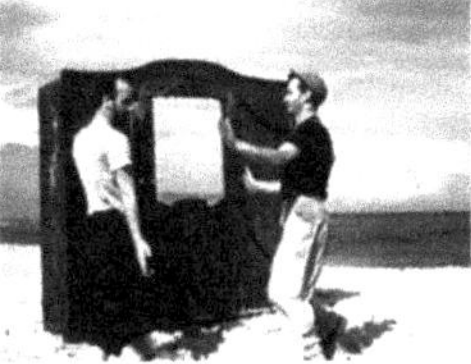

Shot 5 Their dancing continues

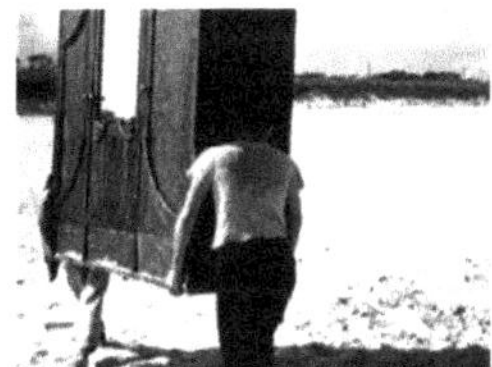

Shot 6 After dancing, they playfully do calisthenics and somersaults in the sand, then pick up the wardrobe and leave the beach, the camera panning back to the sea. (Dissolve.)

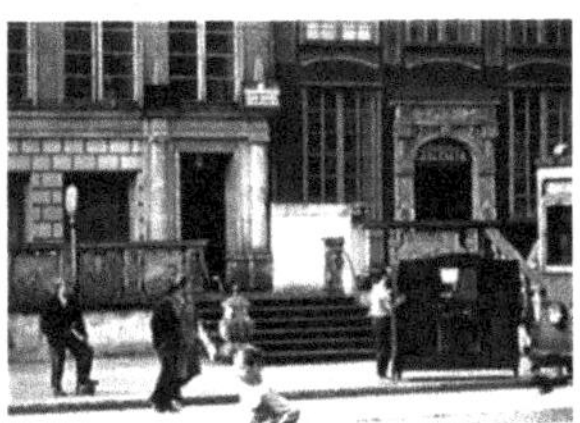

Shot 7 The two men are waiting for a tram, which pulls in to the stop.

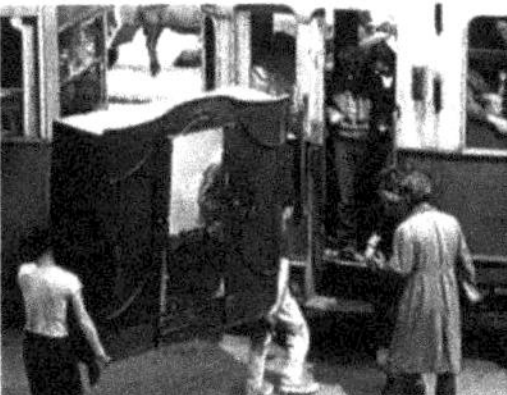

Shot 8 They attempt to board it, but are pushed out by other passengers.

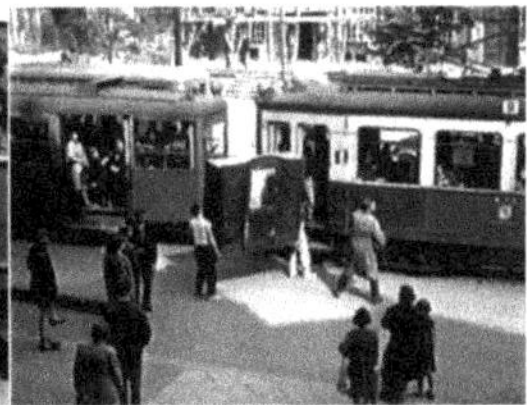

Shot 9 They stand there with their wardrobe as the tram is about to pull away.

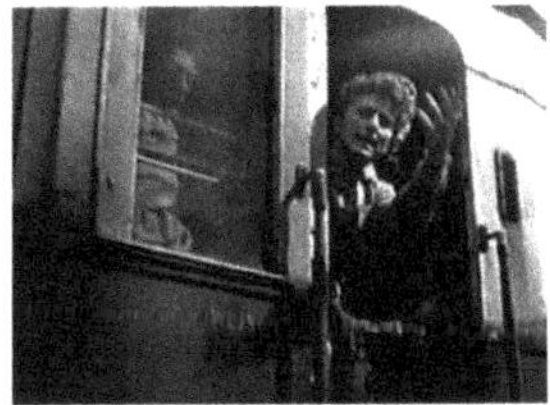

Shot 10 Passengers make indignant gestures at them as the tram pulls out. (Dissolve.)

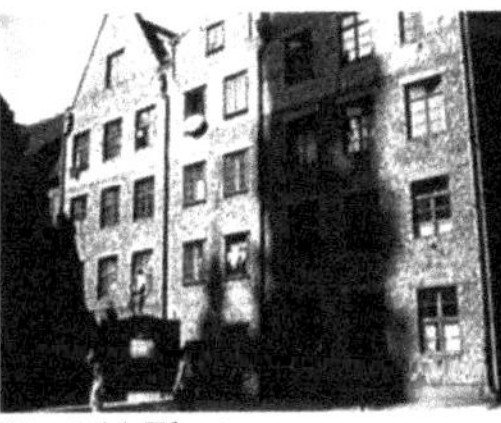

Shot 11 The two men carry their wardrobe past an apartment house. (Dissolve.)

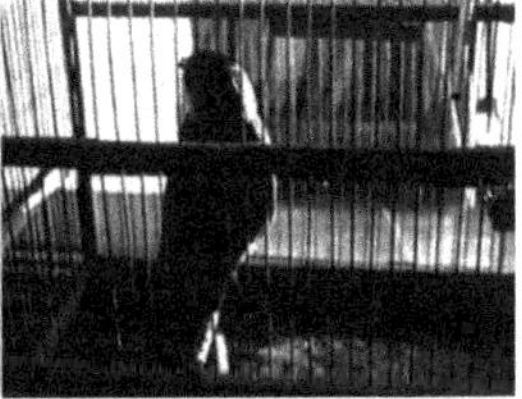

Shot 12 We see a bird in a cage. Tilting upward, the camera shows a girl looking down at the bird. The two men appear behind her.

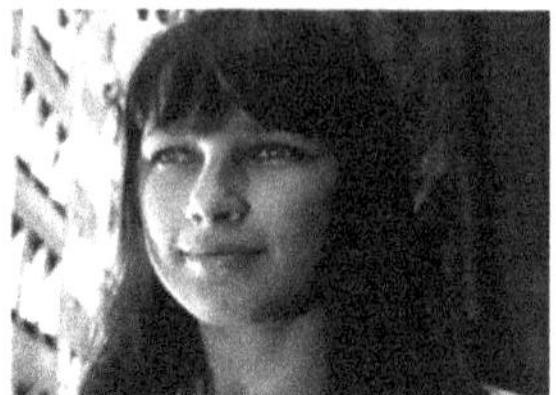
Shot 13 She turns and smiles at the men.

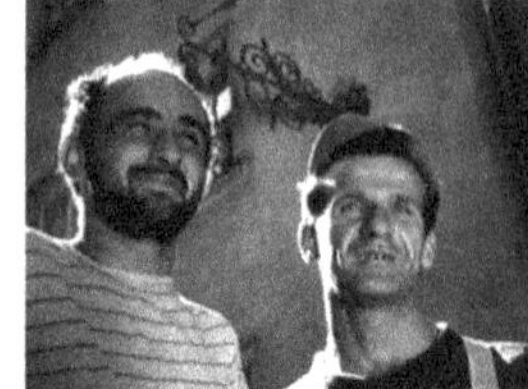
Shot 14 They smile back at her.

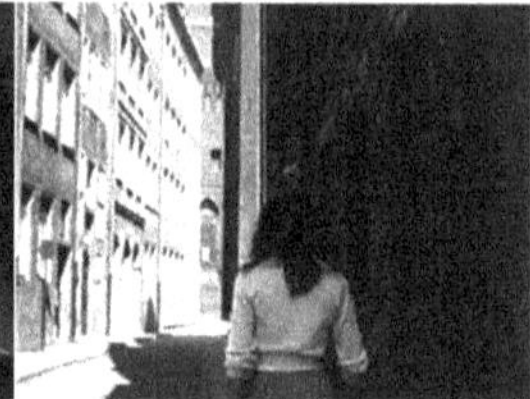
Shot 15 She walks away.

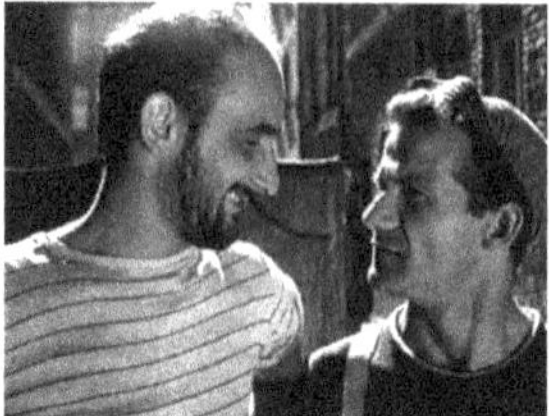
Shot 16 They watch her walk away, then decide to approach her.

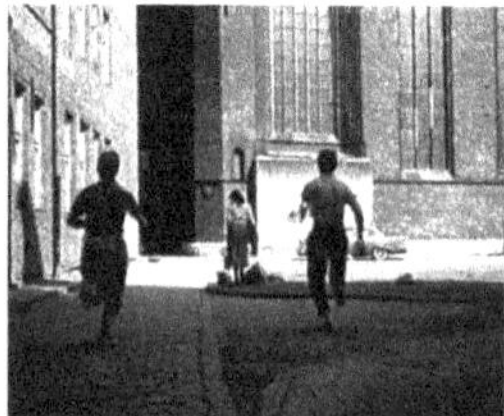
Shot 17 They run after her, introduce themselves with great formality, then ask her to wait while they run back to their wardrobe.

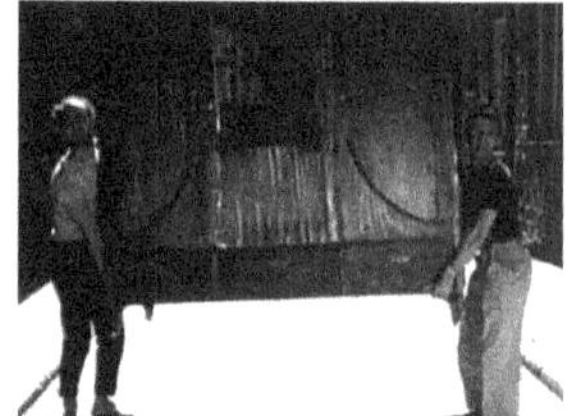
Shot 18 Returning to the spot where they had left the wardrobe, they lift it for her to see.

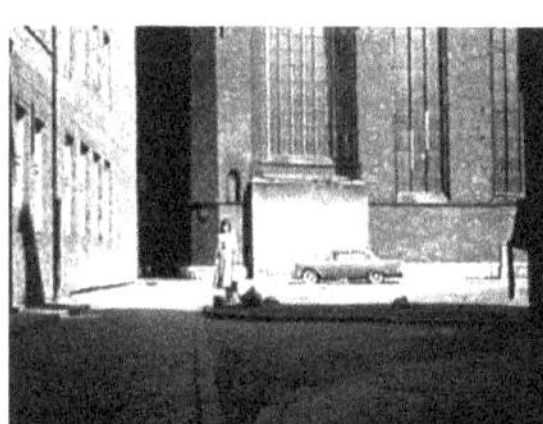
Shot 19 She looks at it, then turns and walks away.

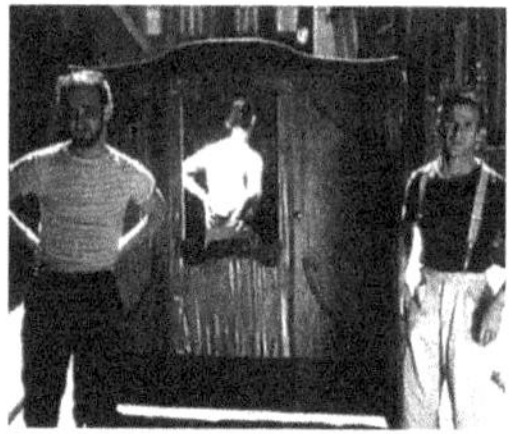
Shot 20 Discouraged, they set it down, their eyes still on her.

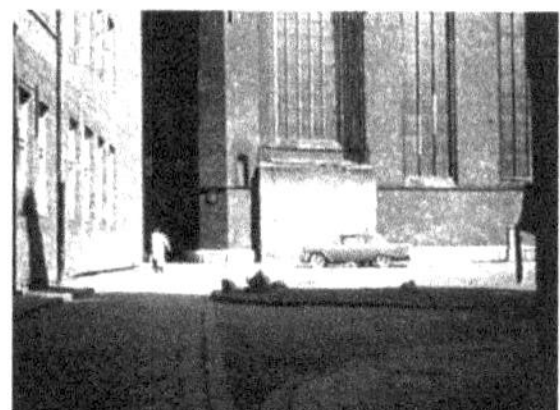
Shot 21 She disappears from view. (Dissolve.)

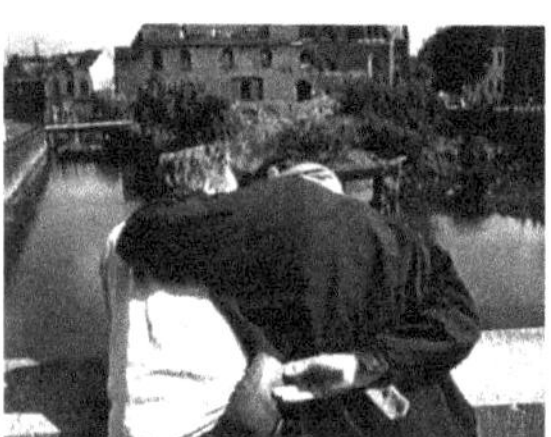
Shot 22 As the two men carry their wardrobe along an embankment, two other men are seen from behind, sitting on a bench, laughing. One has his arm around the other, while furtively stealing his wallet. (Dissolve.)

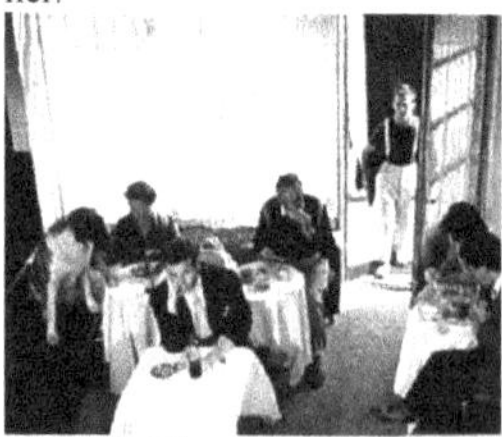
Shot 23 The two men enter a restaurant carrying their wardrobe.

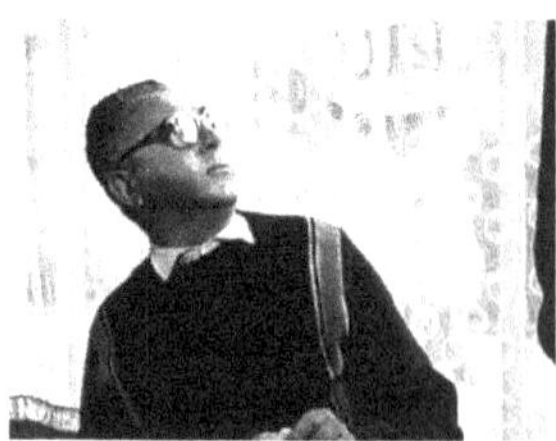
Shot 24 A man eating at a table looks up in shock.

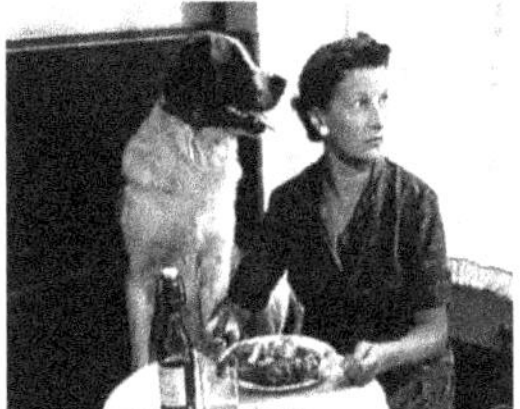
Shot 25 A woman eating, with her dog seated beside her, also looks up in shock.

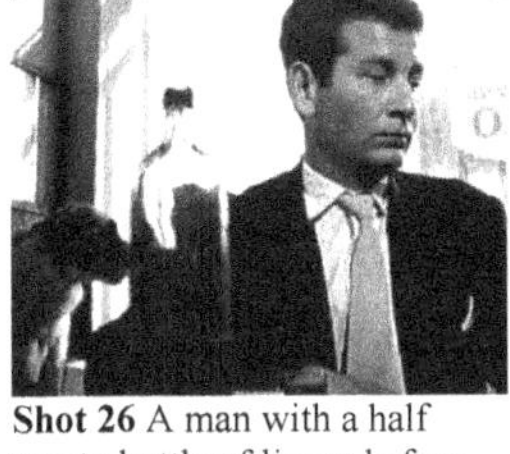
Shot 26 A man with a half empty bottle of liquor before him, turns to look.

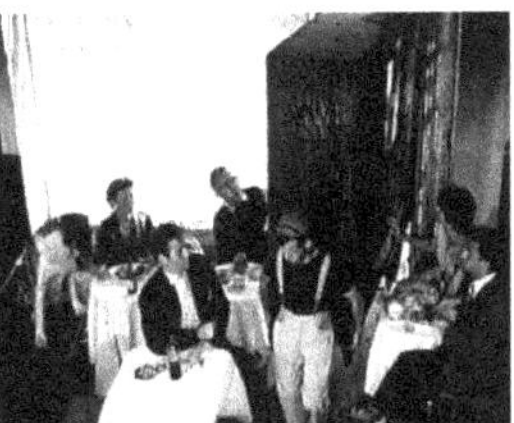
Shot 27 The patrons stare disapprovingly as the two men set down their wardrobe.

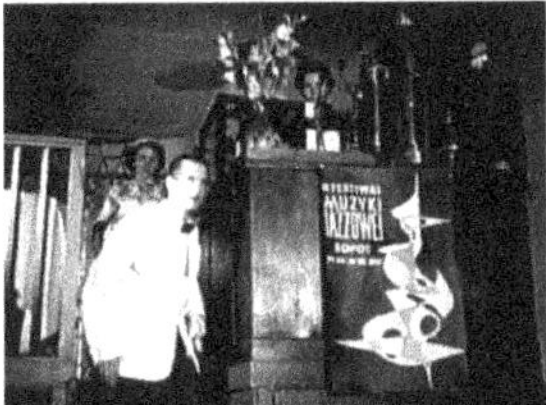
Shot 28 The manager of the restaurant rushes down the stairs.

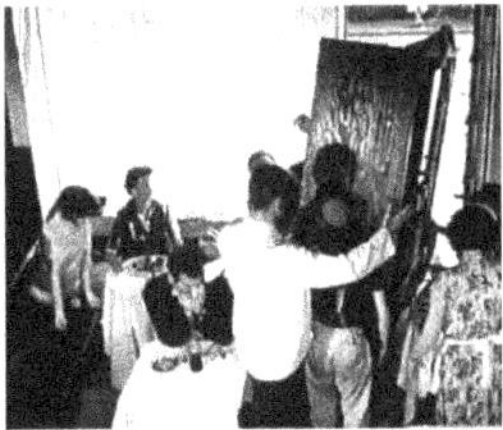
Shot 29 He shows the two men out of the restaurant, to the patrons' satisfaction. The manager then turns to the patrons, deploring the interruption of their meal. (Dissolve.)

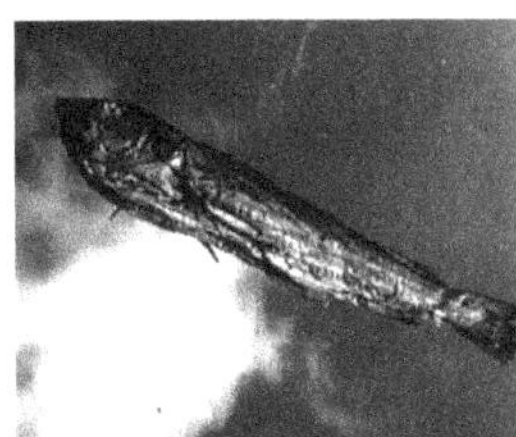
Shot 30a A fish appears to be flying in the sky, with clouds drifting by behind it.

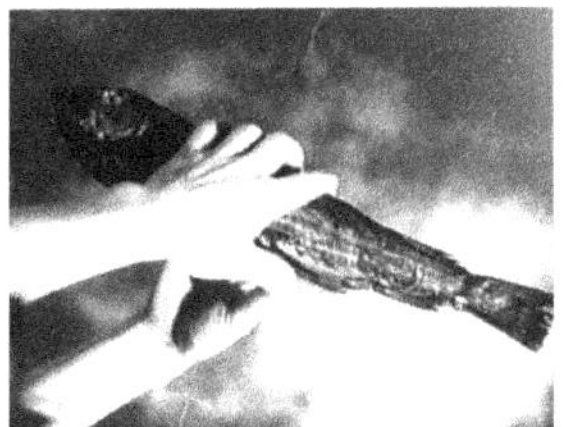
Shot 30b Suddenly, hands reach out and grab the fish.

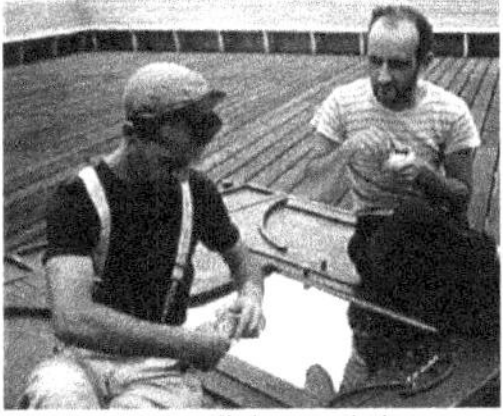
Shot 31 The fish was lying on the wardrobe mirror reflecting clouds. Jakub shares the fish with Henryk.

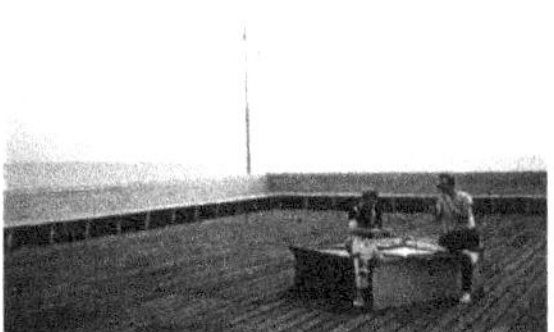
Shot 32 The two men eating, are now seen from a greater distance.

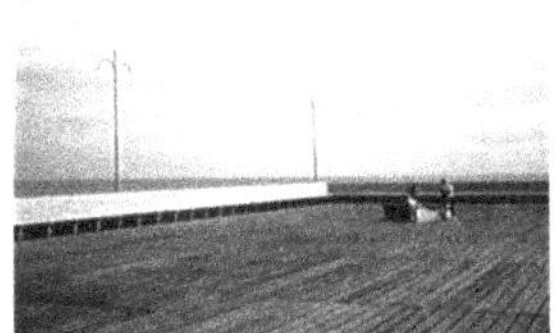
Shot 33 Seen from an even greater distance, they seem to be pointing toward the sky. (Dissolve.)

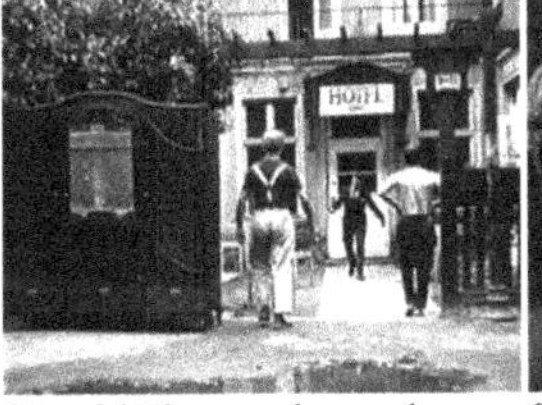
Shot 34 They set the wardrobe down in front of a hotel, which they enter as a dandy exits. He looks at himself in the wardrobe mirror, as the two men bring the hotel manager out to see the wardrobe. When the manager makes repeated gestures of refusal, the two men, dejected, walk toward the wardrobe.

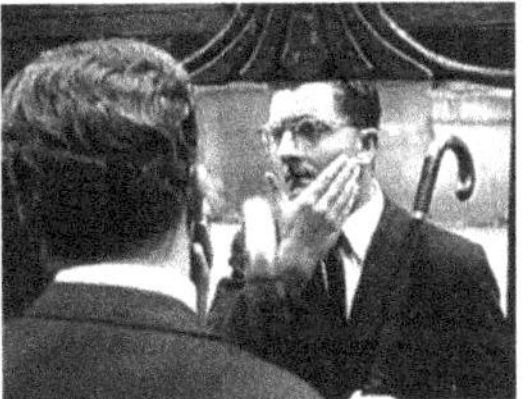
Shot 35 The dandy looks at his face in the wardrobe mirror. As the two men remove the wardrobe, he continues – unruffled – looking at his face in another mirror which happened to be behind the wardrobe.

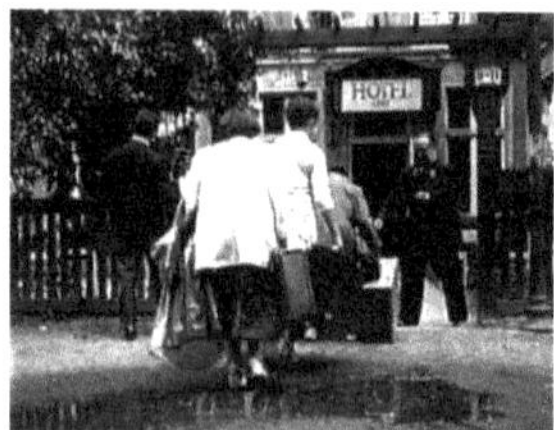

Shot 36 The two men leave the scene. Travellers arrive with suitcases and are welcomed by the hotel manager who helps carry their bags and ushers them into the hotel. The dandy finally tears himself away from the mirror and leaves. (Dissolve.)

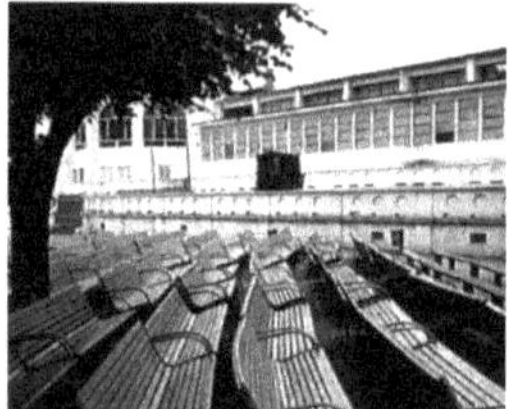

Shot 37 The two men carry their wardrobe past empty benches, toward a deserted bandstand. (Swish pan.)

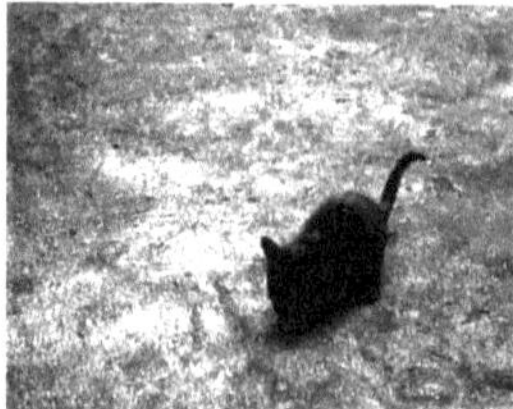

Shot 38 A kitten is licking its paws nearby.

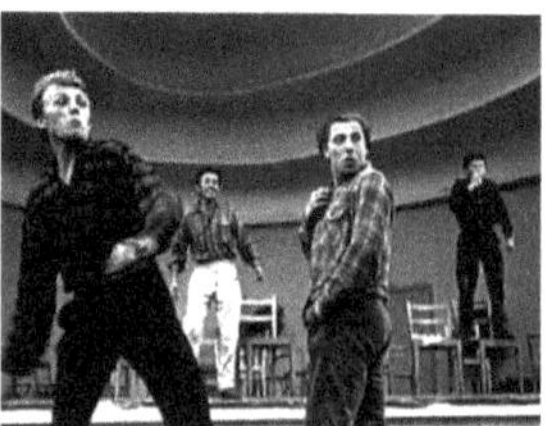

Shot 39 Four young thugs who are eating apples on the bandstand, begin throwing them at the kitten.

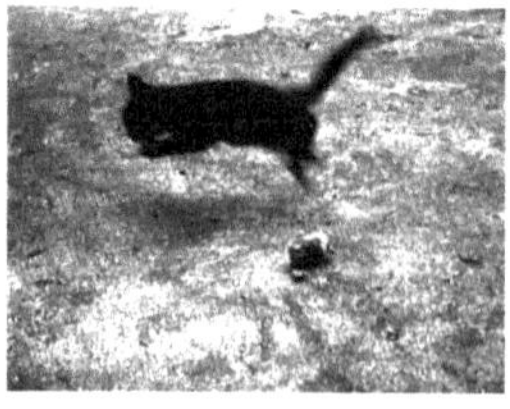

Shot 40 The kitten, struck by an apple, scampers away

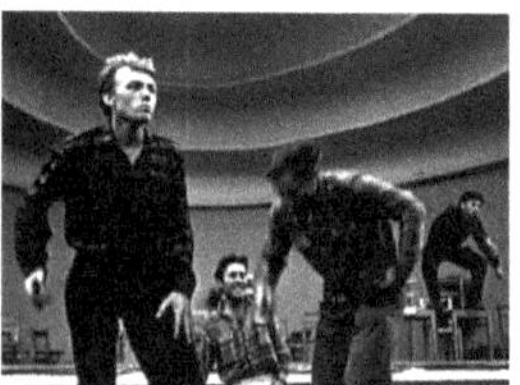

Shot 41 Laughing, the thugs continue to throw apples at it. One of them leans down.

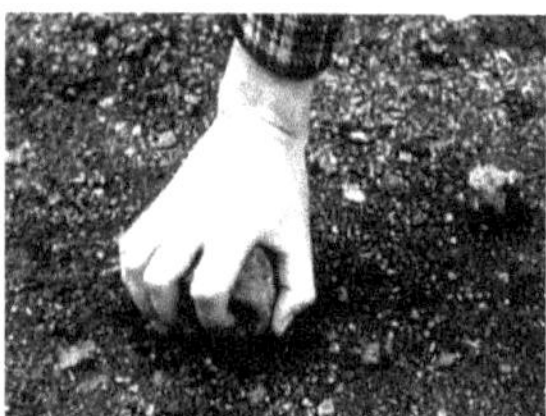

Shot 42 A hand picks up a heavy rock.

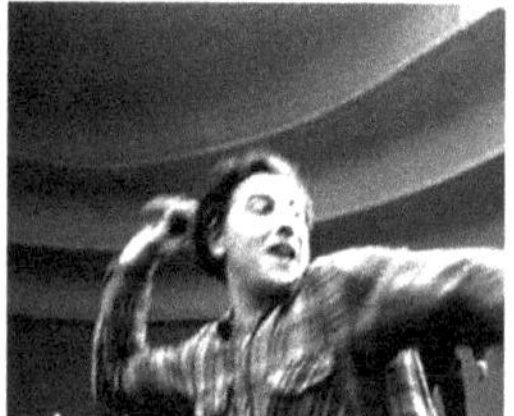

Shot 43 The thug laughingly throws the rock.

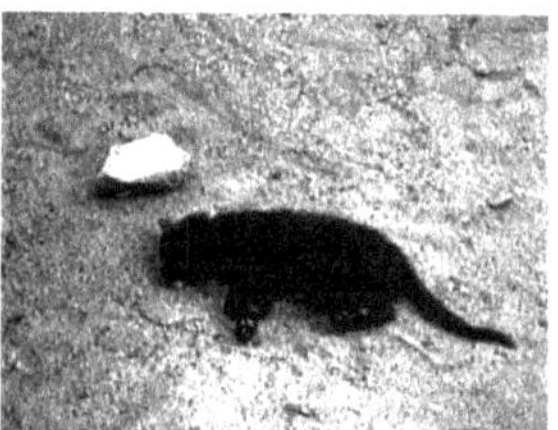

Shot 44 The kitten, which has been struck by the rock, curls up and dies.

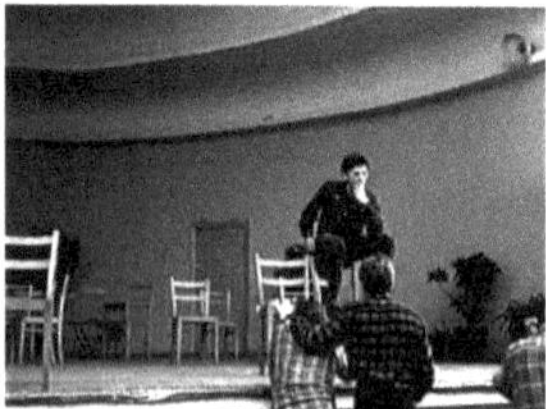

Shot 45 The thugs now eat more apples on the bandstand when the one who had killed the kitten rushes somewhere off camera.

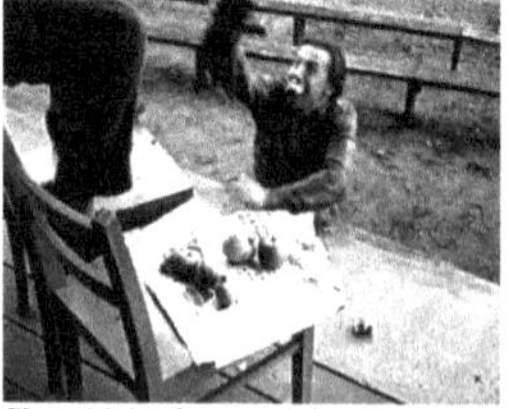

Shot 46 As the remaining thugs continue eating their apples, the one who had left them returns with the dead kitten, which he shoves into the faces of his comrades as a joke. (Dissolve.)

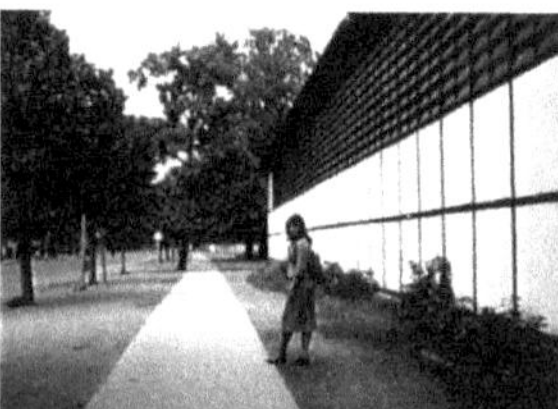

Shot 47 A girl is waiting on the sidewalk, at a deserted spot.

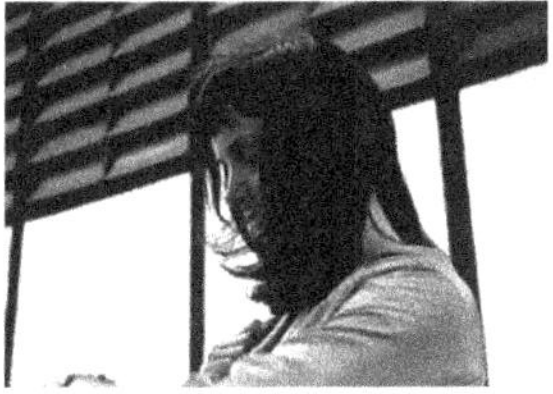

Shot 48 She raises her wrist to look at her watch.

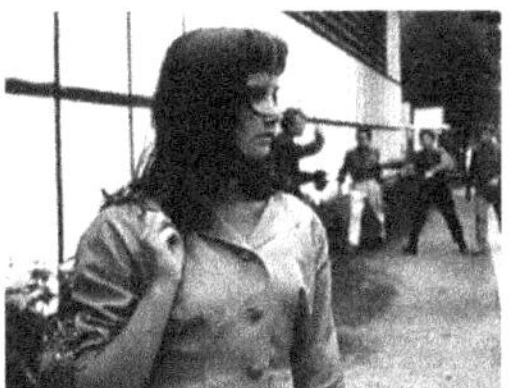

Shot 49 As she looks at her watch, the four thugs approach from behind. The leader has the kitten in his hand as he heads for the girl, who is looking in the other direction.

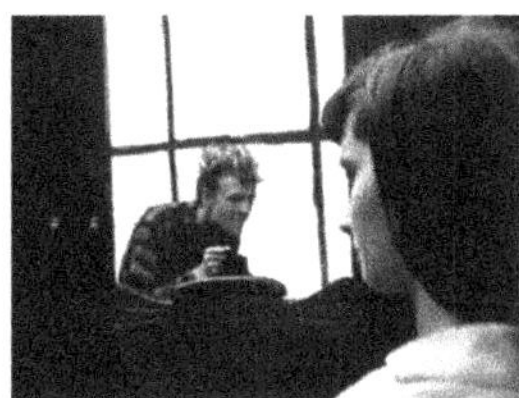

Shot 50 The wardrobe mirror passes just before the girl, and in it, she can see the thug approaching, with the dead kitten in his hand.

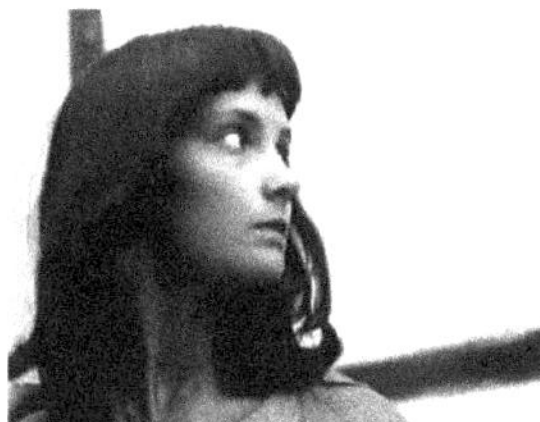

Shot 51 She turns to look at him.

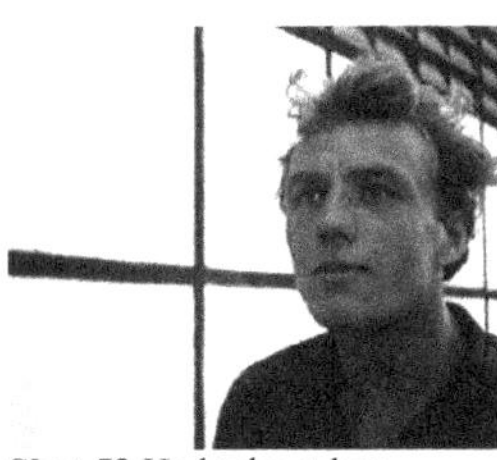

Shot 52 He looks at her.

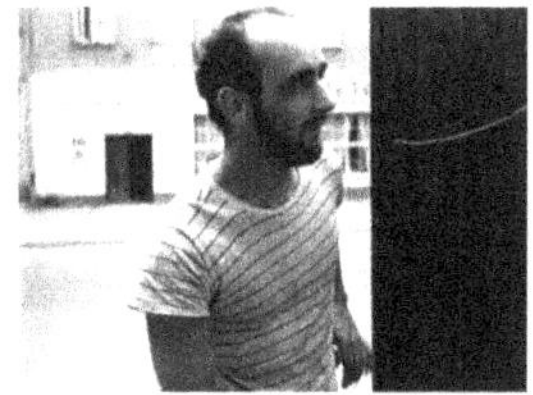

Shot 53 The two men put the wardrobe down on the sidewalk. Henryk looks at the leader.

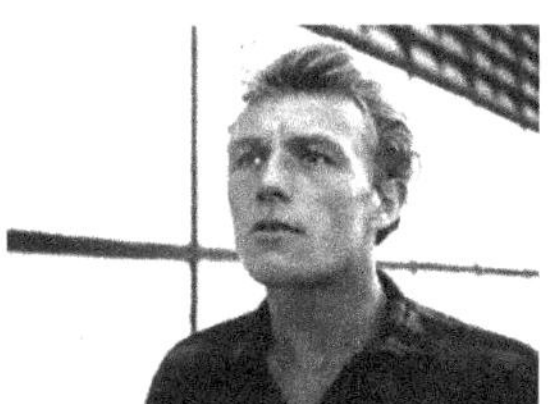

Shot 54 The leader is still looking at the girl, off camera.

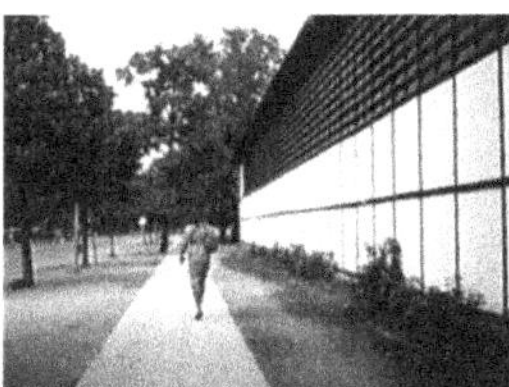

Shot 55 The girl makes a successful getaway.

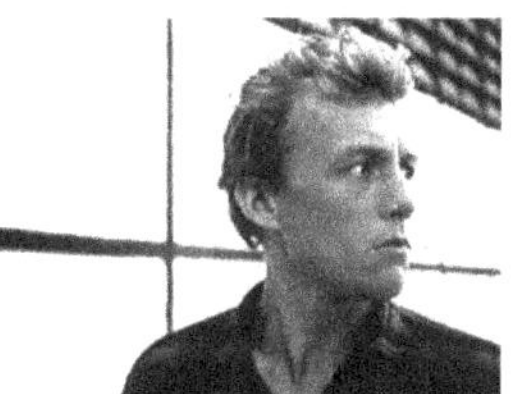

Shot 56 The leader angrily turns to look at the two men.

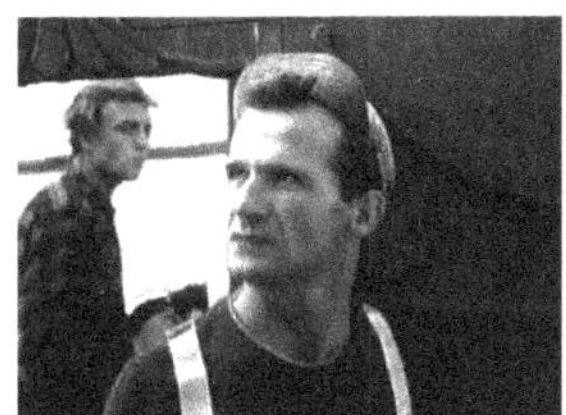

Shot 57 With the leader's reflection in the mirror, Jakub turns to look at him.

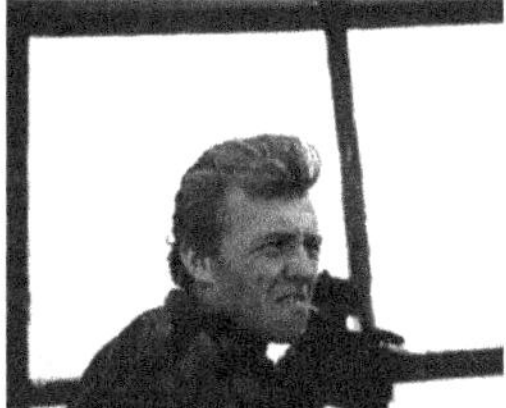

Shot 58 The leader, who is twice his size, looks him up and down, then throws the dead kitten in his face.

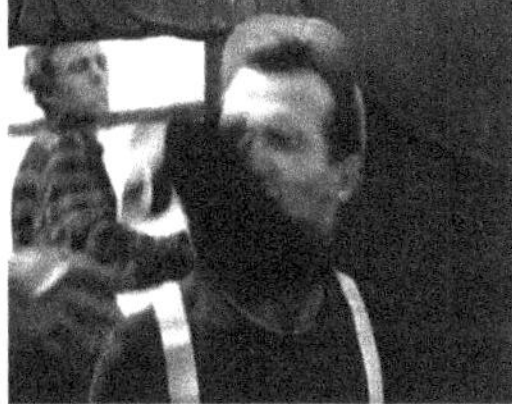

Shot 59 The dead kitten strikes Jakub in the face. He stares at the leader.

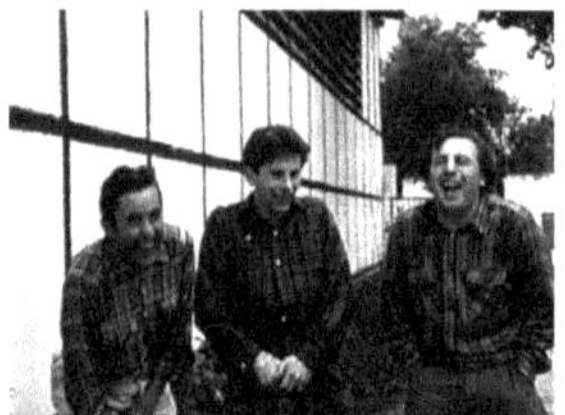
Shot 60 The three other thugs roar with laughter.

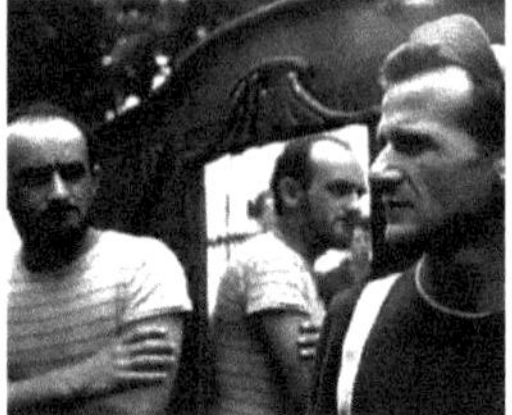
Shot 61 Jakub approaches the leader and slaps him in the face.

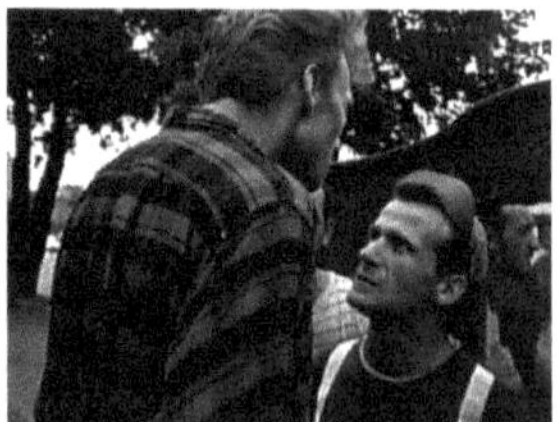
Shot 62 The leader, at least a head taller than Jakub, backs him toward the wardrobe.

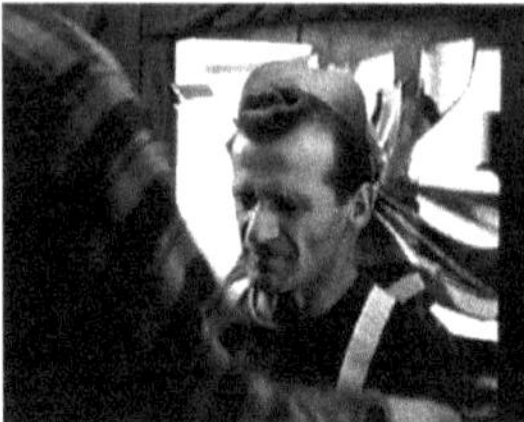
Shot 63 The leader pushes Jakub into the mirror, which breaks as Jakub falls to the ground.

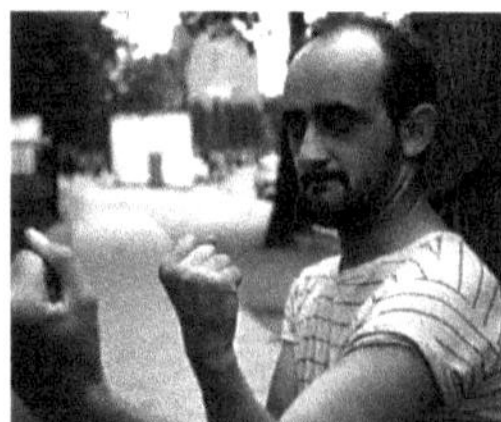
Shot 64 Henryk now rolls up the short sleeves of his polo shirt and moves forward, boxing mode.

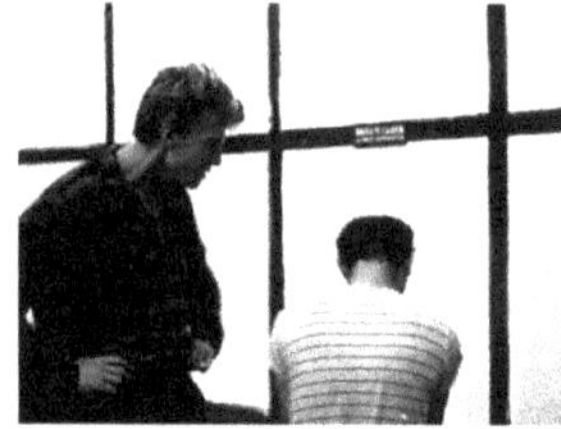
Shot 65 With his head down, he begins boxing maneuvers.

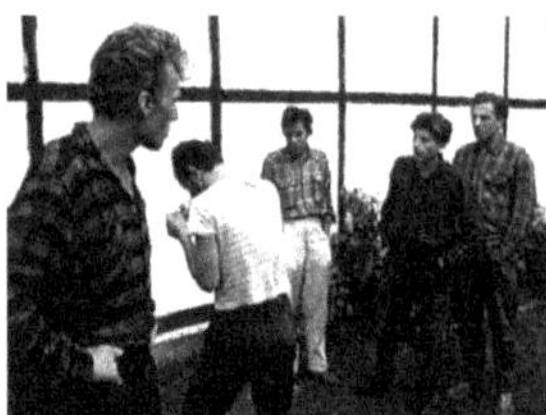
Shot 66 The thugs stand there and watch him, as he boxes without hitting anyone or even seeing what is around him. The leader taps Henryk on the shoulder. When he looks up, the leader punches him in the face and he goes flying backwards.

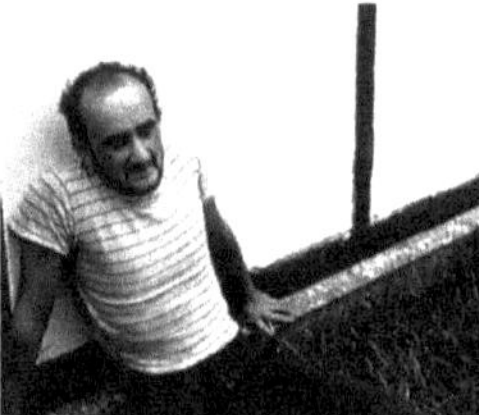
Shot 67 Henryk's head strikes the wall.

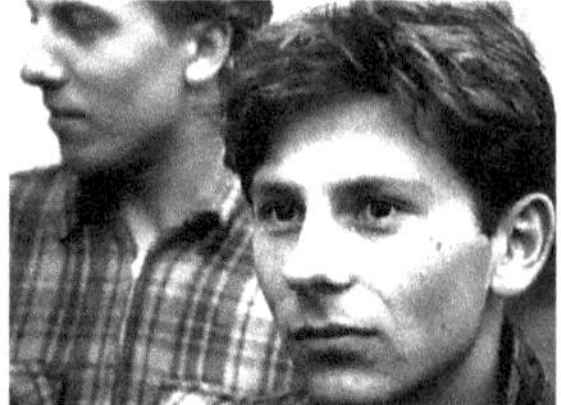
Shot 68 The shortest of the thugs (played by Polanski) looks over at the victim, then up at the leader, asking with a gesture whether he may go ahead and finish the job.

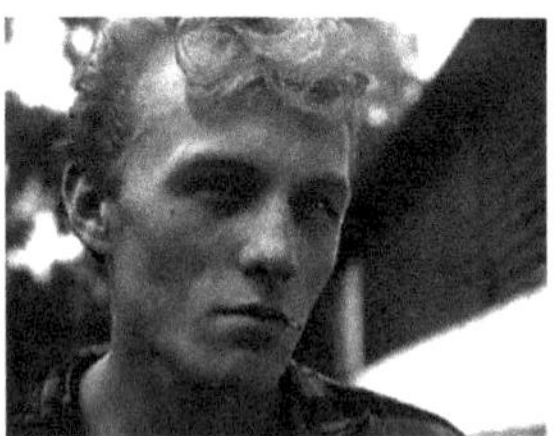
Shot 69 The leader signals "yes" with a movement of his head.

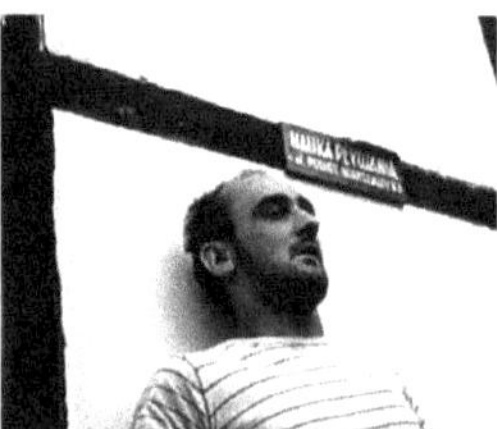
Shot 70 Henryk struggles to his feet.

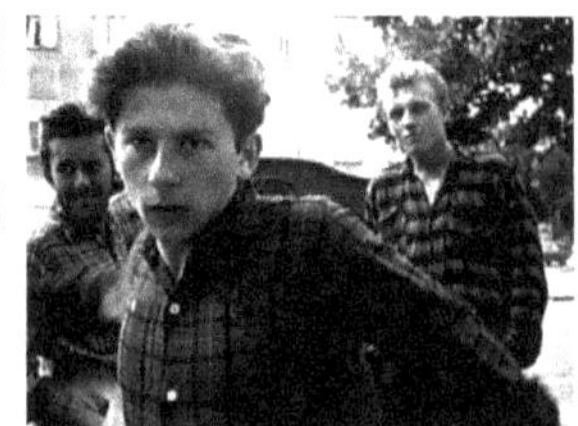
Shot 71 Polanski approaches, readying his fists, and takes a swing.

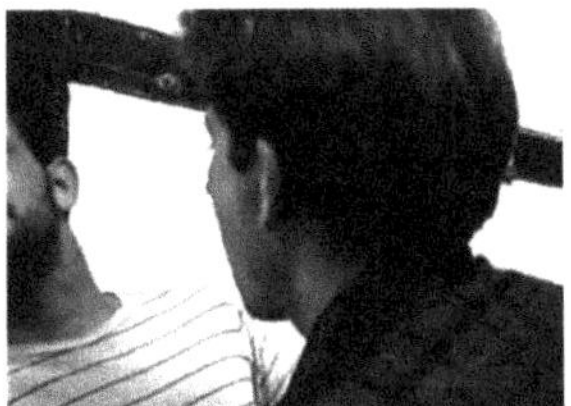

Shot 72 Polanski's fist hits Henryk in the face repeatedly.

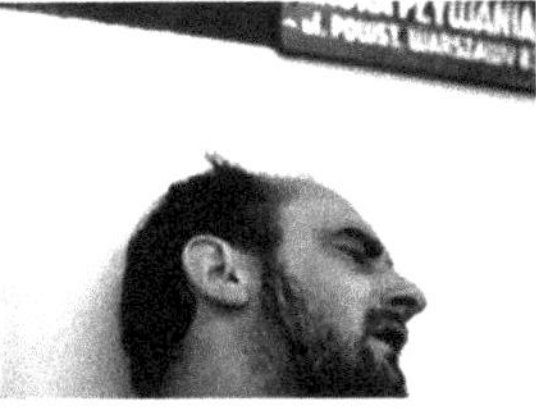

Shot 73 The beating continues.

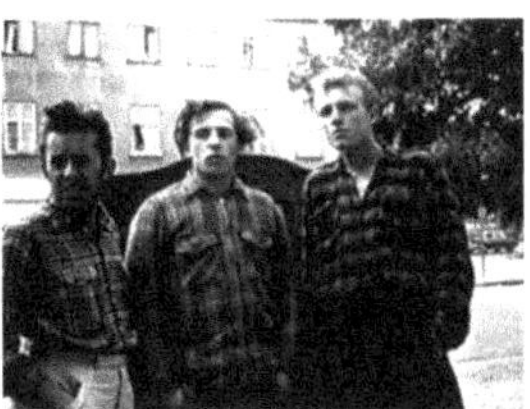

Shot 74 The other thugs look on.

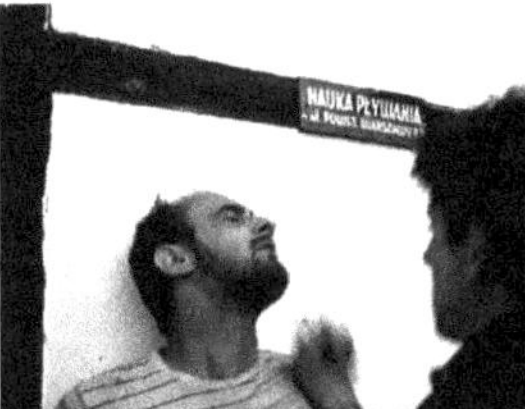

Shot 75 Blows continue to rain down on Henryk, who is now bleeding from the mouth.

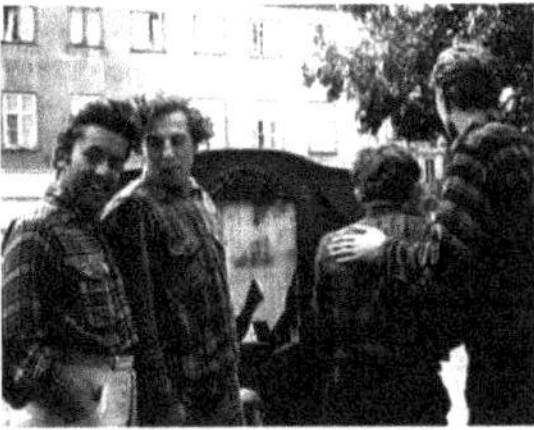

Shot 76 Polanski rejoins his comrades and the four thugs walk away. (Fade to black.)

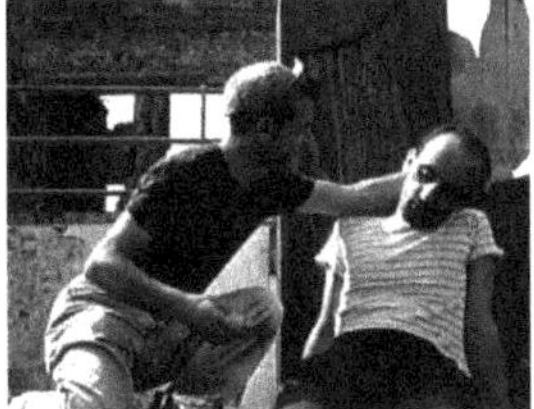

Shot 77 A tin can is hoisted up from the water by Jakub, sitting at the edge of a pier, with his wounded friend.

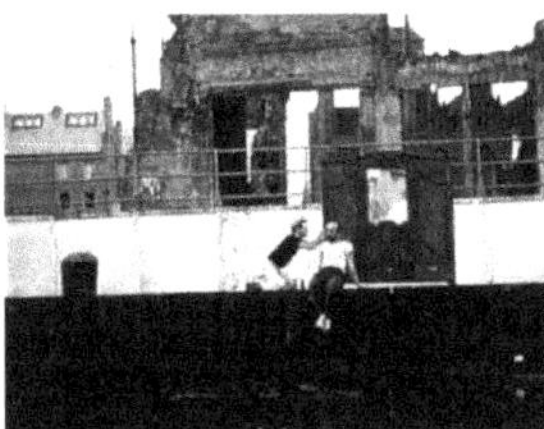

Shot 78 Jakub washes Henryk's wounds. Behind them stands their wardrobe with its broken mirror. (Dissolve.)

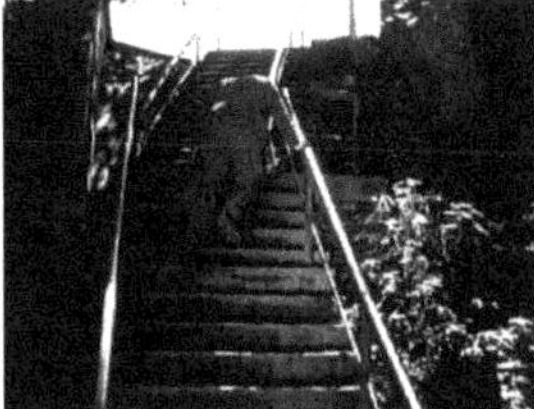

Shot 79 As the two men cross a bridge carrying the wardrobe, a drunk with a briefcase manages to get half way up an outdoor wooden staircase, at which point he spins around and walks down again. (Dissolve.)

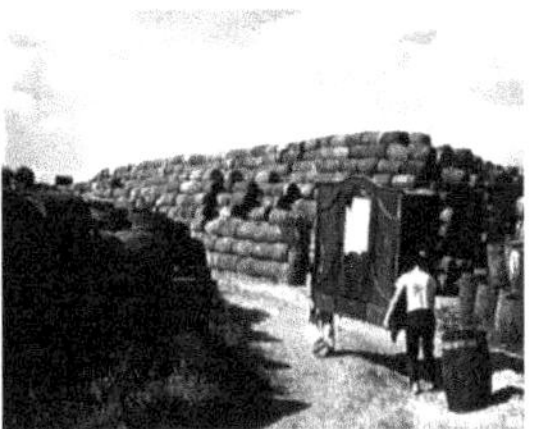

Shot 80 The two men carry the wardrobe into a barrel storage depot. (Dissolve.)

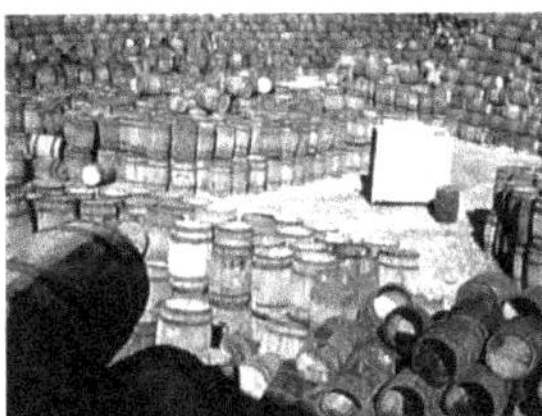

Shot 81 The wardrobe is surrounded on all sides by stacks of barrels.

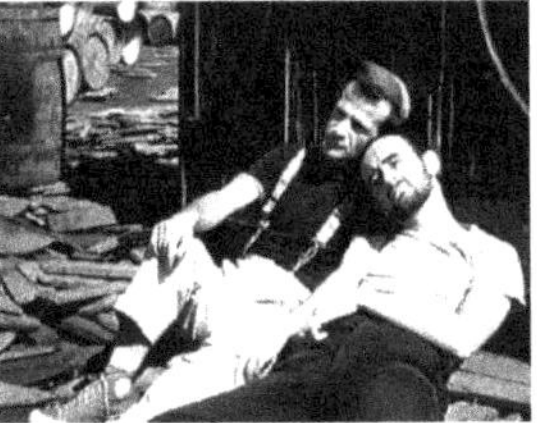

Shot 82 The two men are leaning up against one another. They look upward.

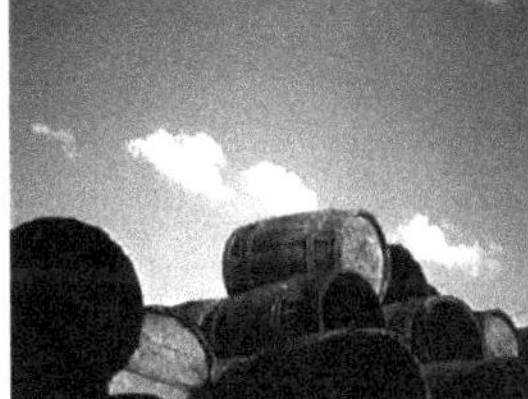

Shot 83 Clouds pass in the sky, over the tops of barrels piled high. (Dissolve.)

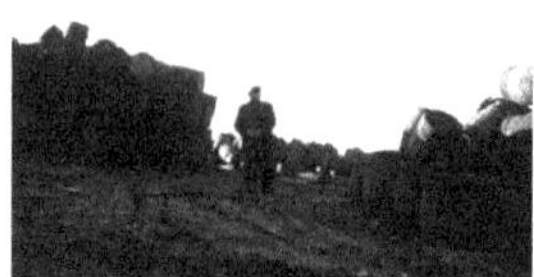

Shot 84 The camera pans, showing eerie stacks of empty barrels, then finally focuses on a guard who has caught sight of something off camera and who walks toward it.

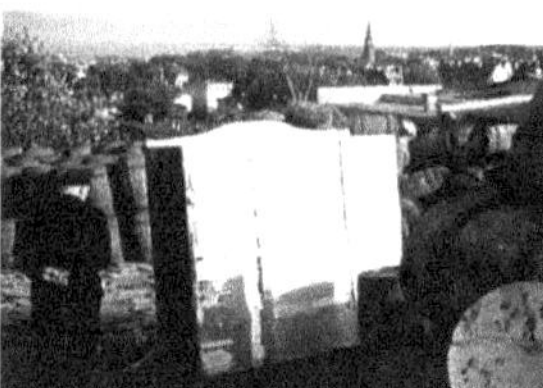

Shot 85 The guard approaches the wardrobe from behind, then passes in front of it.

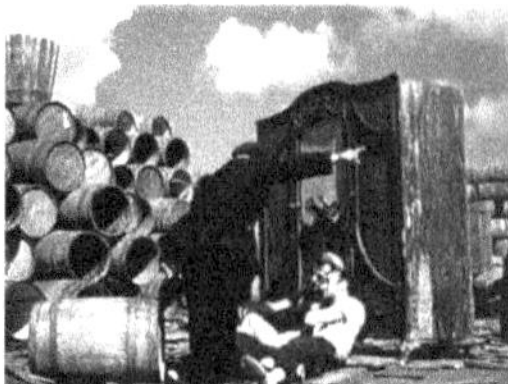

Shot 86 There he finds the two men who are resting and orders them off the property.

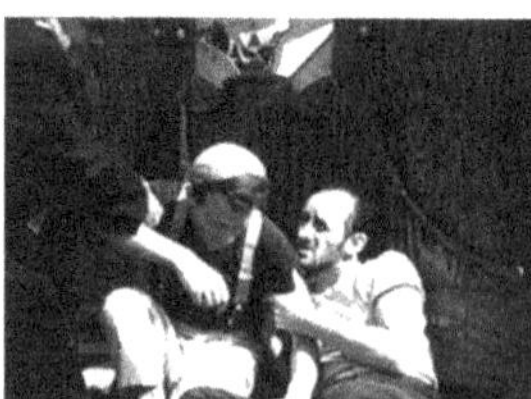

Shot 87 He pulls Jakub up who circles around the wardrobe then sits down again as he pulls Henryk up.

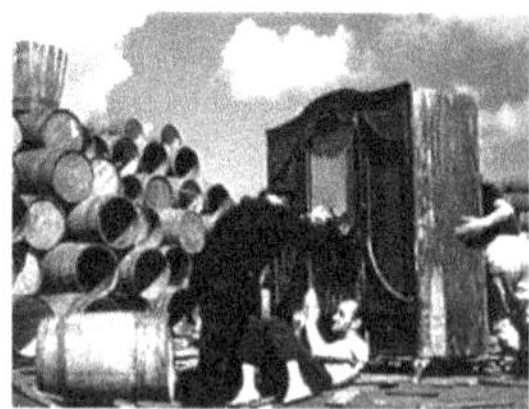

Shot 88 This continues, until Henryk finally pushes the guard away.

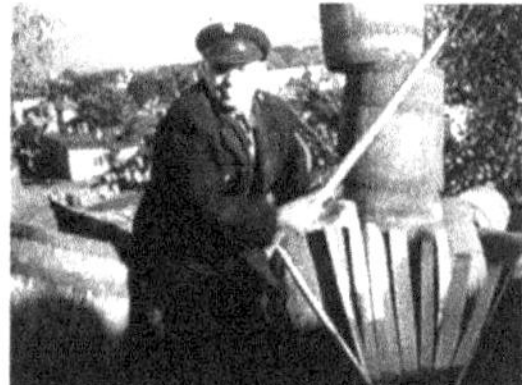

Shot 89 The guard lands in a stack of barrels, which fall about him. He detaches a stave.

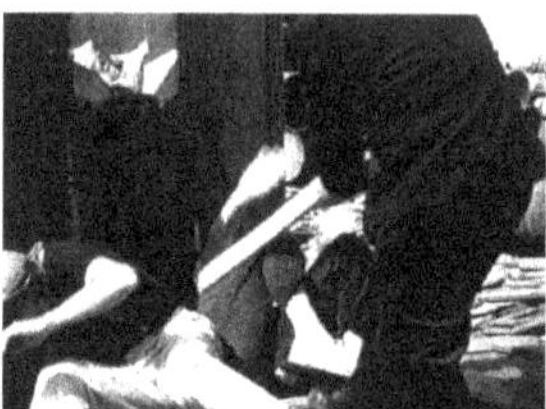

Shot 90 The guard beats the two men with the stave, as they lie on the ground, trying to fend off the blows. (Dissolve.)

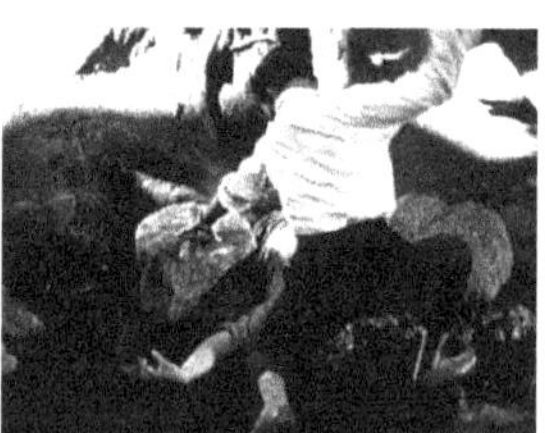

Shot 91 The two men walk in the distance, carrying their wardrobe past the apartment house of shot 11. The camera pans downward, to a nearby stream, where one man strikes another with repeated blows to the head with a heavy rock, the victim audibly groaning. The aggressor then drops the rock and runs away. (Dissolve.)

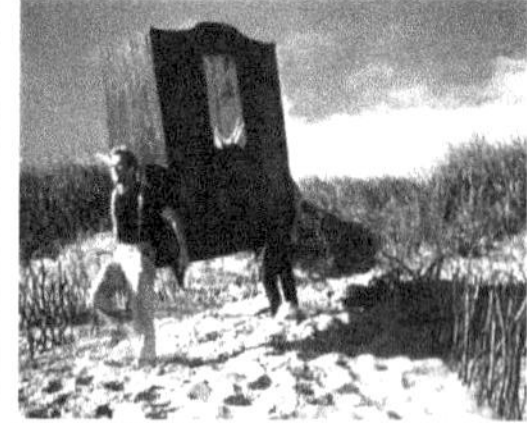

Shot 92 The two men carry the wardrobe down a sand-covered slope on their way to the sea.

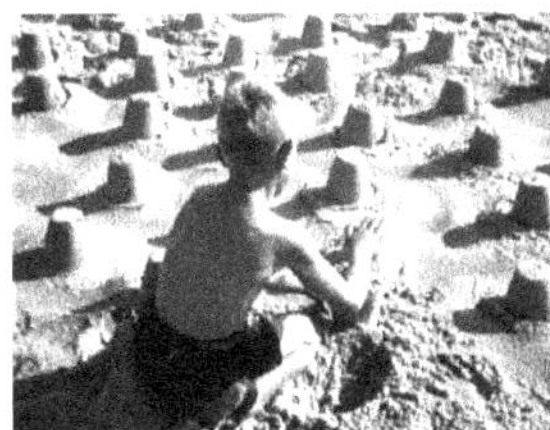
Shot 93 A little boy is making mud pies.

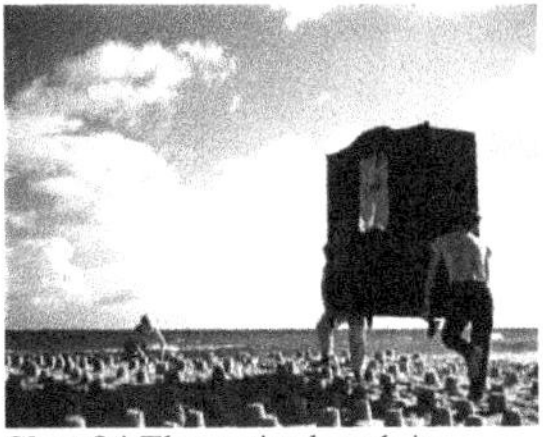
Shot 94 The entire beach is covered with these mud pies. The two men carefully walk so as not to disturb the mud pies.

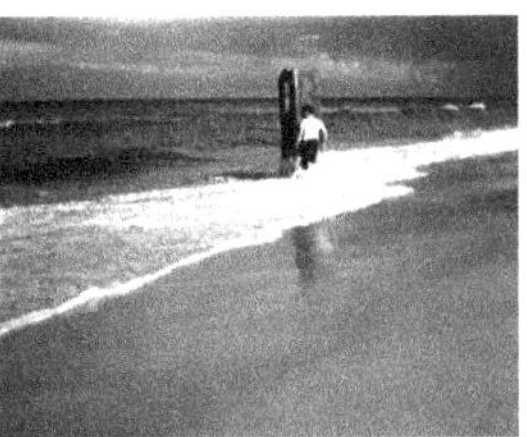
Shot 95 The two men carry the wardrobe into the water, as waves wash up on the beach.

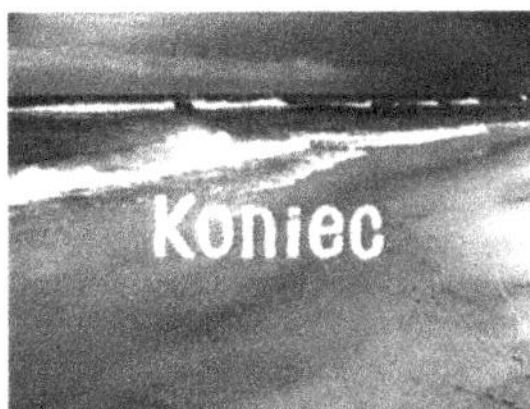

Shot 96 After an imperceptible dissolve, the men and their wardrobe are no longer there as the waves continue washing up on the beach.

YIN OF VULNERABILITY and **YANG OF BEING IN CHARGE**

Henryk and Jakub have a total of six encounters with other characters in the course of this film and are positioned in each case as vulnerable *yin* characters, dependent on the approval of *yang* characters who are in charge of the situation.

Four of those encounters concern specific social spaces Henryk and Jakub either wish to enter but are prevented from doing so (a tram in Shots 7–10, a hotel in Shot 34) or from remaining in a space which they have entered (a restaurant in Shots 22–29 and a barrel depot in Shots 80–90).

One of the remaining encounters involves a girl, first seen looking at a bird in a cage. The two men, to whom she smiles, present themselves and their wardrobe to her. She isn't interested and walks away, to their great disappointment (Shots 12–21).

The other encounter not yet discussed is with the thugs who take out their frustrations on Henryk and Jakub after a young woman, whom the thugs were going to frighten with a dead kitten, sees a reflection in the wardrobe mirror in time for her to make a getaway.

In all six cases, the outcome of the encounter is a defeat for Henryk and Jakub and reconfirms their vulnerability in relation to others who get to decide whether or not the wishes of the two men will be fulfilled.

YIN OF INTERPRETABILITY, YANG OF STRUCTURE and YANG OF CAUSALITY

On at least three occasions, Polanski himself explained the intended meaning of this film, sometimes making it clear that unlike surrealist or experimental shorts, *Two Men and a Wardrobe* did in fact have a meaning. For example, in his early autobiography, Polanski wrote:

> *Two Men and a Wardrobe* is only superficially surrealistic, because it has a content, which surrealism isn't supposed to have. It was the only film I made that 'meant' something. It was about the intolerance of society toward somebody who is different. Though hung up on surrealism, I also wanted to convey a message. The short I aspired to make would have to be poetic and allegorical yet readily comprehensible (1982: 121-122).

This was in sharp contrast, for example, to Bunuel's experimental short film masterpiece, *An Andalusian Dog* (1929), which I described in an earlier piece as an assembly of disturbing bits and pieces of story that successfully resist all attempts to integrate them into a coherent whole (Raskin 2002: 29). One commentator has aptly characterized experimental film as "a cinema that thumbs its nose at meaning" (Noguez 1979: 20, my translation). In combining the radically innovative esthetics of surrealism with the telling of a meaningful story, Polanski brought about an overnight rebirth of the art form and *Two Men and a Wardrobe* is arguably the first modern short fiction film in respects I described in 2002 (30).

Now getting back to the intended meaning of this film, Polanski stated:

> I wanted to depict a society which rejects a human being who is non-conformist or afflicted in its view by some moral or physical defect. And yet all around these two men, terrible and cruel events occur in the city, but no one sees them or wants to see them. It is only these two men and their wardrobe that everyone notices. Neither the pretty girl, nor the hotel manager, nor the watchman at the depot, nor the thugs, nor the indifferent tolerate the unique trio, which will be forced to disappear and to return to the sea from which it had come (Costes 1960: 13-14, my translation).

> [*Two Men and a Wardrobe*] was about the intolerance of society toward somebody who is different. I didn't give them a piano to carry because that would have implied a specific difference that set them apart, like art. They just have a wardrobe. And because of this wardrobe, they can't do what everybody else does. They are persecuted. Meanwhile, bad things are happening all around them, things society accepts or just ignores (Gelmis 1971: 145).

Many commentators shared Polanski's understanding of the film, calling it "an allegory of the conformist society that turns a cold shoulder to anyone 'different'" (Rasmussen 1969: 415, my trans.); a "wry fable about non-conformity" (Sadoul 1972: 201); or a film in which Polanski "concentrated on the burden of non-conformity in a conformist society" (Liehm 1977: 195).

But not everyone decoded the film that way, with the wardrobe embodying the otherness of two outsiders and resulting in a denial of access to a society that demands conformity. Some understood the film as a story about two men who have come from the sea with a precious gift for mankind, only to find that nobody wants it. For example, one commentator wrote:

> Two men emerge from the sea carrying a large wardrobe. They try to give it away and encounter everyone's refusal. Disappointed by this cruel and indifferent world, they return to the sea (J.-G. P. 1975: 52, my translation).

The fullest expression of this 'refused gift' interpretation describes the values embodied by the wardrobe, which:

> successively symbolizes tenderness, love, desire for communicability, purity, the ideal, in other words everything the spectator would want in the way of unselfishness and which, by that token, would – as everyone knows – be useless in our society. The fact that all the characters met along the way refuse the gift or the very presence of this wardrobe, does not speak very well for human nature (Belmans 1971:15, my translation).

This 'refused gift' interpretation could well apply to the encounter with the young woman (Shots 12–30) and with a little good will, even to the meeting with the hotel manager (Shot 34), but there is surely no basis for interpreting the tram, restaurant, thugs or depot sequences in those terms. Yet the concept of the wardrobe as a gift offers an appealing, life-affirming narrative to consider, especially since it could explain why the men travelled from the sea to the city with their wardrobe to begin with. It may therefore continue to have a following, of which I have been a part, even though it is strictly speaking inconsistent with much of the film.

Yet a third interpretive option might be to see the film itself as Polanski's gift, proposing the values embodied by the wardrobe (childlike innocence, playfulness, tenderness, etc.), and

> predicting its own rejection and the return of its maker to the depths of obscurity. Fortunately, this is not what happened, and it is quite possible that, to whatever degree the wardrobe symbolizes the film itself, the viewer is tactically mobilized by the film to prevent the fulfillment of its own pessimistic prophesy (Raskin 2002, p. 32).

The main point I wish to make is that this film requires interpretation and is susceptible of being understood in several different ways, thanks to the richness of the filmic representation – what some might call the "vehicle" – and thanks to the filmmaker's holding back on making his intentions too explicit within the film. Though any given viewer may opt for one or another of the interpretations mentioned above, a sense of the film's *interpretability* – its overall *yin* quality – is inescapable.

And just as the film's overall meaning is left open and interpretable, so is the meaning of a specific element near the film's conclusion, in Shot 93. For some commentators, the boy and the mud pies now covering the beach are positively charged, representing the childlike innocence of the two protagonists themselves (Belmans 1971: 17; Haudiquet 1963: 125). For others, the mud pies are negative in that they block the way to the sea and are either reminiscent of the cement constructions the Nazis built to block the passage of tanks (Idestam-Almqvist 1964: 141-143; Harker 1959: 53-55), or are symbolic of "rigid and repetitive conformism" (Wexman 1985: 24).

Counterbalancing the film's openness to interpretation (*yin*) are such structural properties as seriality and symmetry as well as the film's causal chains, all forms of *yang*.

Seriality is amply represented in the film in at least three forms (not counting the boy's production of mud pies):

- the seriality of defeats suffered by Henryk and Jakub: the tram (Shots 7-10), the girl (Shots 12-21), the restaurant (Shots 23-29), the hotel (Shot 34), the thugs (Shots 47-76), and the barrel depot (Shots 80-90).
- the seriality of evils glimpsed along the way and not involving the two men and their wardrobe (the treachery of the pick-pocket in Shot 22, the vanity of the dandy in Shot 34, the cruelty of the thugs killing the kitten in Shots 42-44, the drunk on the staircase in Shot 79, the murder in Shot 91).
- the seriality of positive values embodied by Henryk and Jakub (their childlike, playful innocence in Shots 2-6, their gentlemanly manners when introducing themselves to the young woman in Shot 17, their sharing of food in Shot 31, their standing up for each other and fearlessly confronting the thug leader in Shots 61-66), Jakub's

caring for Henryk's wounds in Shots 77-78, and finally their not disturbing any mud pies in Shot 94, about which we will soon take a closer look).

Symmetry is found in the film when the ending – the two men's disappearance in the sea with their wardrobe – mirrors the opening shots of them emerging from the sea with the wardrobe. These symbols of birth and death serve as framing pieces, bookending the two men's brief adventure in a world not meant for them.

And while there are moments of causality throughout the film, there is a long causal chain of interlocking causes and effects when the two men encounter the thugs and repeatedly the effect of one cause becomes the cause of the next effect:

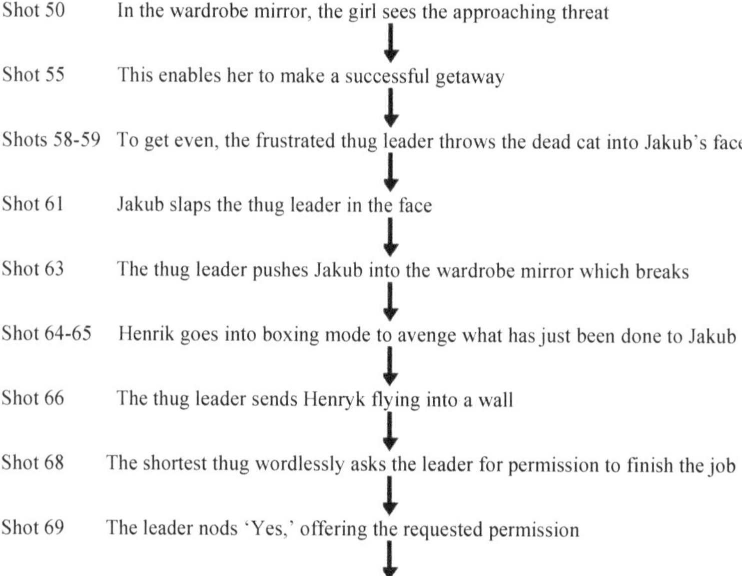

In addition to the causality embedded at this micro level in the beats of the action, there is also a broader causality in play when the six defeats suffered by Henryk and Jakub cumulatively result in the protagonists' decision to return to the sea.

YIN OF OMISSION and YANG OF CRAFTING THE PRODUCTION

That there is no dialogue in *Two Men and a Wardrobe* is the result of a principled decision on Polanski's part. When asked about this absence of dialogue, the filmmaker replied:

...I think that in a short it's unpleasant to use dialogue. It's like a *piece* of a feature film. [...] When you use people in a short, if they talk you expect it's going to last for two hours. It's not natural, not proper, to the form (Gelmis 1971: 145).

Not using dialogue as a storytelling resource is *yin*, a holding back, an omission, which Polanski manages beautifully by having characters communicate with each other via body language. For example, in Shot 68 when the thug he plays in the film wants to take over the beating of Henryk, he looks over at the victim then up at the leader with a questioning nod of his head, to which the leader can simply nod "yes" in Shot 69.

However, the *yang* that more than makes up for the omission of dialogue is the brilliant music written for the film by Kryzsztof T. Komeda and performed by the composer's Sekstet Komedy. Polanski described Komeda as "our guru. We worshipped him for his modern pieces. Without him my short would never have come into existence." For Polanski, the music was "the catchy, lilting accompaniment that contributed so much to [the film's] atmosphere" (Polanski 1982: 124), while for a commentator named Paul Davay the music was "full of melancholy" and the parts "for accompanied clarinet or piano alone were especially moving" (cited in Belmans 1971: 15, my trans.).

This music is an important element in the *yang of crafting the production.*

YIN OF NON-DOING and YANG OF DOING

Near the end of the film, in a scene we have already discussed, something Henryk and Jakub do *not* do is important for the viewer to notice and consider.

Having decided to return to the sea after their sixth and final defeat, and making their way across the beach which is now covered by hundreds of mud pies made by a little boy playing in the sand (Shot 93), the two men do *not* disturb any of the mud pies. Instead, they carefully weave a path between the sand constructions (Shot 94). This *yin of non-doing* is significant because it shows that despite the beatings and other defeats they have suffered, they have not become embittered or insensitive to the feelings of others

Hence their doing while non-doing in Shot 94 – making their way to the water but not treading on any of the mud pies in the process.

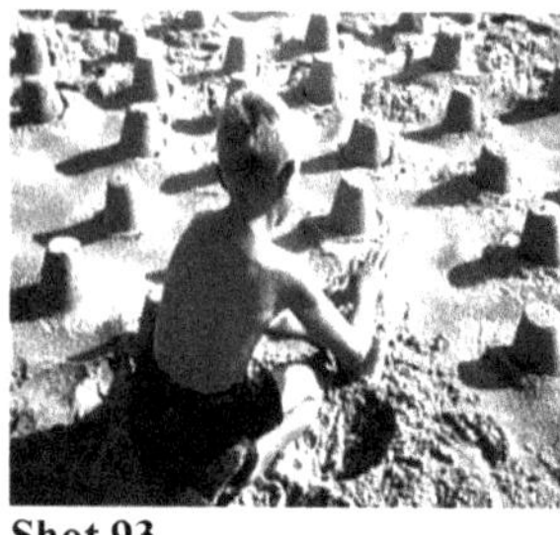
Shot 93

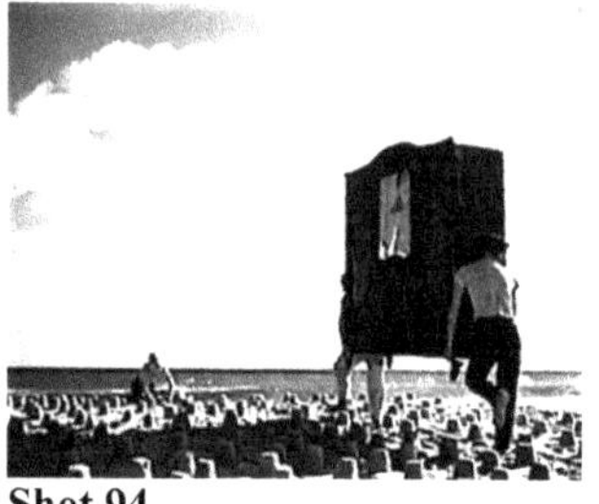
Shot 94

Shot 94 was badly misread by one commentator, the highly distinguished founder of the Belgian Cinémathèque, who wrote:

> The final image, easily symbolic, has a rare eloquence about it: the two men cross the beach once again, kicking in the numerous mud pies that had been built by the children, while returning to the sea (Thirifays 1958, my translation).

An extra shot – high angle, down onto the feet and sand – could have shown more clearly that the men were carefully avoiding the mud pies.

The *yang of structure* (serialities and symmetry), *yang of causality*, and inclusion of Komeda's music in the *yang of crafting the production*, are all played off against the *yin of interpretability* and the *yin of omission*, as described above, with other *yin yang* complementarities – the *yin of vulnerability* and *yang of being in charge*, the *yin of non-doing* and *yang of doing* – also contributing to the richness and balance of this film.

SHORT FILM 2

The Office / Urzad

Krzysztof Kieslowski, Poland, 1966, 6 minutes, B/W

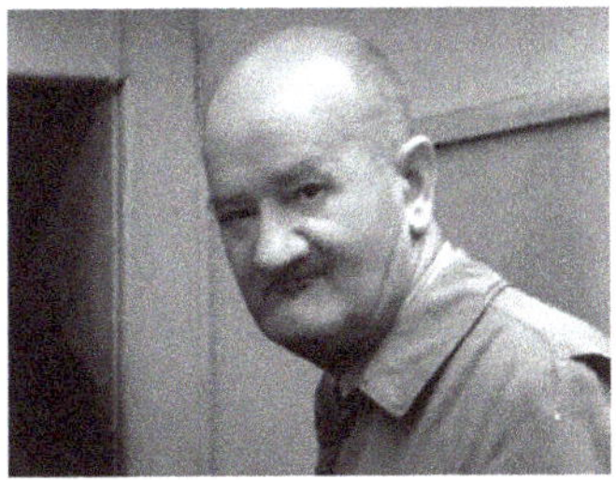

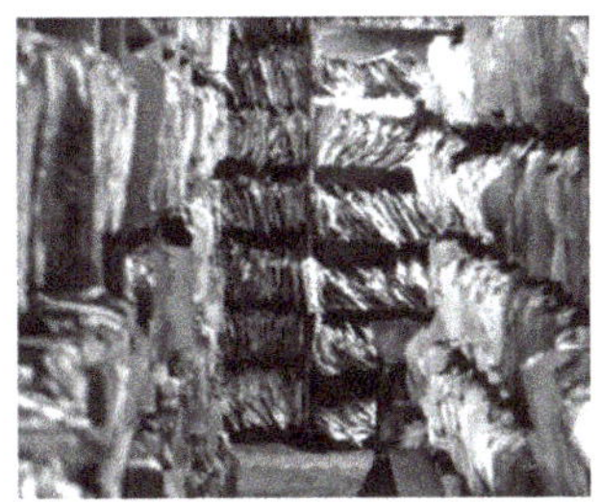

Direction and screenplay	Krzysztof Kieslowski
Cinematography	Lechoslaw Trzesowski
Editing	Janina Grosicka
Sound	Marta Stankiewicz
Production manager	Tadeusz Lubczynski
Production company	Lodz Film School, PWSTiF
Academic advisors	Jerzy Bossak, Kazimierz Karabasz, Kurt Weber

Link to the film: https://www.youtube.com/watch?v=sKqIf-TsEO0

Despite its extraordinary qualities, *Urzad* is often overlooked in discussions of Kieslowski's films. The director himself makes no mention of it in the interviews that were the basis for *Kieslowski on Kieslowski*, ed. Danusia Stok (London/Boston: Faber and Faber, 1993). And *Urzad* was not included in the 2-DVD set of Kieslowski's documentaries. This film proves that a documentary doesn't have to run 90 min. in order to treat an issue in a powerful and enduring manner.

Synopsis

The setting is a government office in which elderly people apply for their pensions. With little empathy or patience, the clerks (two younger women) working there point out errors in the applications, if for example a client brought two certificates instead of one to prove a claim (Shots 1 and 2), or if a school had used a square stamp to validate a form when a round one was expected (Shot 16), and send the petitioners away requiring that additional forms be filled out. Occasionally the clerks take a break making tea (Shots 42–43), while their clients are asked to wait (Shot 44) and stand around in silence until the clerks are ready to speak with them again. The first 52 shots are all made in the public area of the government office, in which the clients await their turns at counters where windows separate them from the clerks. From Shot 53 to the film's final shot, Shot 64, we see mainly an archive room, undoubtedly accessible only to staff. As the shots made in this room show thousands of folders crammed onto shelves and gathering dust, we hear a clerk's voice repeating a total of six times (Shots 54, 56, 59, 60, 61, 62) that a petitioner must show "what you've been doing throughout your lifetime."

A shot-by-shot breakdown of *The Office*

What follows is merely a schematic outline of the film, making it possible to refer to specific shots by number.

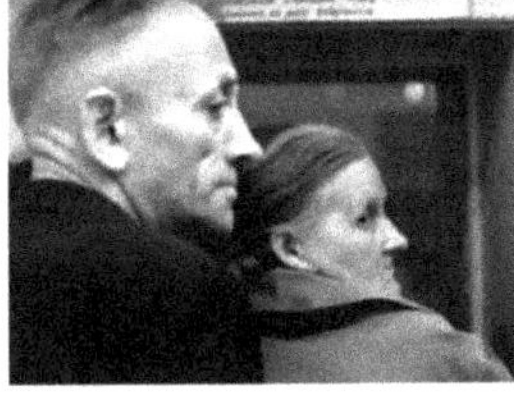
Shot 1

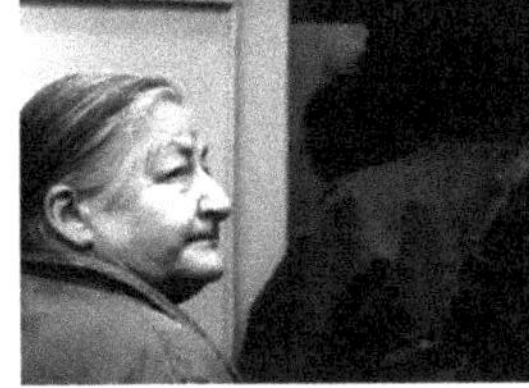
Shot 2

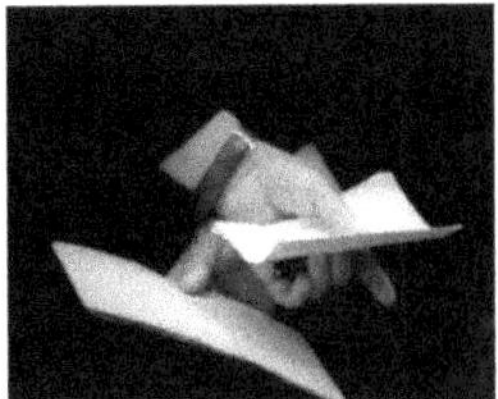
Shot 3

CLERK: You should bring a certificate from work.
CLIENT: But I've already brought one.
CLERK: This certificate?
CLIENT: Hold on, may I have a closer look, because I can't see it well without my glasses.
CLERK: Since we have two different certificates... we can't authorize them. They're not valid. We have to fill in the missing information ourselves, explain things.
CLIENT: But listen, I've brought a small one.
CLERK: But what I'm saying is that if we have two different certificates, madam, we can't pay you your disability payment...in a beneficial way for you.

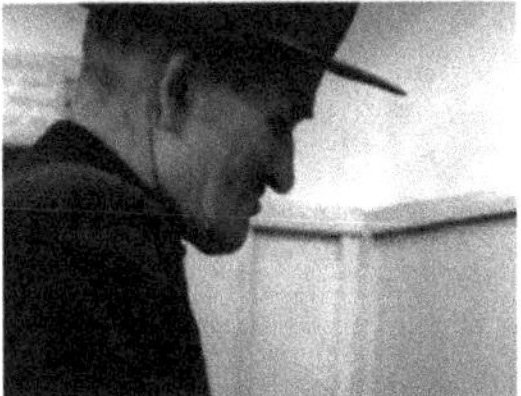
Shot 4

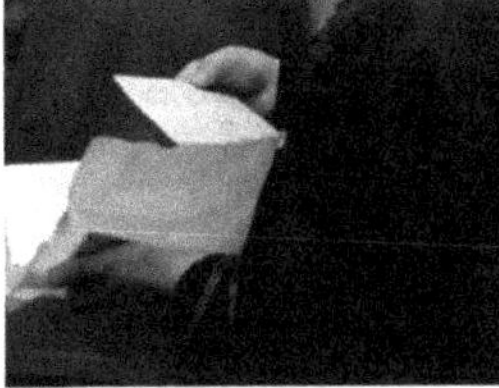
Shot 5

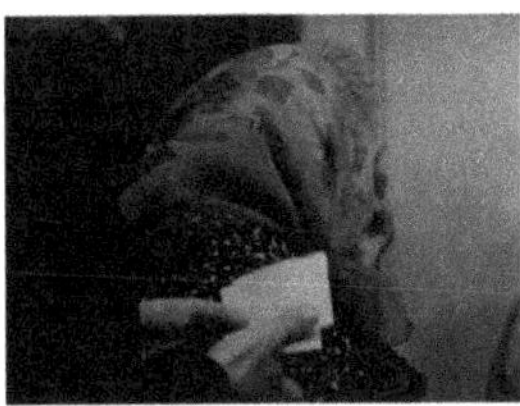
Shot 6

CLIENT: But I've already delivered the paper I was required to bring.
CLERK: So as I have been telling you, they're two different ones.
CLIENT: So, now yet another one?
CLERK: Yes, you now have to bring a certificate to cancel the previous one.

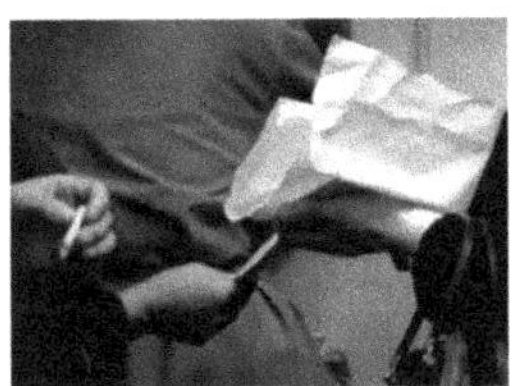
Shot 7

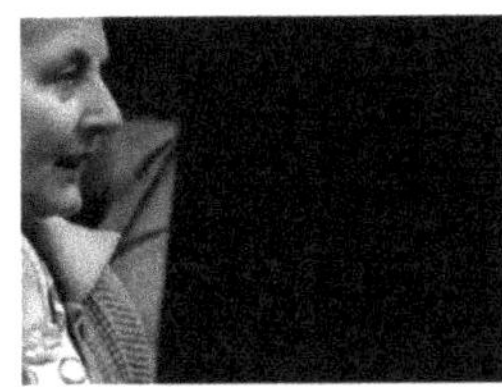
Shot 8

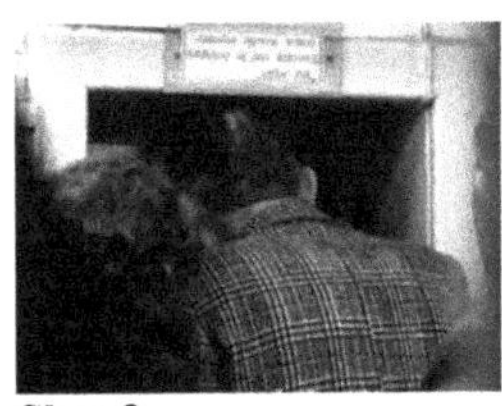
Shot 9

CLIENT: That's not possible. So now I have to go there to get it? That's not possible.

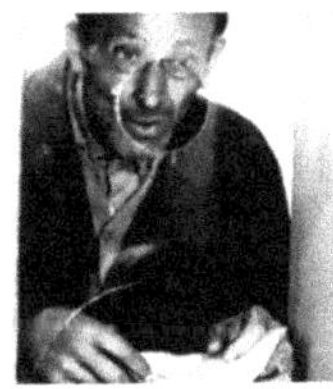
Shot 10

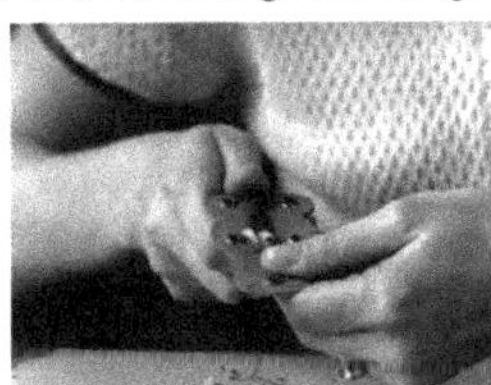
Shot 11

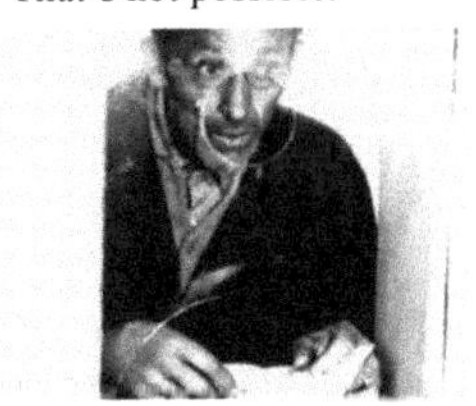
Shot 12

CLIENT: Madam, I...
CLERK: Please wait... [On telephone] Pensions, may I help you? Which district do you belong to? You will get the forms there. These are special forms. There are a few questions there and you have to answer them.... You're welcome.

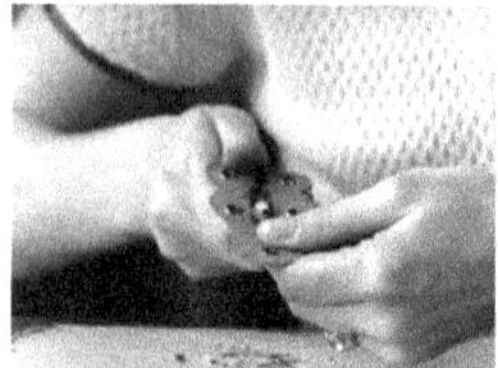

Shot 13
CLIENT: I sent a certificate saying that my daughter goes to school. I was asked to send one and I did it.

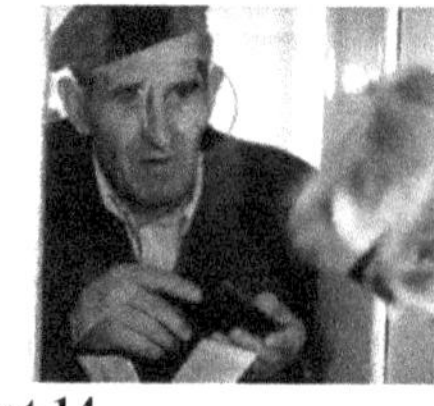

Shot 14
CLERK: Yes, because your daughter is sixteen now, the payment has been withdrawn.
CLIENT: I haven't heard from anyone so I had another certificate ready in case it was needed.

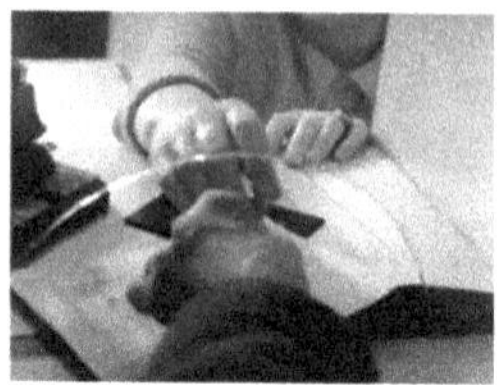

Shot 15
CLERK: Mister, doesn't the school have a round stamp?
CLIENT: Yes it does.

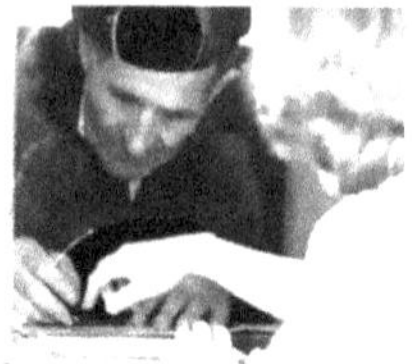

Shot 16
CLERK: So the certificate has to be stamped with the round stamp.

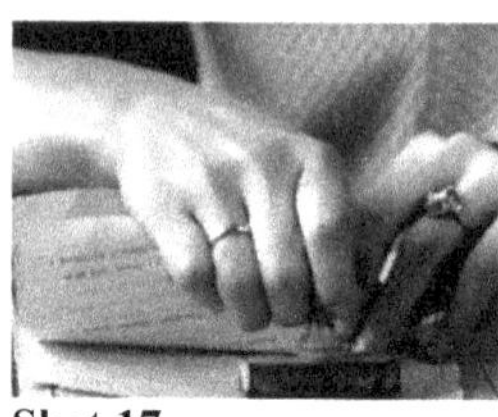

Shot 17
CLIENT: Good, as a precaution I took the one with a round stamp.

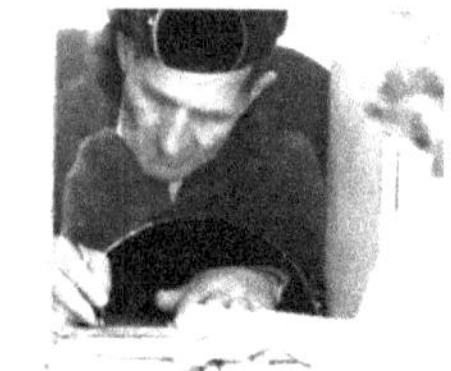

Shot 18
CLERK: Well, you should have given in the one with the round stamp in the first place.

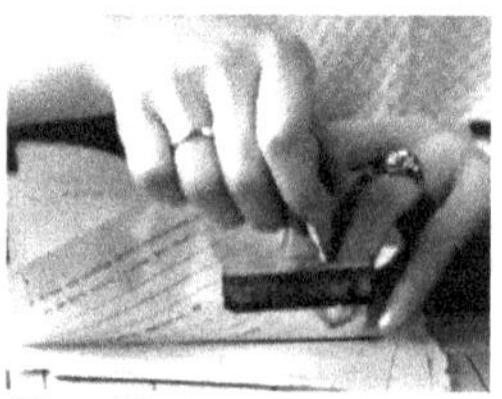

Shot 19
CLIENT: At first I didn't know that they wouldn't recognize the one with the square stamp.

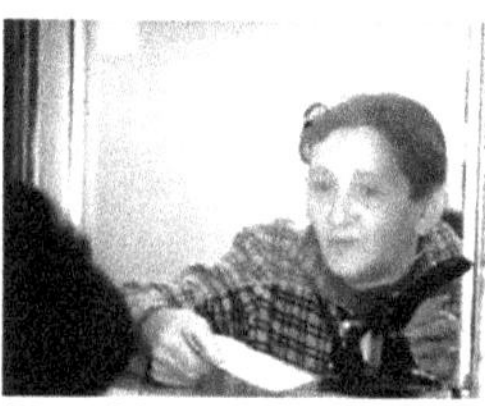

Shot 20
CLIENT: Madam, I want to ask you...

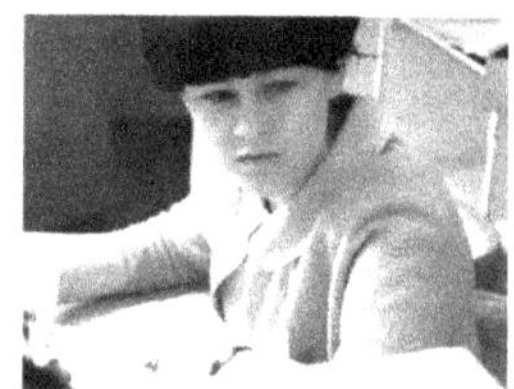

Shot 21
CLIENT: ...because you know I got the pension from the court.
CLERK: Have you got the pension postal order?

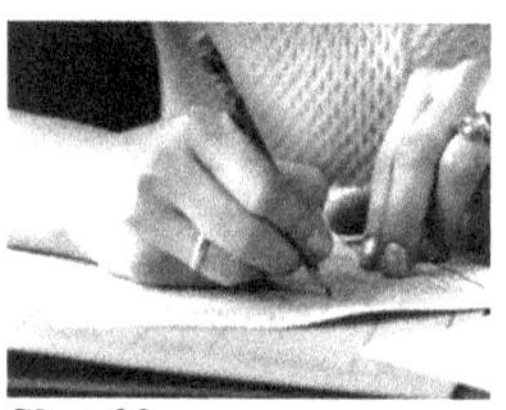

Shot 22
CLIENT: Actually the court rendered its verdict granting me 108 zloties more per child.

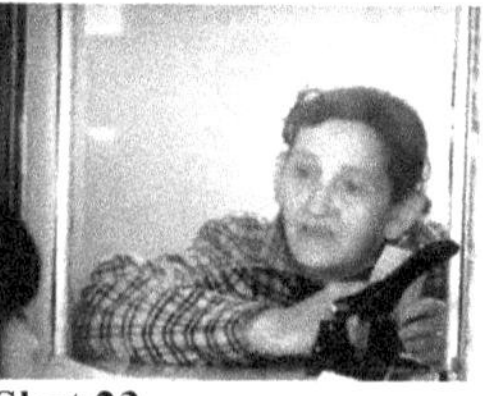

Shot 23
CLERK: We don't deal with such cases here.

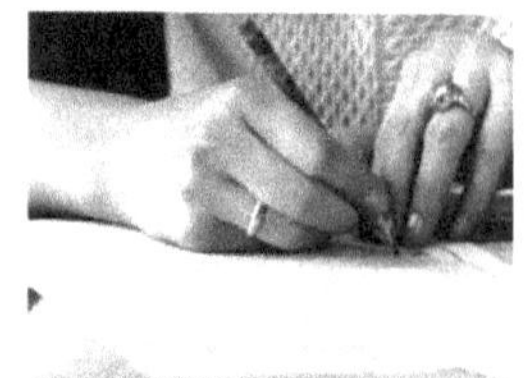

Shot 24
CLIENT: But it seems to me that the court will send it here.
CLERK: Madam, there isn't anything from the court here.
CLIENT: But you'll probably get it. You will get it, madam.

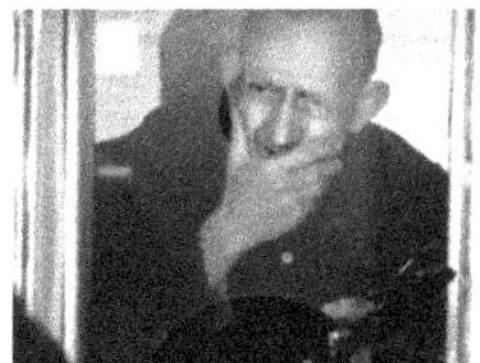

Shot 25
CLERK: Why are you submitting this here?
CLIENT: I wanted to find out…

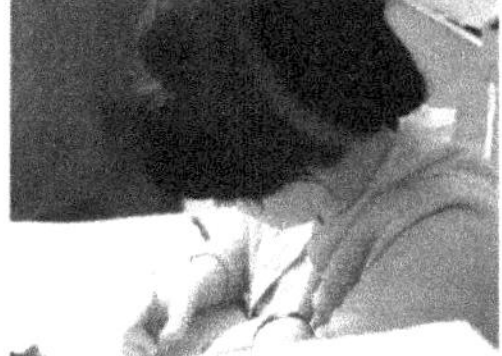

Shot 26
CLERK: Yes, and now what do you want?
CLIENT: I don't know how to do it.

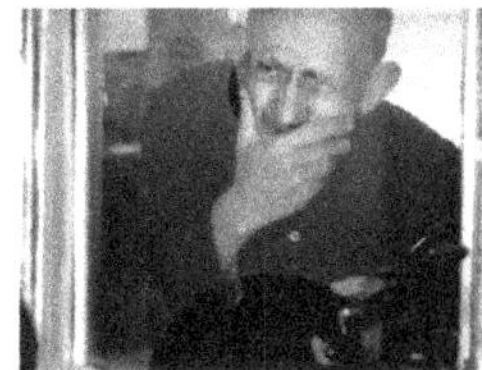

Shot 27
CLERK: When did you see the commission? Have you got the pronouncement from the district commission?

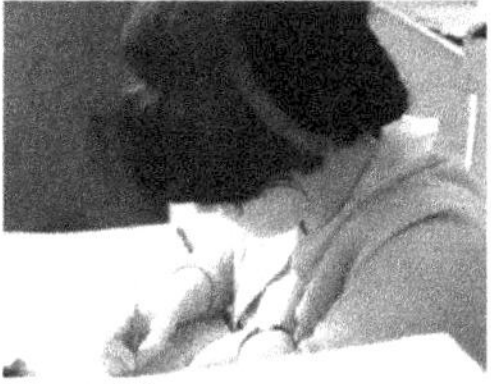

Shot 28
CLIENT: Is it this white one?

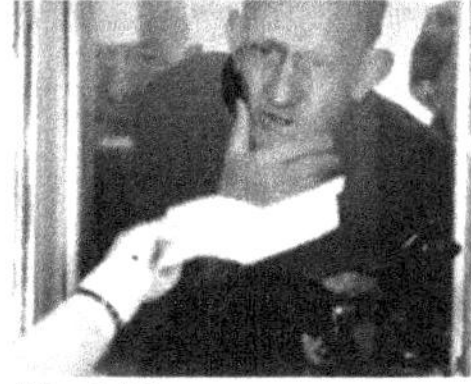

Shot 29
CLERK: This is the pronouncement from the commission, not the decision.

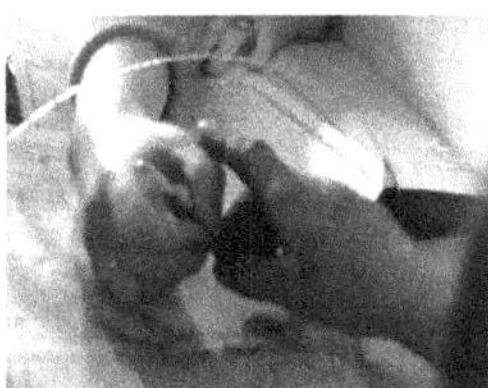

Shot 30
CLERK: You had the right to make a claim to the provincial administration within 14 days.

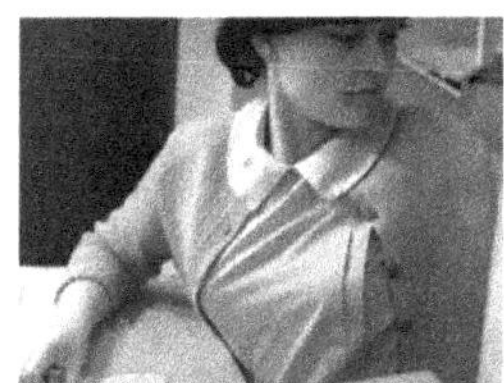

Shot 31

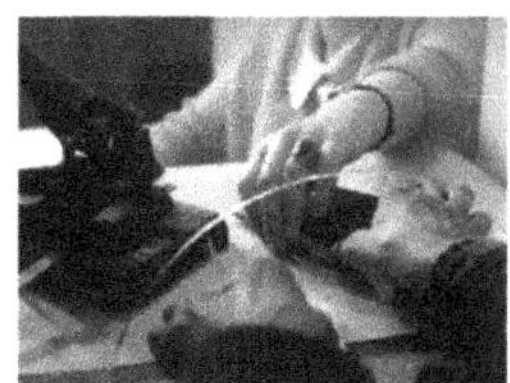

Shot 32
CLERK: And you have made a claim, haven't you? So now you can only appeal this decision to the court.

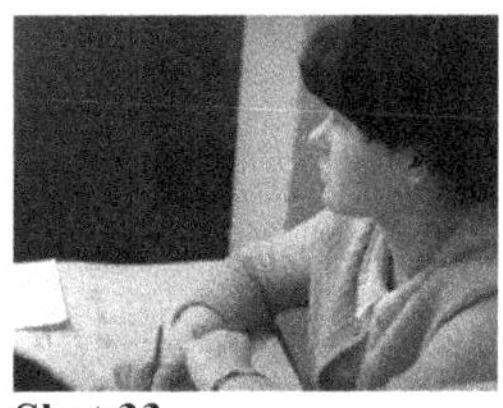

Shot 33
CLIENT: I've just arrived for my mother's funeral and have just buried her.

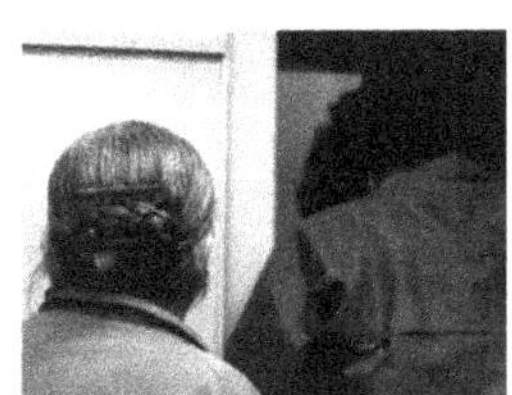

Shot 34
CLIENT: As she was a pensioner, can you tell me if I can get the money for the funeral straight away?

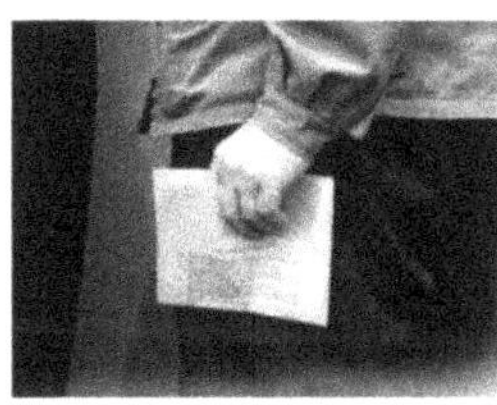

Shot 35

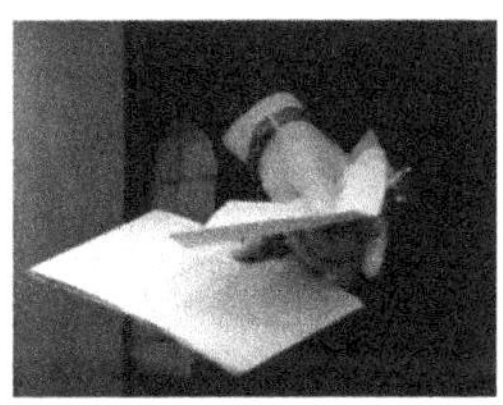

Shot 36
CLERK: When did your mother die?
CLIENT: On the 25th

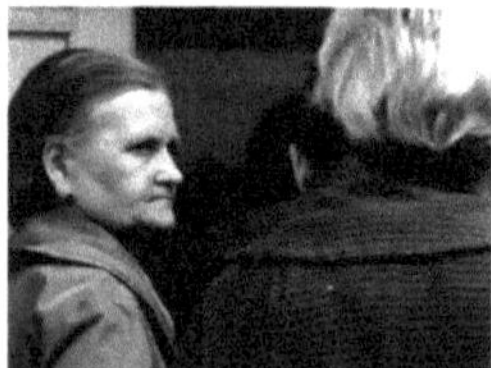

Shot 37
CLERK: No.

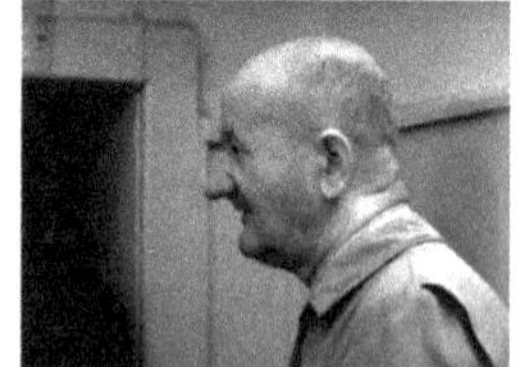

Shot 38
CLERK: Next, please.
CLIENT: Why didn't I get my back payments?
CLERK: Madam, in order to explain this to you, I would have to read you the verdicts...

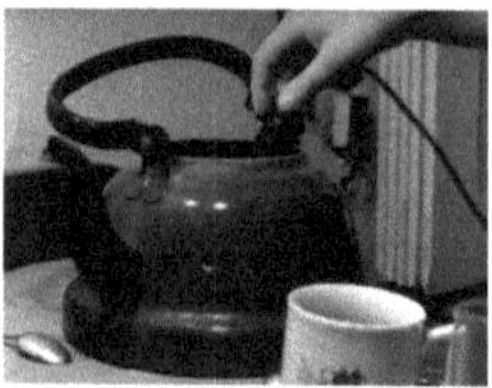

Shot 39
CLERK: ...of both the court and the tribunal.

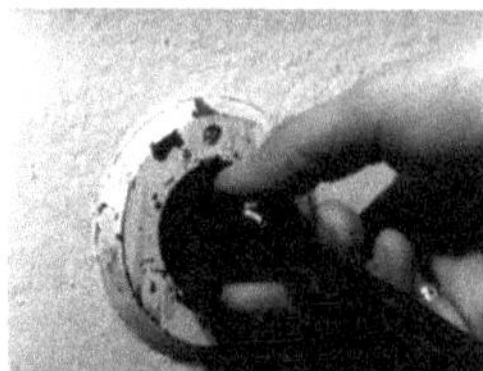

Shot 40
CLERK: Yes, the case was presented to the court because we had cancelled your pension. And you appealed to the court?

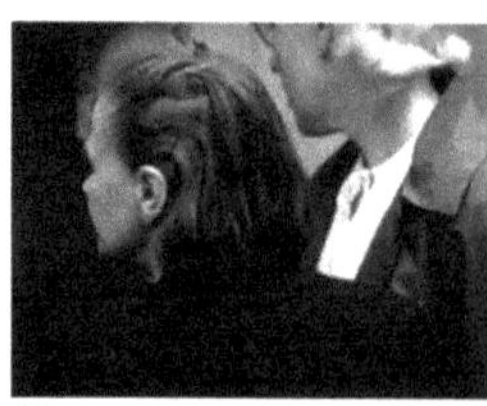

Shot 41
CLERK: The court granted you the pension but we didn't agree with the verdict

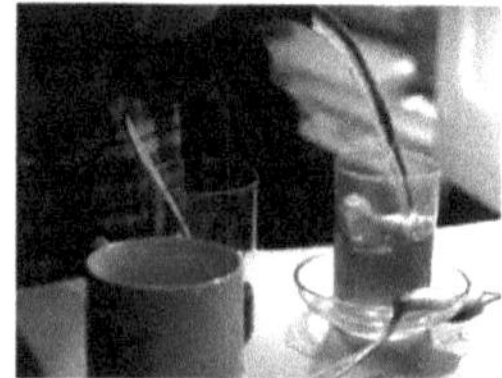

Shot 42
CLERK: ...of the court so we appealed to the National Insurance Tribunal.

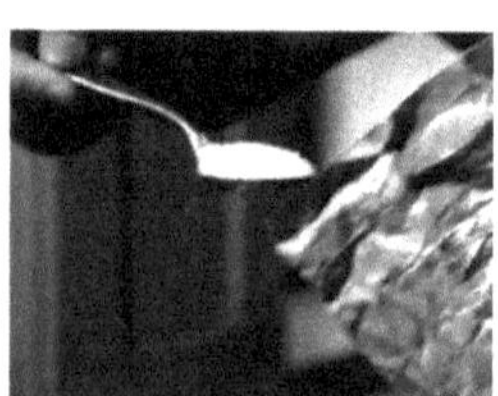

Shot 43a

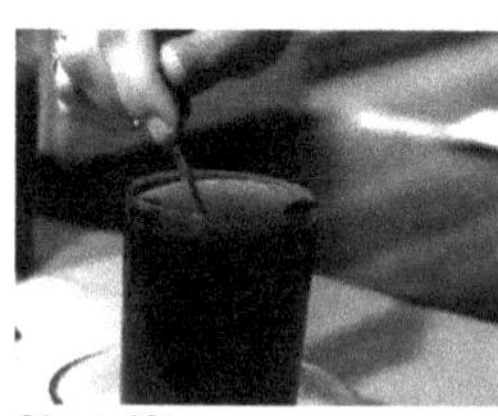

Shot 43b
CLERK: The Tribunal reversed the court's decision and the pension was stopped.
CLIENT: But the court granted me the pension and though it was due me, it wasn't paid.

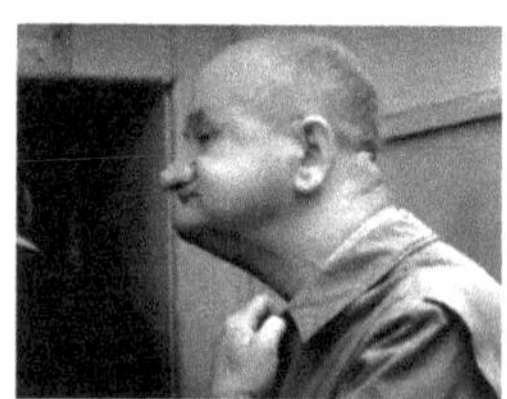

Shot 44
CLERK: Could you please wait?

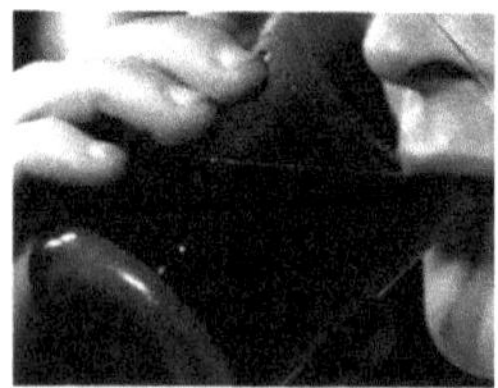

Sho 45

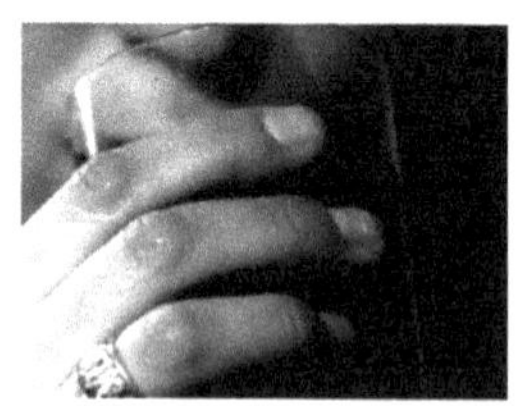

Shot 46

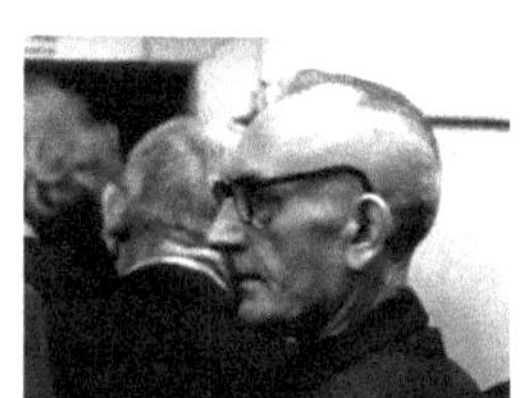

Shot 47

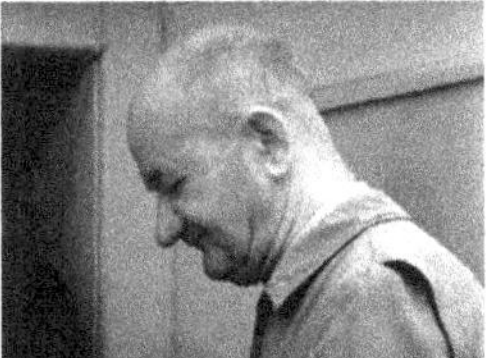
Shot 48

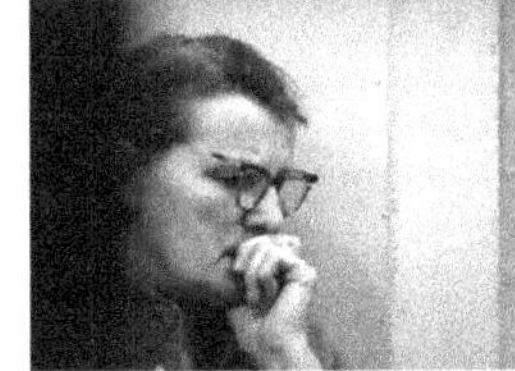
Shot 49

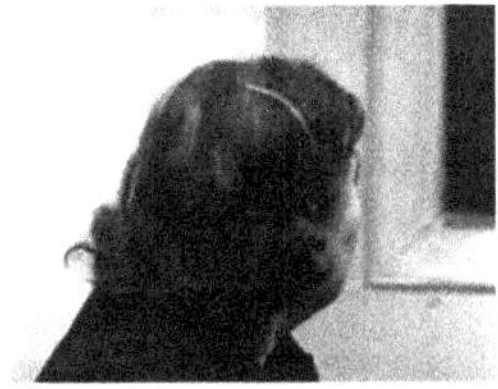
Shot 50

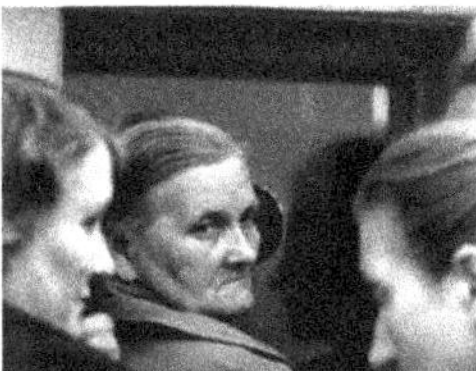
Shot 51

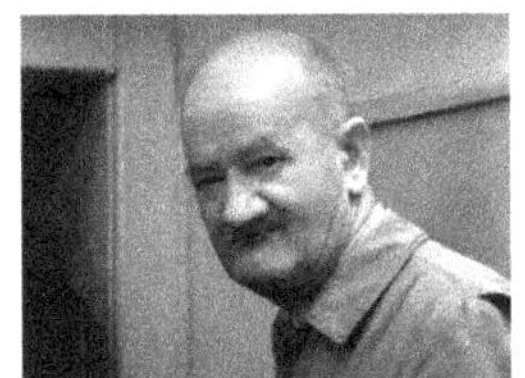
Shot 52
CLERK: Yes please.
CLIENT: Could you please tell me, madam, my husband has just left the hospital. The papers are here. And I'd like to know when he's going to be paid his pension because I have no money to live on.

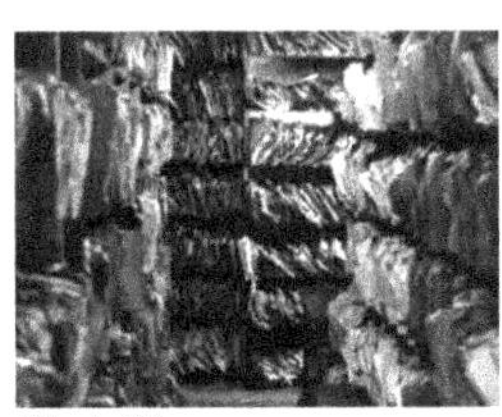
Shot 53
CLERK: Now you can submit a new application.
CLIENT Yes, now I have already two slips.

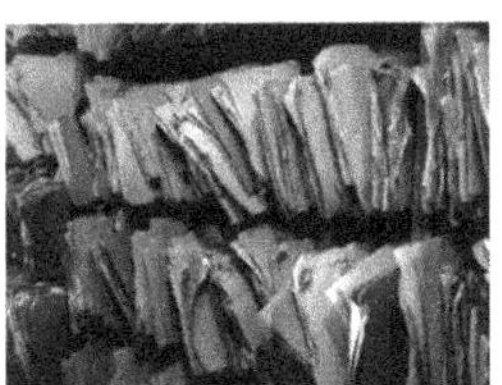
Shot 54
CLERK: There's a special form in which you specify what you have been doing throughout your lifetime.

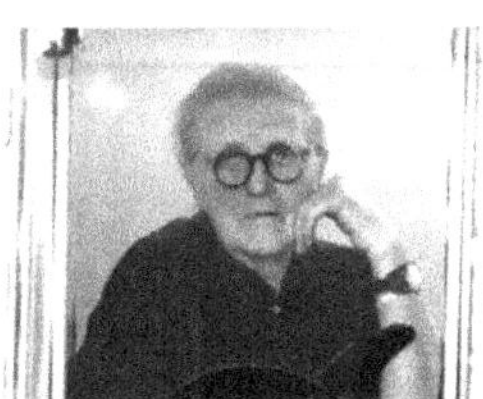
Shot 55
CLERK: So you should write that "From this date … to this date … I worked in these places. I have no documents."

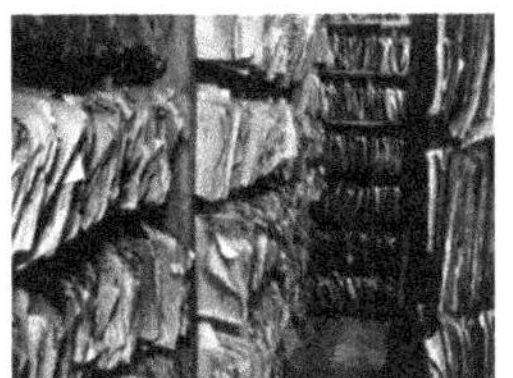
Shot 56
CLERK: What you've been doing throughout your lifetime. Where you were working, which workplaces…

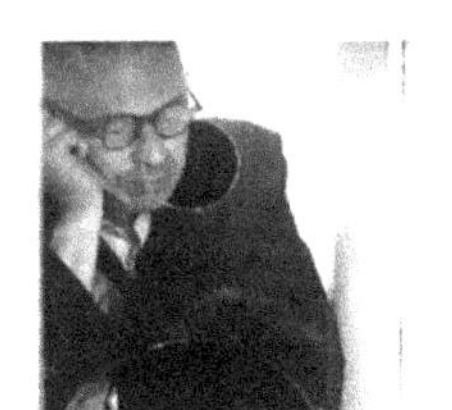
Shot 57

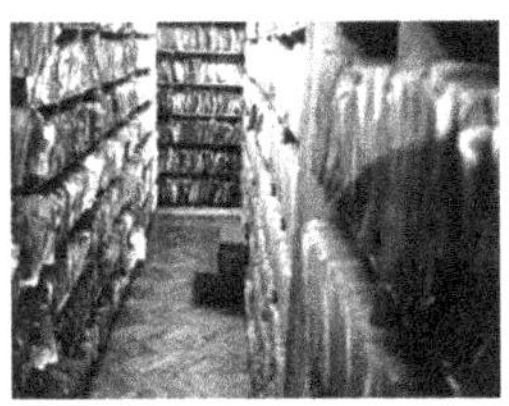
Shot 58
CLERK: Fill in this form yourself and answer all the questions 'yes' or 'no.'

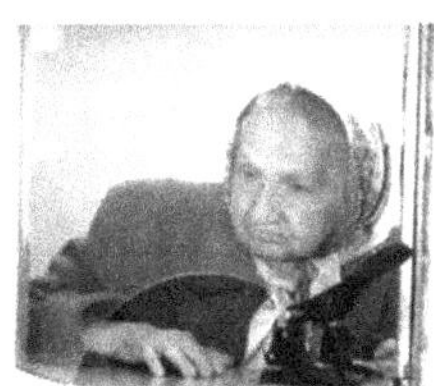
Shot 59
CLERK: And here in this form you specify what you have been doing throughout your lifetime.

Shot 60
CLERK: There is a form in which you say what you've been doing throughout your lifetime.

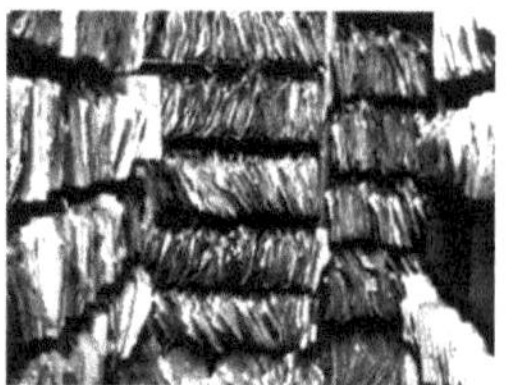

Shot 61
CLERK: ...and you say what you've been doing throughout your lifetime.

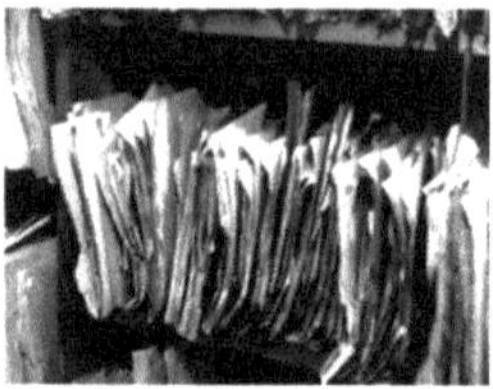

Shot 62
CLERK ...what you've been doing throughout your lifetime...

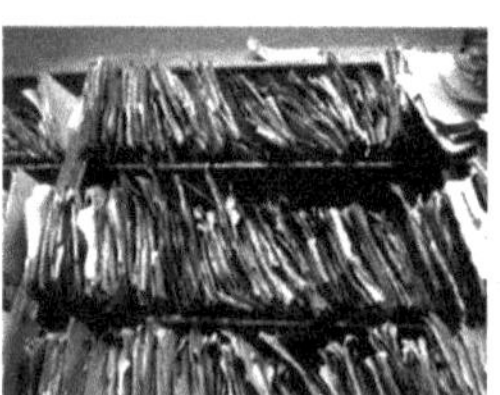

Shot 63

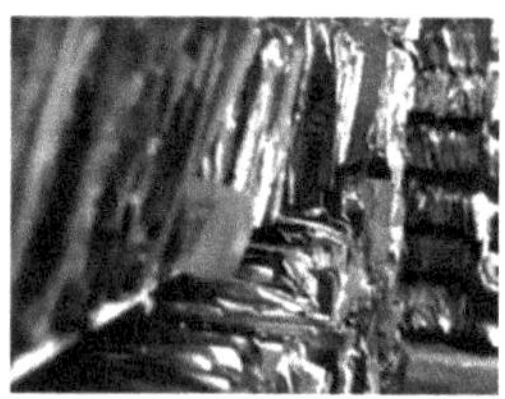

Shot 64a

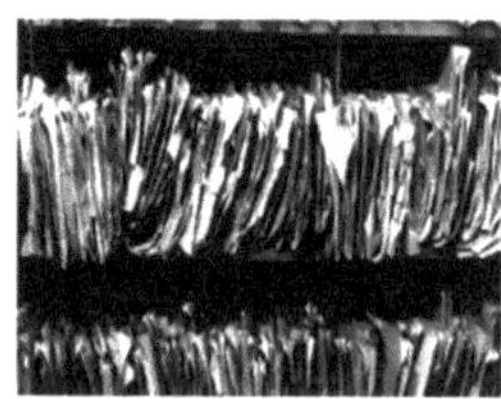

Shot 64b

YIN OF VULNERABILITY and YANG OF BEING IN CHARGE

This film is populated by two sets of characters who meet at the government office. Embodying the *yin of vulnerability* are the elderly clients who have come seeking payments to which they are entitled and which will probably be denied to them by the two younger clerks who enjoy the *yang of being in charge*. The clerks generally find fault with the clients' documentation, which for example may have been mistakenly validated with a square stamp instead of a round one. The clients are dependent on the clerks and have no choice but to follow their instructions and comply with their demands. And there is no trace of empathy in a clerk's dismissive treatment of a client who, for example, has just buried her mother (Shots 33–37).

Though the boundaries between documentary and fiction are more porous than was once believed, there is nothing in the scarce material on *The Office* to suggest that Kieslowski in any way prompted either clerks or clients to say or to do anything he had scripted for them or that they would not have otherwise done if he weren't there. It is therefore reasonable to assume that the interactions between clerks and clients as depicted in this film are authentic and free of any interference on the part of the filmmaker.

YIN OF INTERPRETABILITY and YANG OF STRUCTURE

The editing of this film is disjunctive, in the sense that image and voice are put together in the editing process as Kieslowski chose, rather than as dictated by the recorded material. Shot 14 is one of the few shots in *The Office* in which sound and image are synchronous, with the lip movements of the person shown on screen clearly in sync with the utterances we hear spoken. As I have suggested in an earlier piece, the disjunction of sound and image

> gives the viewer an opportunity to make his or her own connections between what is said and what is seen, as a step toward constructing a meaning for the film as a whole. In this way, the film is unusually rich in subtext, due not only to the resonances of the individual spoken and visual elements in themselves but also to the disjunctive relationships between those elements. Further contributing to this richness of subtext is

the absence of any guiding commentary addressed to the viewer and telling him or her how to understand what is going on (Raskin 2006: 81).

At no point in this film do we hear the voice of the director himself or of a surrogate, guiding our understanding and helping us to make sense of what we are shown, as is the case for example in Alain Resnais' masterpiece, *Night and Fog* (1956), in which the narration, written by Jean Cayrol and delivered by Michel Bouquet, helps the viewer to grasp the intended point of the film in its final moments: that the threat of the death camps is far from over and that we ourselves may be carriers of the contagion.

With *The Office*, the task of working out the film's intended meaning is left entirely to us by a director who holds back even as the film ends, leaving it to us to connect the dots and make whatever sense we can of the juxtaposed images and voices.

The remainder of this discussion will focus on the final sequence, the start of which I will place at Shot 52, when dialogue resumes after a stretch of seven shots with no voices heard.

There are two noteworthy *serialities* to point out in this final sequence:

- Audio: Instructions to the clients are now repeated six times. Clients are to write down in special forms "what you have been doing throughout your life" (Shots 54, 56, 59, 60, 61, 62).
- Video: We see nine shots of folders gathering dust on shelves in the storage room (Shots 53, 54, 56, 58, 60, 61, 62, 63, 64).

These *serialities* constitute a *yang of structure* that can serve as a counterweight to the *yin of interpretability*. But do we have an interpretive option for connecting the audio and visual serialities of this final sequence?

One such option would be to assume that if the clients comply with the instructions they are given, and take the trouble of writing down everything they have been doing throughout their lives, those forms may simply be placed unread on the dust-gathering shelves, which would make the very act of writing those autobiographical pages an almost comically absurd exercise in futility. Without mentioning that interpretive option, Ib Bondebjerg has aptly characterized this final sequence as the most explicitly Kafkaesque portion of the film (2002: 79).

One remaining complementarity worth mentioning concerns the storage room and the public part of the office, which constitute *loci* of *yin* and *yang*, respectively – with hidden realities (files gathering dust on shelves) in the one and appearances of a functioning support system in the other.

SHORT FILM 3

Andy Warhol Eating a Hamburger.
Jørgen Leth, Denmark, 1982, 4 min. 28 sec., color.

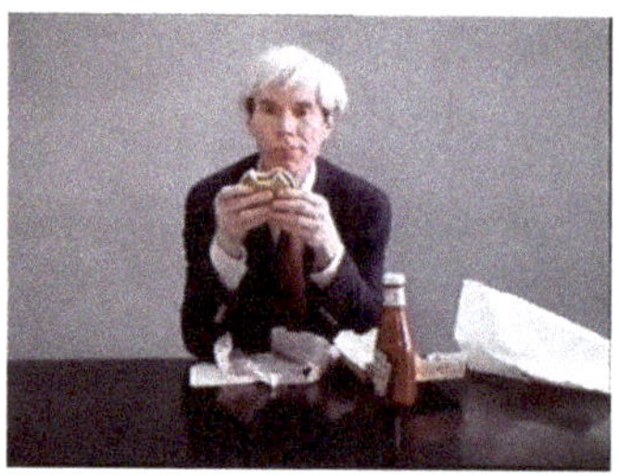

Director: Jørgen Leth
Writer: Ole John
Cinematographer: Dan Holmberg
Production and Distribution: Sunset Productions and Statens Filmcentral

Link to the film:
https://www.youtube.com/watch?v=H-t-IxJctVM

Though originally a segment of Jørgen Leth's anthology film, *66 Scenes from America* (1982, 42 min.), *Andy Warhol Eating a Hamburger* has taken on a life of its own and can now be considered a short film in its own right. In 2019, part of it was used in a Superbowl ad, and there are countless parodies of it on YouTube, some funnier than others. Iggy Pop eats a hamburger in one of them. They show to what an extraordinary degree this little film has become a familiar enough part of popular culture in America for people to enjoy playing with the concept and imagery.

Synopsis

Seated at a table with a Burger King bag and bottle of ketchup just to his left, Andy Warhol looks at the camera then removes a napkin and cardboard Whopper box from the bag. He opens the box, removes and unwraps the burger, lifts the top half of the bun off the burger, then picks up and opens the ketchup bottle. He manages with difficulty to pour some ketchup onto the wrapping paper (under his breath saying "It doesn't come out"), puts the bun back on the burger which he dips into the ketchup and takes a bite. While chewing he replaces the cap on the ketchup bottle, soon wipes his mouth with a napkin and continues eating. After a while, he removes the remaining top half of the bun and folds the bottom half over what is left of the burger and continues eating. He drops a bit of unfinished burger onto the paper, wipes his mouth, packs everything up into the bag, wipes his mouth again, drops the last napkin into the bag which he crumples, puts the crumpled bag and ketchup bottle out of the way, and with hands folded, looks into the camera. Then for about 45 awkward seconds, his eyes wander and he looks uncomfortable, as though not quite knowing what to do with himself. Finally he says, "Uh, my name is Andy Warhol and I just finished eating a hamburger." After another beat, we hear Jørgen Leth (off camera) saying "Burger, New York."

Schematic breakdown of ***Andy Warhol Eating a Hamburger***, which consists of a single, unbroken shot.

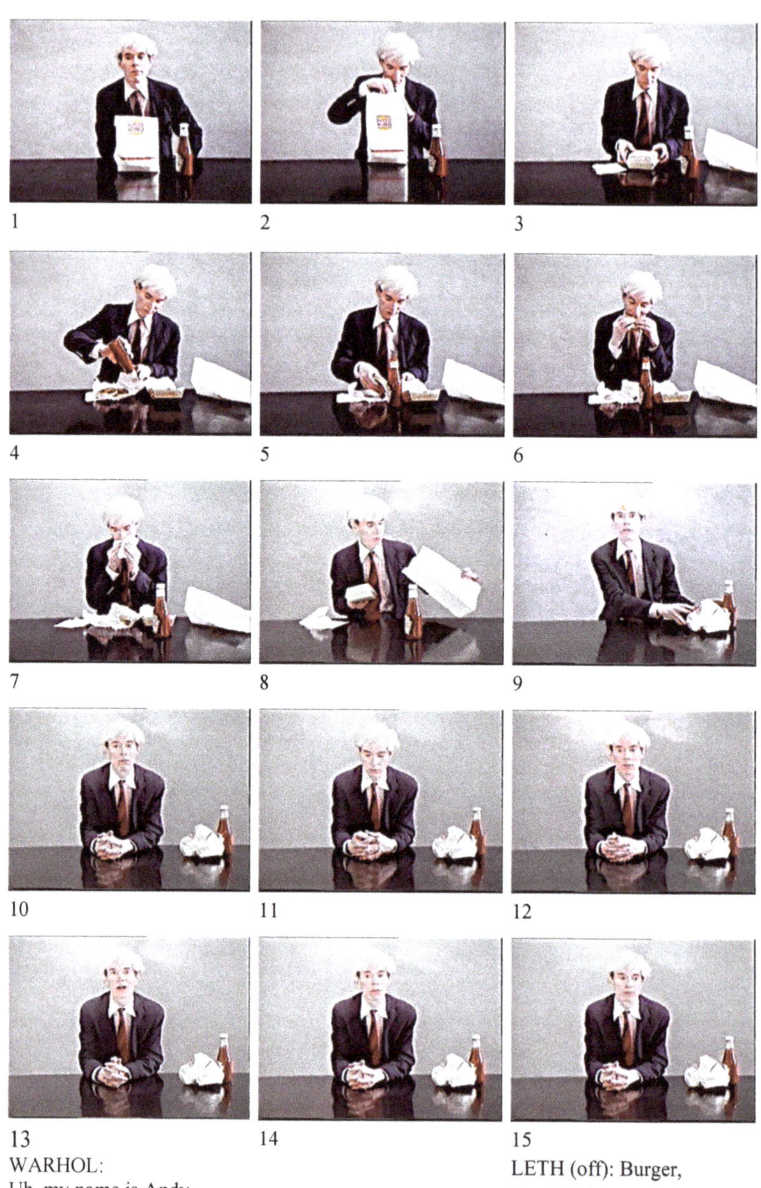

1 2 3

4 5 6

7 8 9

10 11 12

13
WARHOL:
Uh, my name is Andy Warhol and I just finished eating a hamburger.

14

15
LETH (off): Burger, New York.

YIN OF WELCOMING THE GIFTS OF CHANCE and YANG OF CRAFTING THE PRODUCTION (for the filmmaker)

When Jørgen Leth and his crew met with Andy Warhol at The Factory and the conditions for the shoot were finalized, it was agreed that the film would be a single continuous take, with no possibility of a second try or any editing.

During the shoot, not everything went as smoothly as planned. Leth regretted providing a new bottle of ketchup, since it didn't pour easily when Warhol tried to shake some drops out of it (Frame 4). And Leth regretted not providing something for Warhol to drink.

But what was most unexpected was the approximately 45-second pause between the moment Warhol had cleared the table (Frame 10), and the moment he spoke his one line (Frame 13). During those 45 seconds – undoubtedly the most riveting portion of the film thanks to its almost agonizing awkwardness – Warhol fidgeted and appeared lost, not knowing where to look or what to do. Finally he spoke his line, "Uh, my name is Andy Warhol and I just finished eating a hamburger."

As it turns out, that long pause was unintended. Leth explains:

> Warhol happens to misunderstand what he's supposed to do, so there's a long pause after he's finished eating his hamburger during which time he simply sits there, ready. His eyes flicker around and he doesn't utter the sentence immediately after he's finished eating as I'd expected him to do. He sits there and we see the concern in his eyes, the suspense almost kills us, although we feel compassion too in a way. At last, after a noticeable pause, he says the phrase and the explanation for the delay is that he was waiting for a cue. Now this delay gives the scene a quite different dimension, I think (Hjort and Bondebjerg 2000: 70-71).

Leth considered this delay to be "an involuntary and perfectly wonderful gift, which precisely makes me believe in the magical significance of chance." Unlike other filmmakers who make a point of controlling their productions in accordance with preordained rules, Leth is a great believer in letting chance work its magic. The statement cited above continues this way:

> I like to think of many of these [chance occurrences during filming], which are inscribed within the film, as comprising a kind of mysterious trace, that is at some level, as I've already suggested, I really believe in a kind of magic of the film material […] I've been committed to the idea of controlling things up to a certain point. And beyond that point I prefer some uncharted territory, so that chance and circumstances can play a role. That openness is tremendously important, because it also explains why I, at some deep level, refuse to operate with banal dramaturgical principles. It's very important to me that my films be moved by a different kind of spirit, that their pulse be different. […]

Whenever appropriate, Jørgen Leth gladly lets go of his control of the production process, of his crafting of that process, to allow for the gifts of chance to work their magic, when unplanned events occur during a shoot and bring his film to life in entirely unexpected ways.

YIN OF NON-DOING and YANG OF DOING
(for the actor)

Now let's consider the shoot once again, but this time from the perspective of the actor, Andy Warhol, rather than the filmmaker.

For Warhol, the 45 seconds were a period of holding back, of non-doing, as he waited for his cue. He chose to wait but probably thought he had no choice in the matter, until he reached the point where he could no longer believe a cue could still be on its way and *non-doing* gave way to *doing*.

SHORT FILM 4

With Raised Hands / Z podniesionymi rekami

Mitko Panov, Poland, 1985, 5 min., b/w

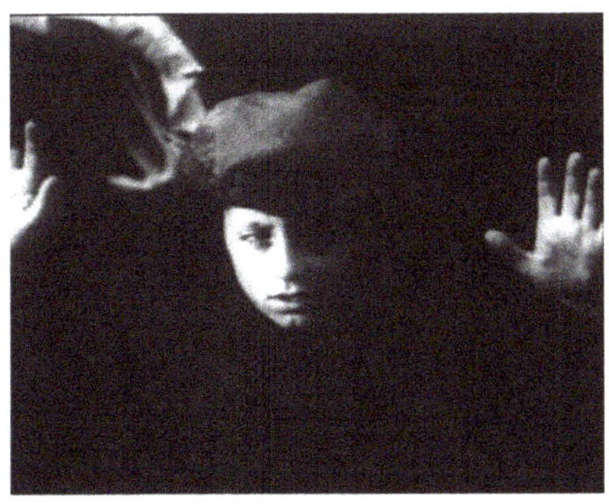

Direction and screenplay	Mitko Panov
Cinematography	Jarek Szoda
Film Editor	Halina Szalinska
Music	Janusz Hajdun
Production	PWSFTv&T (National School for Film, Television and Theater), Łódź, Poland
Cast	Etel Szyc, Monika Mozer, Jaroslaw Dunaj

Link to the film: https://vimeo.com/36044164

Golden Palm for Best Short Film, Cannes Film Festival, 1991.

Synopsis

This is an imagined reconstruction of the scene in which the iconic SS-photo on the following page was made and of what may have happened afterwards to the boy in the picture. A camera is set up and SS soldiers roughly push prisoners into place for the photo. A little boy is singled out for attention by the trooper in charge who picks up the boy's cap from the ground, places it firmly on his head and holds the boy's arms in the air. The boy runs to his mother and is pushed back into place, then coaxed and threatened to put his hands up, which he finally does, as in the well-known photo, to the trooper's satisfaction. A gust of wind suddenly blows the boy's cap off his head. After looking at the photographer and trooper in charge, he walks out of frame in the direction in which his cap was blown. He finds the cap, far from the scene of the filming, but before he can pick it up, it is blown away by another gust of wind, to a place even further away from the scene of the filming. Just as he reaches it, it is yet again blown further away. Finally, the boy grabs his cap and puts it firmly on his head. Off in the distance, the photographer is still visible to the boy. A girl at the scene of the filming tries to catch sight of the boy and the photographer then does so as well. But neither can see him now, as he is walking through an unguarded ghetto gate to freedom. When he is outside the gate and we can no longer see him, his cap goes flying up into the air and comes down again. Then once again it is thrown up into the air, but this time does not come down. Cars of a train now streak past and finally the iconic photograph fills the screen, with the final credits superimposed over the lower half of the image.

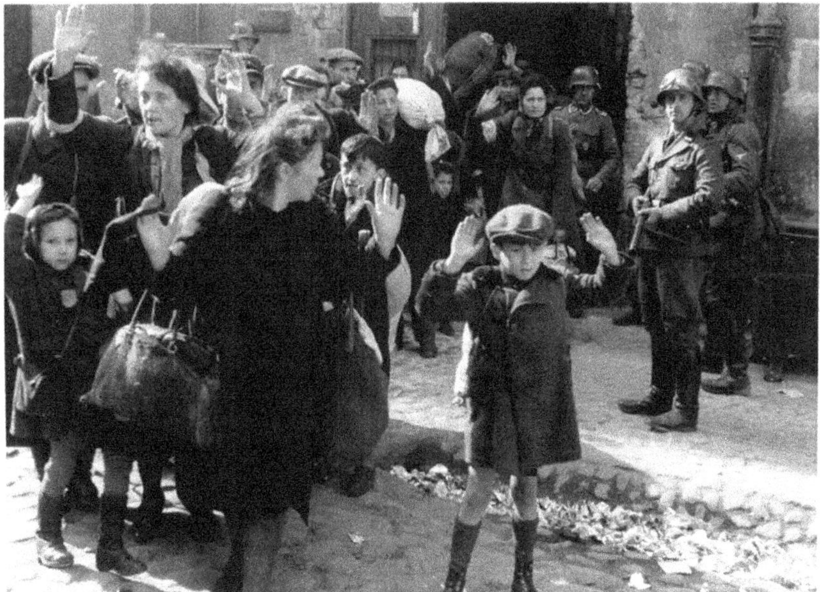

Figure 1. Widely considered the most iconic Holocaust photograph, this picture was taken by an SS photographer in 1943 and was one of 53 photos used in the "Stroop Report," a souvenir book made in only three or four copies when the Ghetto uprising was finally crushed after holding off the German forces far longer than expected. The identity and fate of the boy in the photo remains uncertain. For further details, see Raskin 2004.

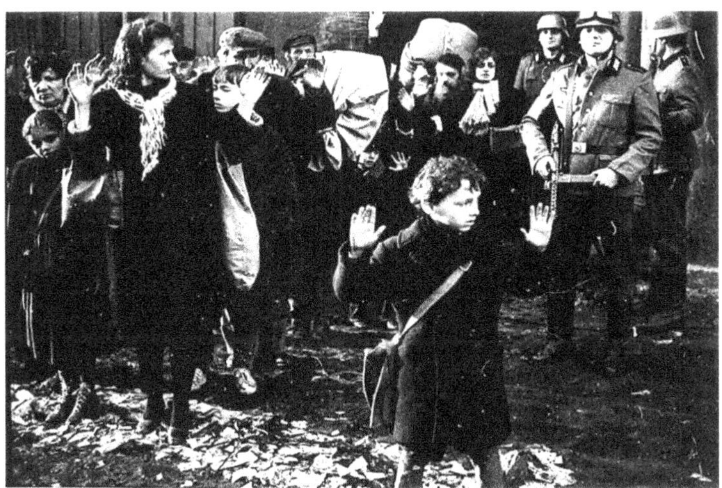

Shot 15. A frame in *With Raised Hands* nearly matching the SS photograph, but with the boy's cap missing due to a gust of wind.

Shot-by-shot breakdown of *With Raised Hands*

What follows is merely a schematic outline of the film, making it possible to refer to specific shots by number.

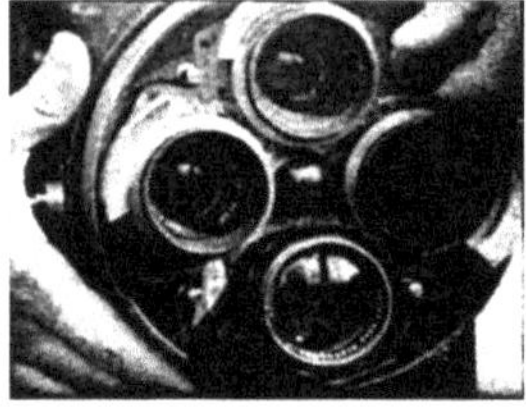

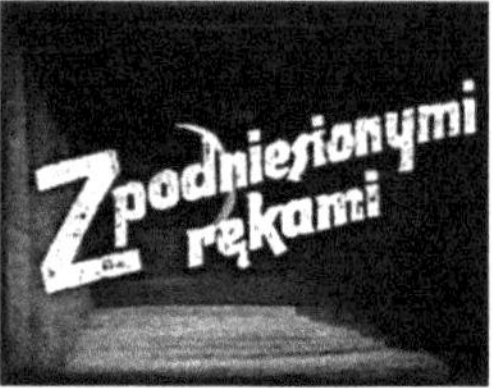

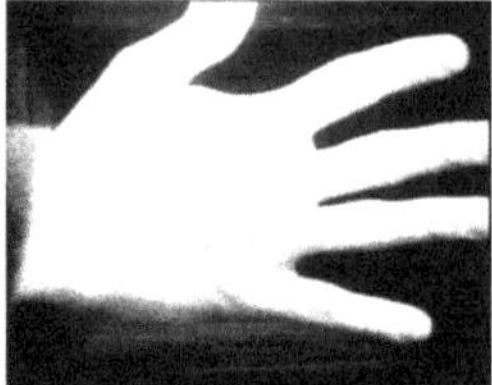

Shot 1 Hands adjust the turret of a wartime movie camera and affix a square lens shade to the camera. The title appears momentarily on screen, after which the photographer places his hand in front of the lens and the screen goes black.

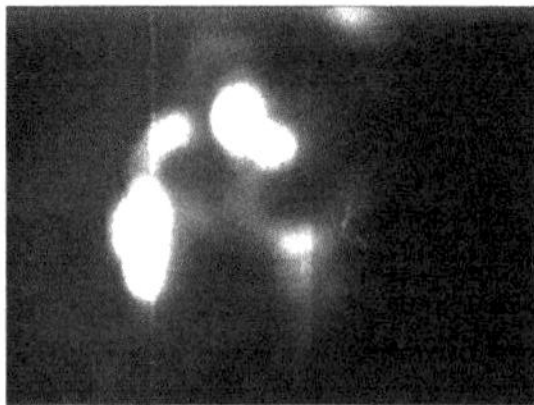

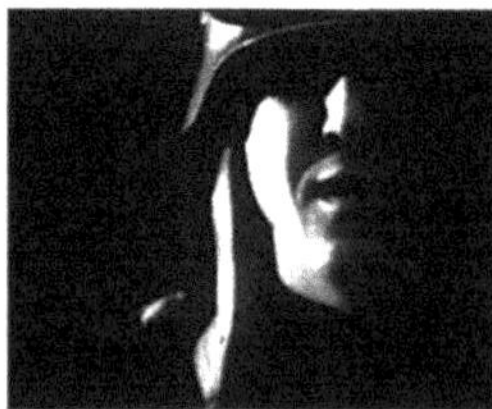

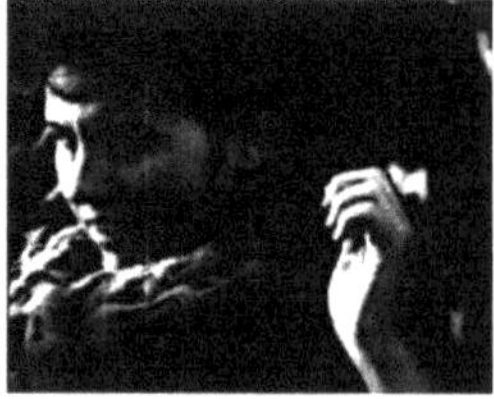

Shot 2 A woman with her hands raised as she approaches the camera. An SS trooper in charge, with motorcycle goggles on his helmet, suddenly appears, looks around then straight into the lens and smiles to the photographer, after which he looks downward, coaxing someone off-camera to do something. The trooper now moves out of frame, no longer eclipsing the woman who was standing behind him and facing away from the camera. She now turns toward us, still with her hands raised.

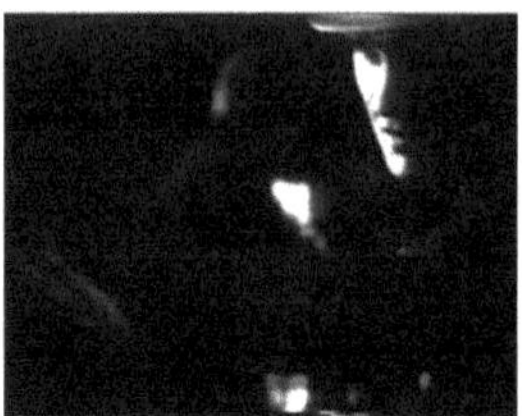

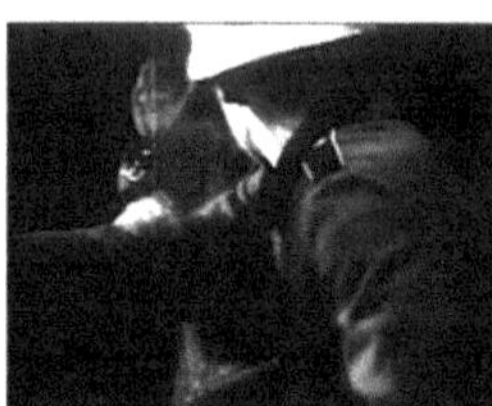

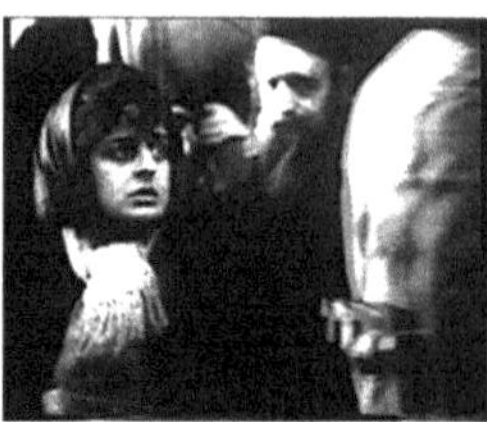

Shot 2 (cont.) The woman is roughly pushed along by another soldier and she is soon followed by other captives – women, children and older men – all roughly made to move along.The screen suddenly goes black.

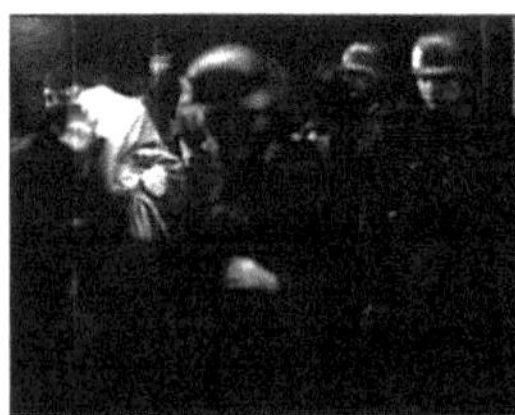

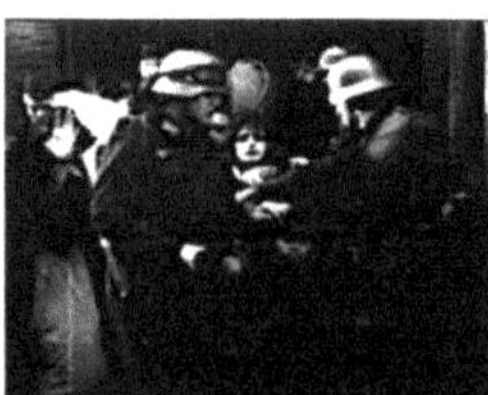

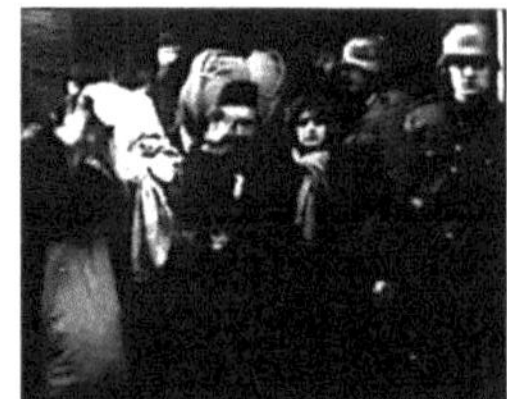

Shot 3 Again, an image is rotated upward, indicating that the turret is turned, now showing a wider shot. The first trooper pushes a little boy into our field of vision and picks up the boy's cap from the ground, planting it firmly on the boy's head, and holding the boy's arms up in the air. But the boy runs to his mother, clinging to her, as she continues to hold her hands up. When the soldiers pull him away from her, she tries in vain to hold onto him. He gets away from the soldiers and runs out of frame, the first trooper running after him. The screen goes black again.

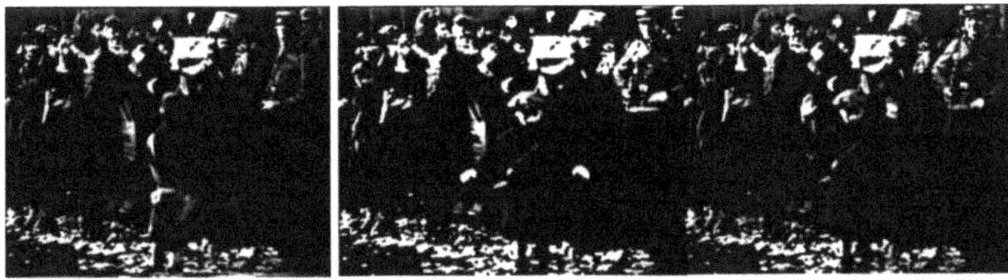

Shot 4 A new image is rotated downward and the photographer's face momentarily fills the screen as he looks into his camera. Once the photographer is out of frame, we see the trooper pushing the little boy back to the desired spot. The boy faces him, with his back to us, as the soldier coaxes him once again and finally threatens him by brandishing his submachine gun. Resigned, the boy turns around, facing the camera and raising his hands. The trooper beams and the picture – modeled on the 1943 photograph – is briefly frozen.

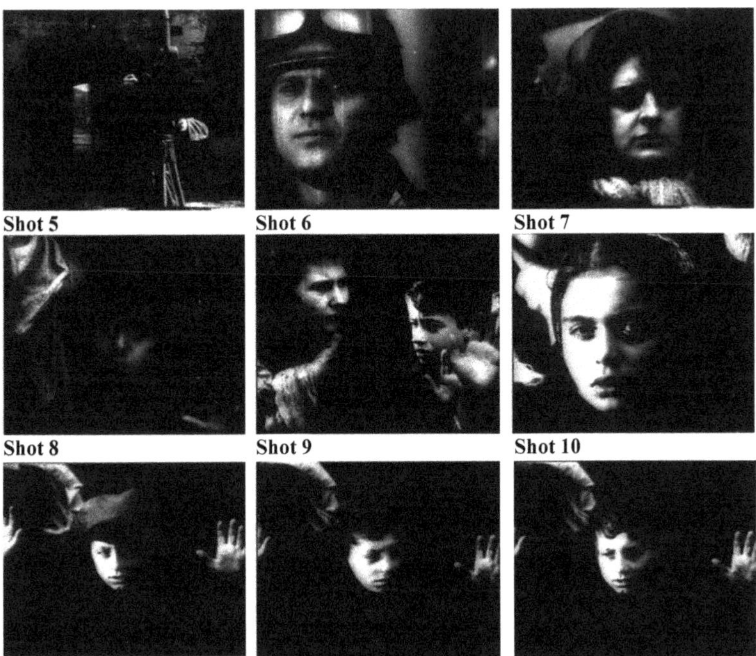

Shot 5 **Shot 6** **Shot 7**

Shot 8 **Shot 9** **Shot 10**

Shot 11 A gust of wind suddenly blows the boy's cap off. He looks to our right, in the direction of the cap, then back toward the photographer, as if to ask what he should do.

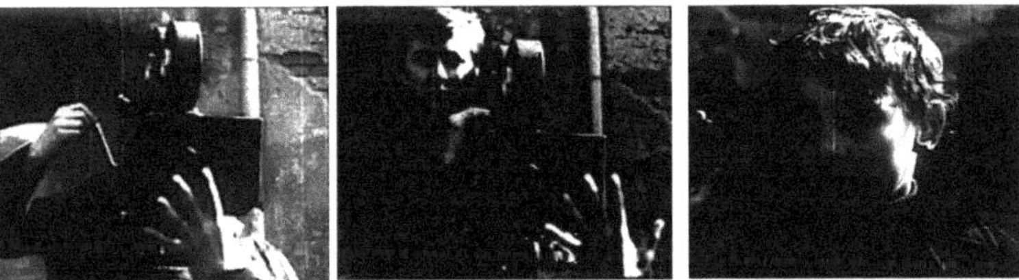

Shot 12 The photographer stops cranking his camera, looks in the direction the cap was blown, then at the boy. With a panning movement, the camera then returns to the boy, still standing bare-headed and not knowing what to do.

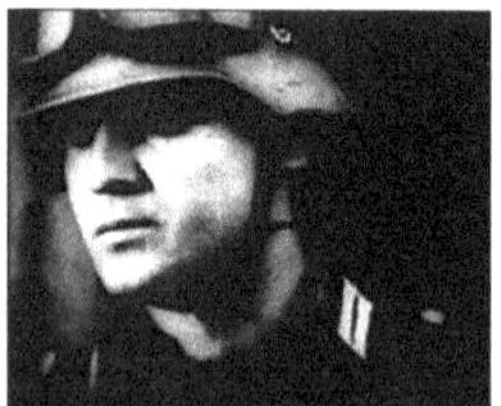
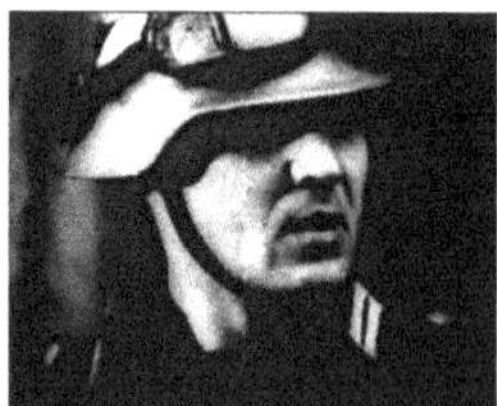
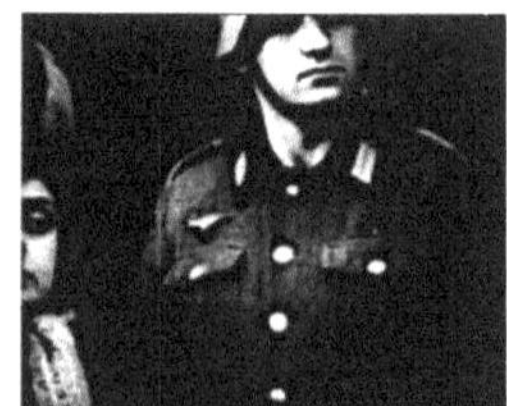

Shot 13 All eyes seem to be on the main trooper, but he just stands there, waiting. The camera pans left, past the other soldier...

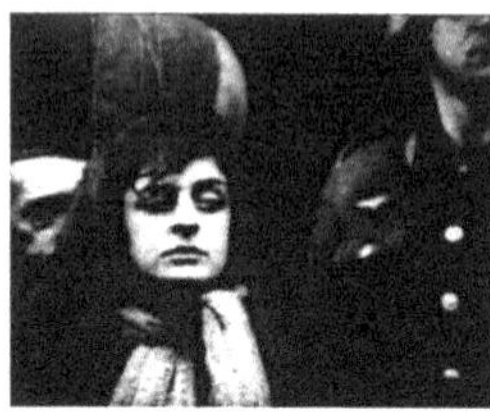
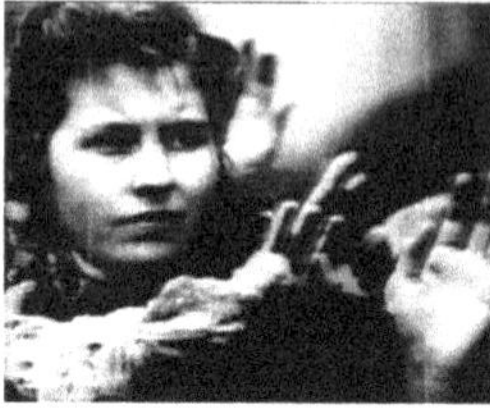
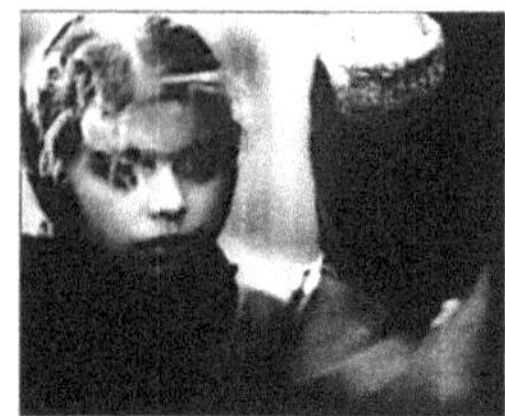

Shot 13 (cont.) ... past the boy's mother and other women and children, standing with their hands raised. As it passes the boy, we see only his raised hands, and from their movement, we can see that he is turning around. After showing the little girl, standing at the end of the row of prisoners...

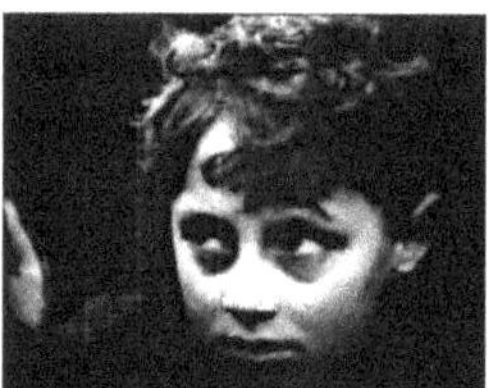

Shot 13 (cont.) ... the camera changes direction and returns to the boy, who once again looks toward the photographer.

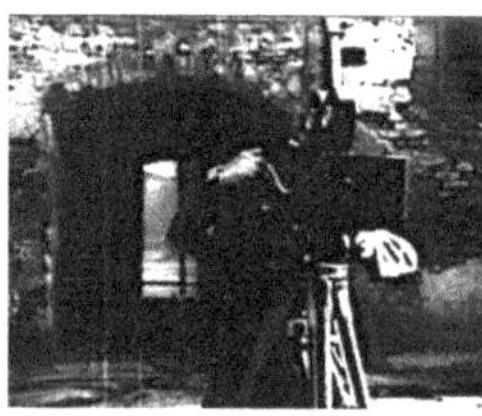

Shot 14 The photographer is cranking his camera

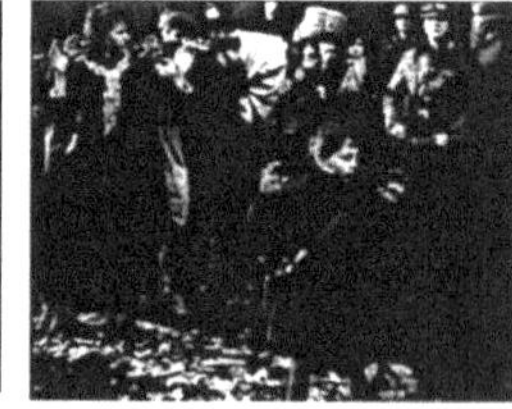

Shot 15 The boy looks at the trooper in charge, who simply stands and waits. The boy walks out of frame in the direction of his hat...

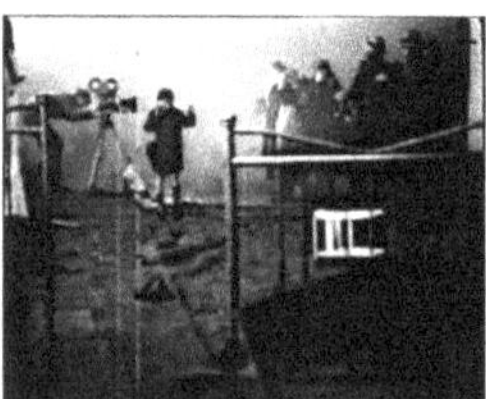

Shot 16 The boy leaves the scene of the filming, walking cautiously at first with hands up, then when he spots his cap, running forward toward it.

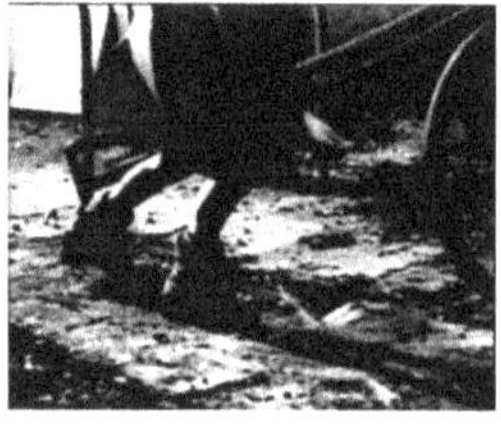

Shot 17 The cap, lying on the pavement, is suddenly blown away by another gust of wind, just as the boy reaches it. A swish-pan begins.

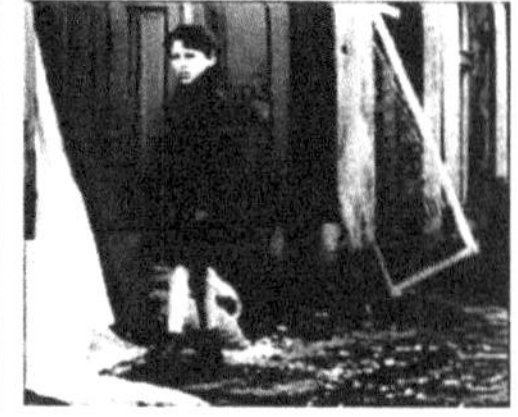

Shot 18 A new swish-pan brings us to the boy's new location, even farther from the scene of the filming, which he now looks at from a distance.

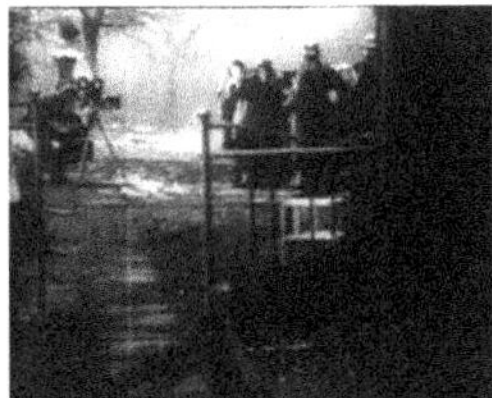

Shot 19 The scene of the filming, from the boy's point of view.

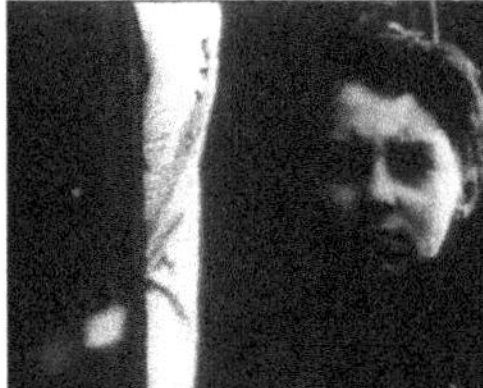

Shot 20 The boy looks at the distant scene, then bends down to pick up his cap.

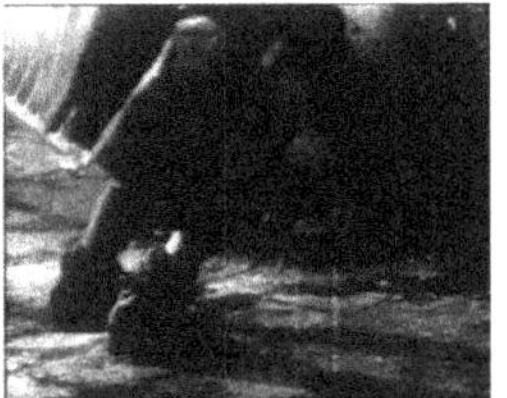

Shot 21 Once again, the cap is blown away by a new gust of wind, just as the boy reaches for it. A swish-pan begins.

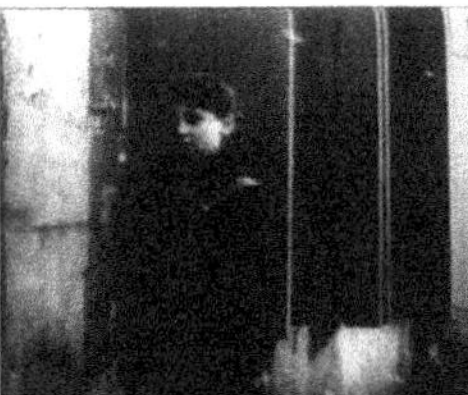

Shot 22 A new swish-pan takes over seamlessly, and once again, the boy turns to look at the distant scene he has left.

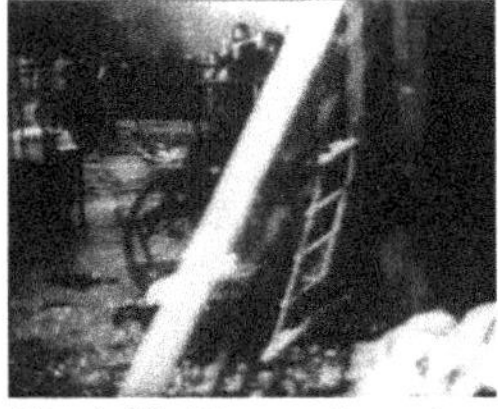

Shot 23 We see from the boy's point of view the distant scene of the filming, once again.

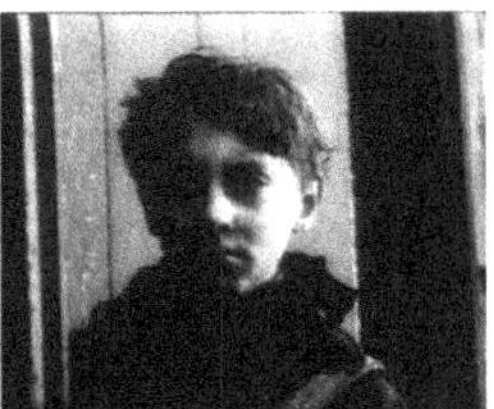

Shot 24 After looking, he turns and runs after his cap once again.

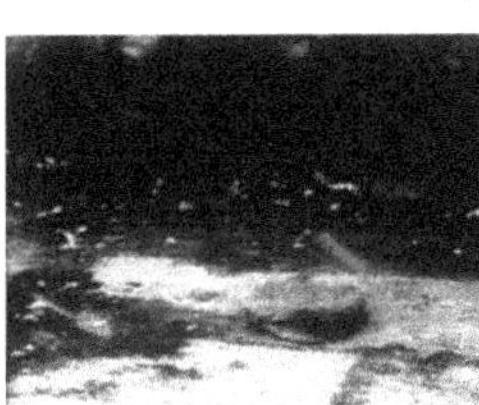

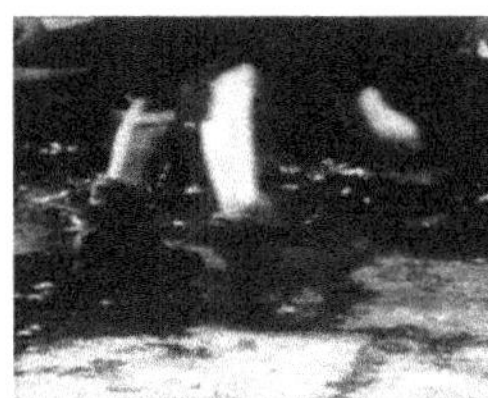

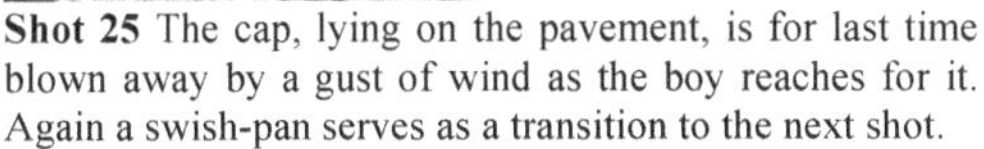

Shot 25 The cap, lying on the pavement, is for last time blown away by a gust of wind as the boy reaches for it. Again a swish-pan serves as a transition to the next shot.

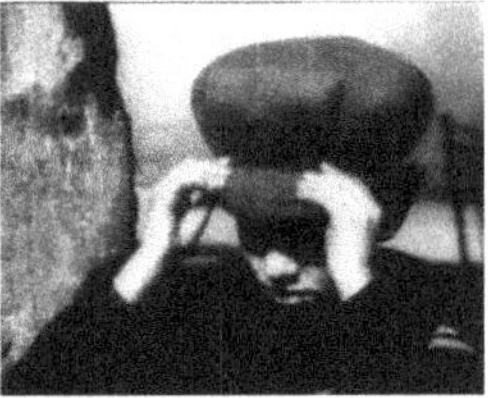

Shot 26 This time the boy manages to grab the cap and puts it firmly on his head. Again he watches.

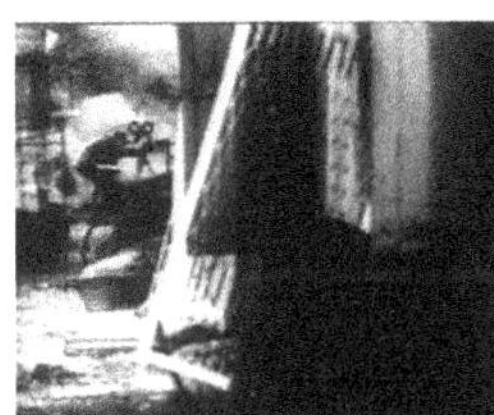

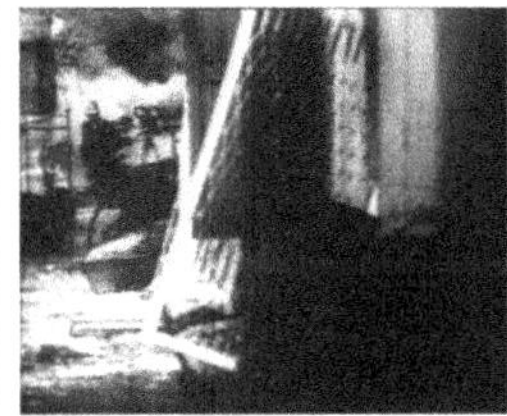

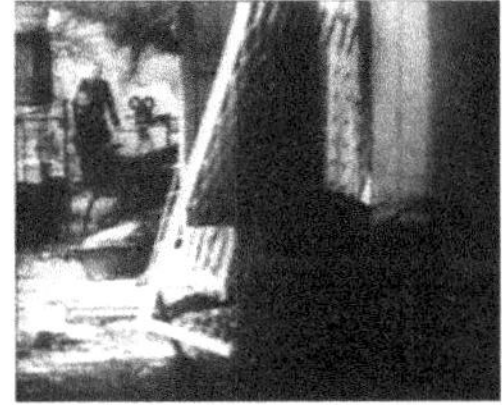

Shot 27 The boy's point of view: the photographer is still cranking his camera, but when the little girl appears in frame and looks for the boy, the photographer also stops what he is doing and looks as well.

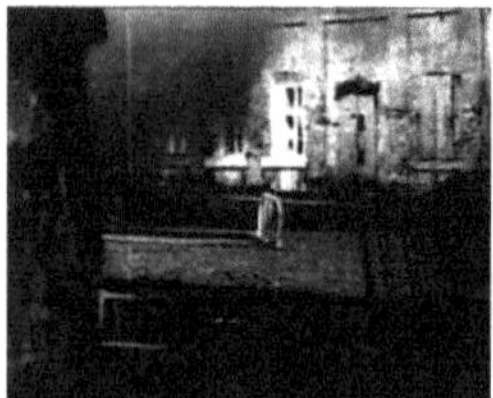

Shot 28 From the point of view of the photographer and little girl: the boy is gone. Billows of black smoke (from the burning buildings) fill the air.

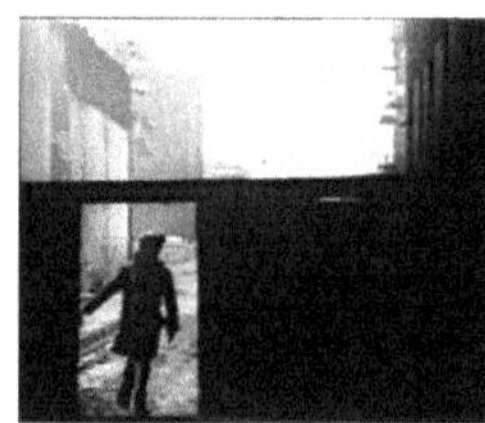

Shot 29 The boy on his way out of the Warsaw Ghetto.

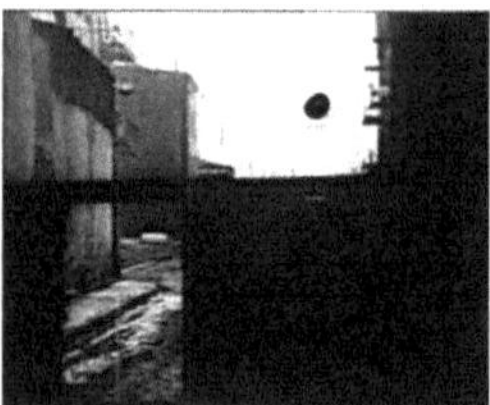

Shot 29 (cont.) Once on the other side of the gate, the boy can no longer be seen. But his cap suddenly appears, thrown up in the air.

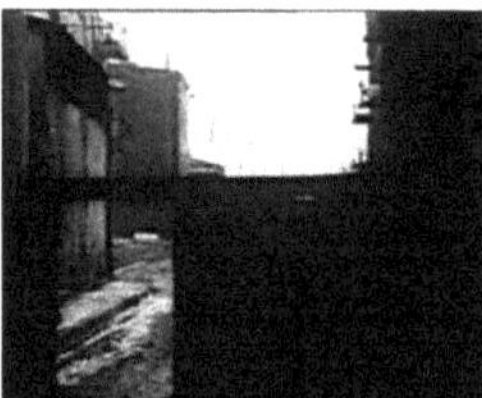

Shot 29 (cont.) After coming down from its flight, the cap is once again thrown into the air, so high that it is out of frame, and this time it doesn't come down. This picture with nothing more happening persists for several seconds.

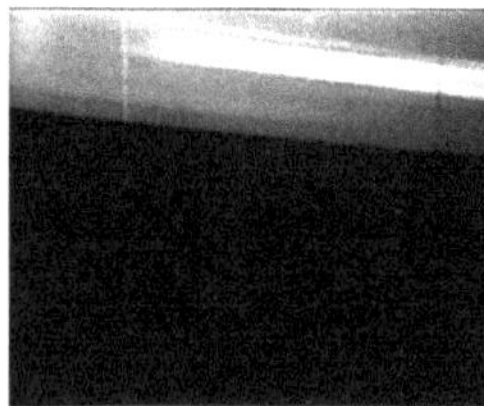

Shot 30 The cars of a railroad train streak by.

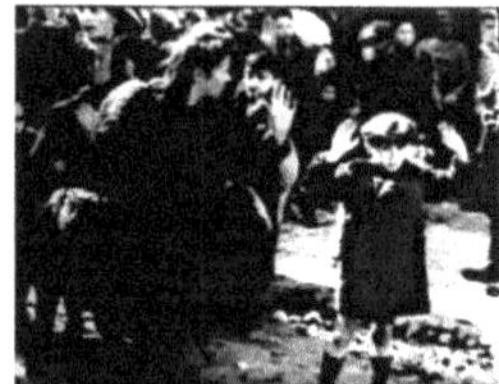

Shot 31 The 1943 photo now appears on screen and remains in view with the end credits superimposed over the lower half of the picture.

In the 1943 photo shown on p. 65, the boy with his hands raised and the oversized cap appears to have been of special interest to the SS man whose submachine gun is pointed in the boy's direction. That SS trooper, named Josef Blösche, was spotted after the war and tried for his crimes, which included participation in the shooting of more than 1000 Jews in the courtyard of a building complex in the Warsaw Ghetto on April 19, 1943 – a possible indication of the fate that the prisoners in the photo would soon meet (Raskin 2004: 97). Incidentally, while serving in the Warsaw Ghetto, Blösche had no motorcycle, which means that the goggles he wore on his helmet were chosen solely for the look they gave him, a matter of self-presentation. For simplicity's sake, I will refer to the character modeled on him in the film as "the trooper."

In Shot 3, the trooper picks up the oversized cap from the ground and plants it firmly on the boy's head, which is where he wants it to appear in the trophy photo. The other thing the trooper wants is for the boy to put his hands up, as a sign of surrender. This is undoubtedly what the trooper was coaxing the boy to do in Shot 2, and more visibly in Shots 3 and 4, finally succeeding after threatening to shoot the boy for not complying. When he has gotten the boy to look as he does in the photo, the trooper beams (Shot 4).

Considering the extreme *vulnerabilty* of the child at the hands of killers who may well go on to stage a mass execution once the trophy images have been recorded, the *yin of not being there* could be a matter of survival. Four well-timed gusts of wind blow the boy's cap off his head (Shots 12, 17, 21, 25), each offering an opportunity for him to distance himself from the locus of danger. Though hesitant at first, he *seizes* all of these *opportunities*, which bring him progressively further away from the scene of the filming, and ultimately to an unguarded gate through which he exits the ghetto.

We don't see his face as he walks through the portal but can soon deduce what he must be feeling when we see the cap flying above the ghetto wall, which means that he must have tossed it into the air to celebrate his freedom and also the cap itself, whose absences had led the way to his own *not being there* in the ghetto. In commenting on his choice to render that moment as he did, the filmmaker stated:

> I am generally a great fan of film lapses. I like films in which more is hinted than told. I jokingly call them 'interactive films' because they don't spell everything out for you, but leave a lot to your imagination. That way you can also do your own share in making the film (Raskin 2004: 129).

And an extra twist is gratifying though inexplicable: when tossed in the air a second time, the cap doesn't come down (Shot 29). It is gone, missing for good, an ultimate expression of the *yin of not being there*.

Our attention when watching this film is focused on the fate of the boy with the oversized cap. However, the story's underlying dynamics, enabling it to function as well as it does, involve an interplay of at least three forms of *yin* (*vulnerability, not being there, interpretability*) with at least three forms of *yang* (*causality, seriality, seized opportunities*).

SHORT FILM 5

Derailment / Avsporing

Unni Straume, Norway/France, 1993, 7 minutes, b/w

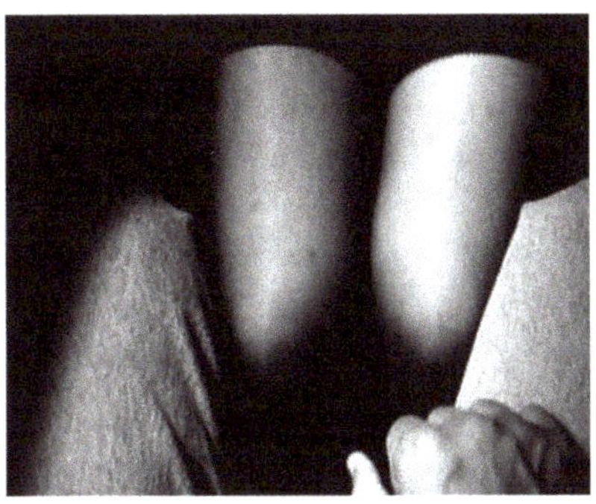

Director and Screenwriter	Unni Straume
Cinematography	Harald Paalgård
Editing	Unni Straume
Producer	Marianne Slot Nielsen
Assistant director	Aamund Johannson
Lighting	Olivier Guillaume
Music / Sound design	Rolf Wallin
Sound recording	Carle Lange
Sound mix	Gunnar Meidell
Production	Unni Straume Filmproduksjon and K-FILMS, Paris
The Woman	Anne-Lise Berntsen
The Man	Tom Remlov

Link: https://www.youtube.com/watch?v=TbO-HcUudaA

Official selection at the Cannes Film Festival in 1993.

Synopsis

At a platform of the Paris metro, a woman is among the travelers waiting for the next train. When it pulls in, she boards the train and advances in a car, looking for a vacant seat. She seats herself facing a sleeping man, and inserts her knees between his to make room for her own legs, prying his legs open in the process. She settles into her seat and studies the man's face. She pulls the hem of her skirt down toward her knees and turns toward the window, possibly lost in thought. She closes her eyes and a new scene appears as in a dream or memory: we see the exterior of an apartment building. A closer shot shows white voile curtains swayed by the breeze in open windows. Now inside an apartment, a curtain is swaying before a mirror. Lying in bed and looking a bit dazed, the woman slowly turns her head toward her right and smiles radiantly at the man, also lying in bed, and looking toward her. A curtain brushes lightly over a broken flower pot lying on the floor. Now the woman, still lying in bed, turns her head in the other direction and smiles. Suddenly we are back in the metro, where the sleeping man awakens, gradually gets his bearings and looks down. He sees the woman's knees nestled between his legs, then looks up at her face. She is still asleep. He smiles and she slowly opens her eyes, eventually seeing him smiling at her. She smiles back, then looks away, lost in thought. The man is now standing, ready to leave the car. He looks back at her. She is now standing as well, looking at him. The scene shifts to a metro station, in which we see the man – presumably through the woman's p.o.v. – as he is walking toward an exit. He stops to have one last look, presumably at the woman, then disappears from view. We then hear resonant footsteps in the same passageway.

Shot-by-shot breakdown of *Derailment*

What follows is merely a schematic outline of the film, making it possible to refer to specific shots by number.

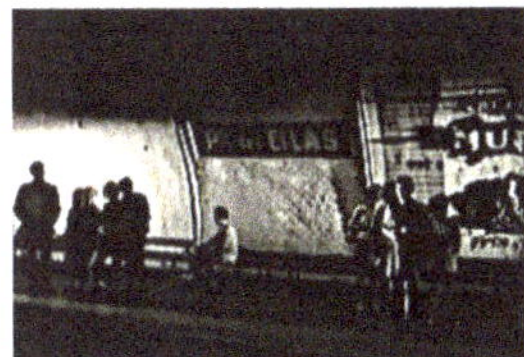

Shot 1 A platform in the Paris metro. A woman steps forward into the light.

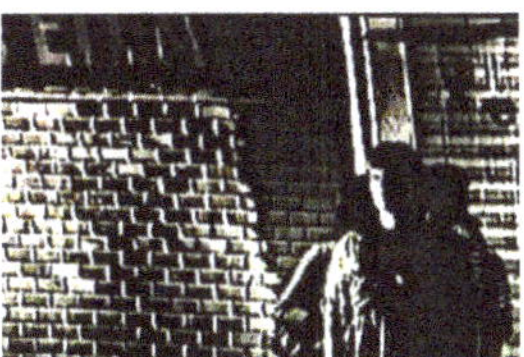

Shot 2 Closer shot of the woman, who can still be seen through the windows of a train pulling into the station and who boards the train along with the other waiting passengers.

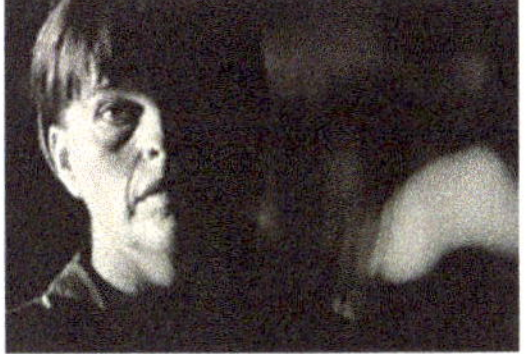

Shot 3 The woman advances in the car, looking for a seat.

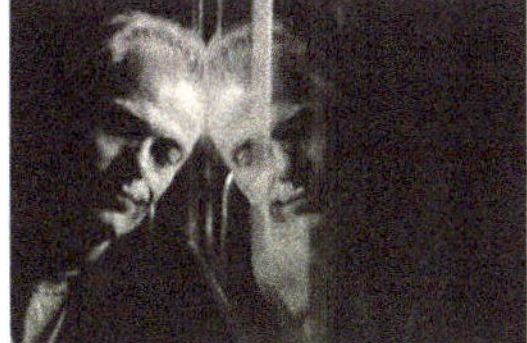

Shot 4 (Her p.o.v.): She searches for a seat, her eyes finally settling on a man sleeping with his head leaning against the window.

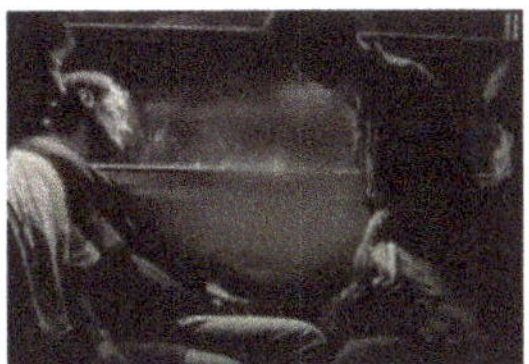

Shot 5 She seats herself, facing the sleeping man.

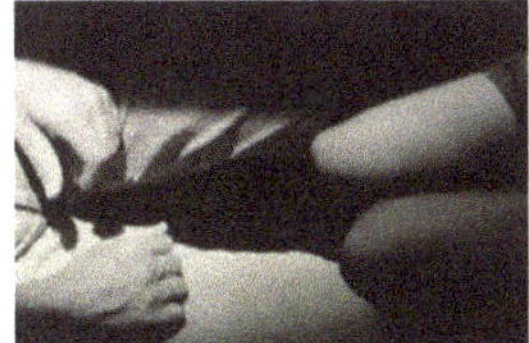

Shot 6 To make room for her own legs, she inserts her knees between the sleeping man's, prying his legs open in the process.

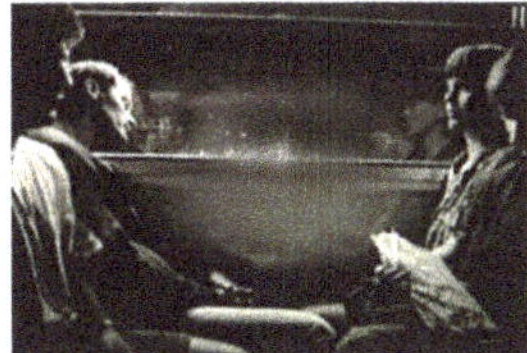

Shot 7 She settles into her seat.

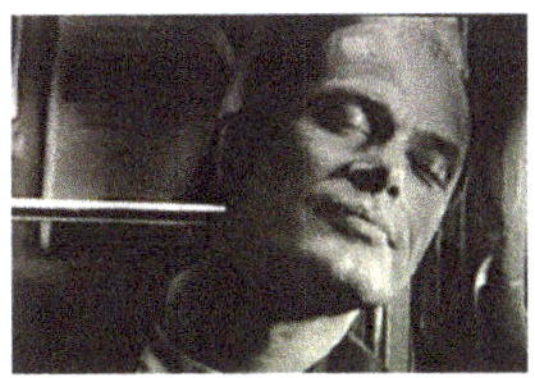

Shot 8 Her p.o.v. of the sleeping man.

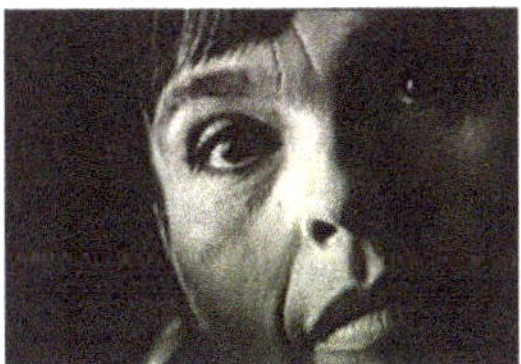

Shot 9 She studies his face.

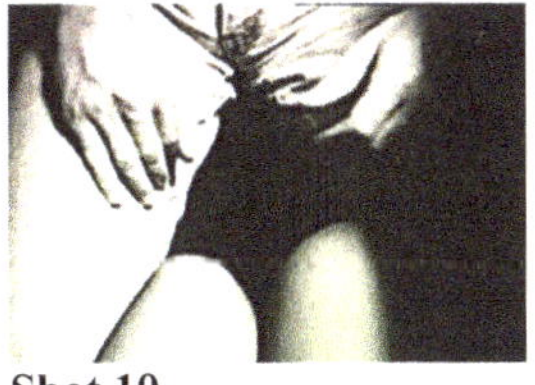

Shot 10

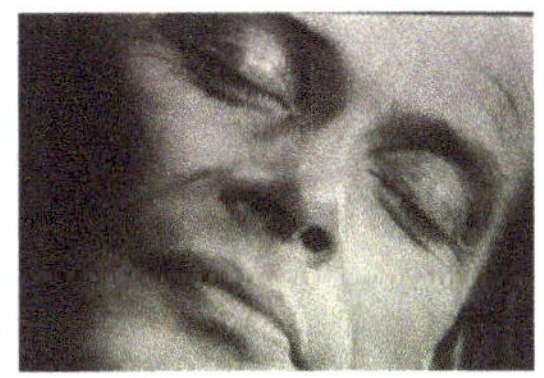

Shot 11

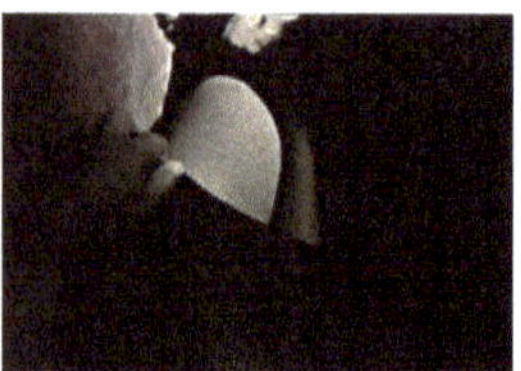

Shot 12 She pulls the hem of her skirt down toward her knees.

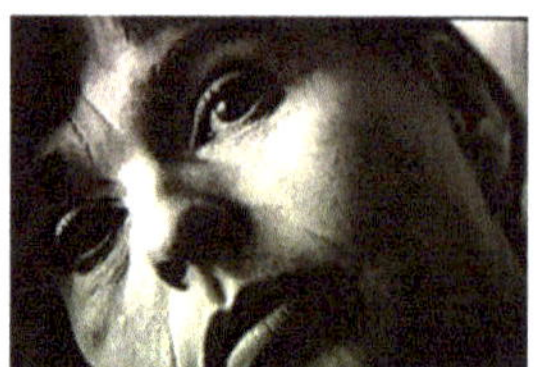

Shot 13 Still studying his face. She then looks toward her right, possibly at his reflection in the window or simply lost in thought.

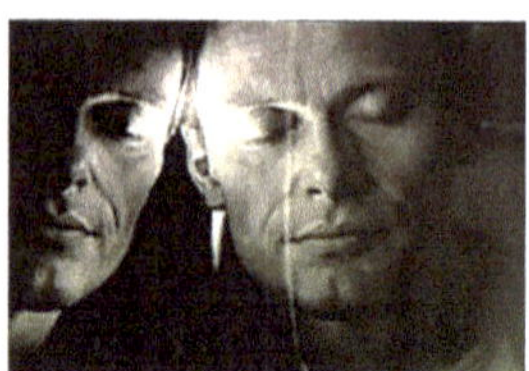

Shot 14

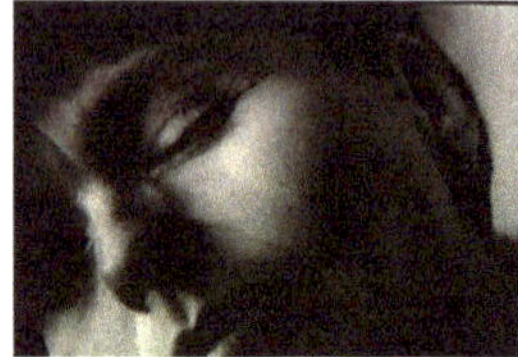

Shot 15 She closes her eyes.

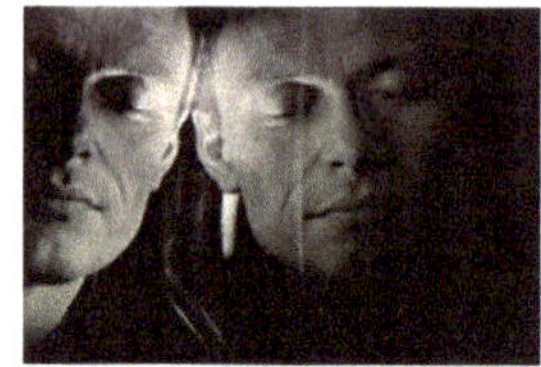

Shot 16

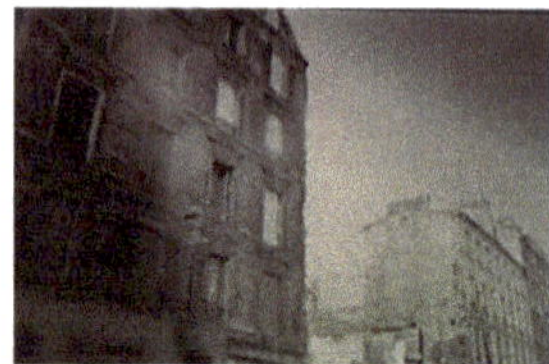

Shot 17 As in a dream or memory: the exterior of an apartment building appears.

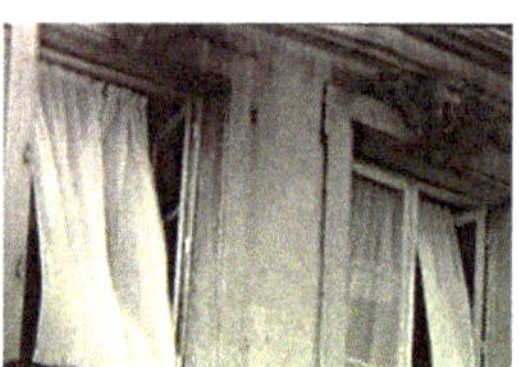

Shot 18 White voile curtains are swayed by the breeze in open windows.

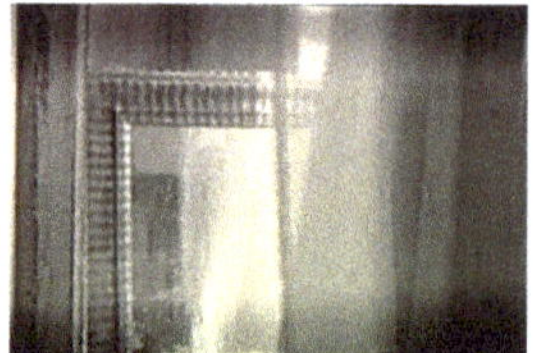

Shot 19 A curtain sways before a mirror inside an apartment.

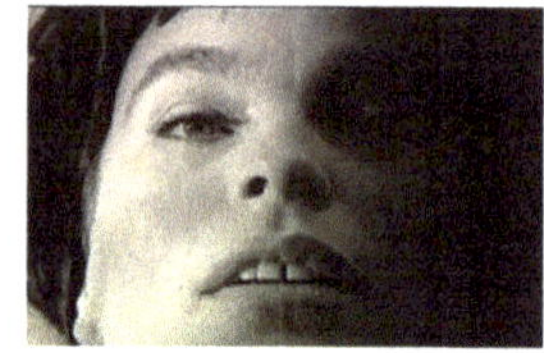

Shot 20 Lying in bed and looking a bit dazed, the woman slowly turns her head toward her right.

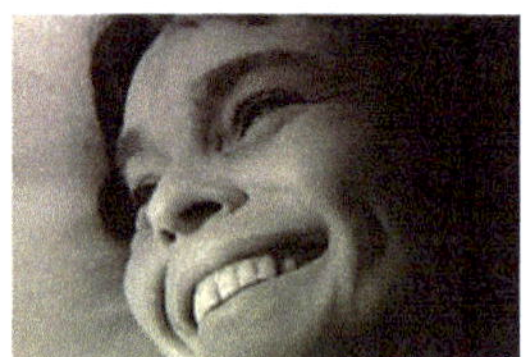

Shot 20 (cont.)

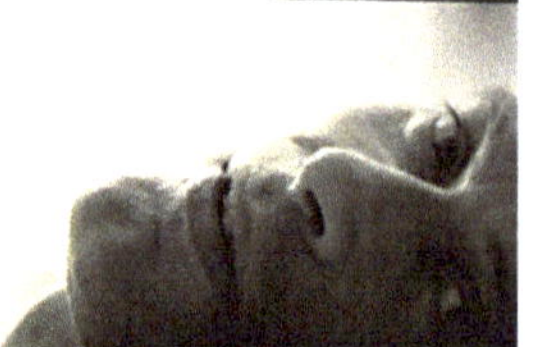

Shot 21 The man is looking back at her.

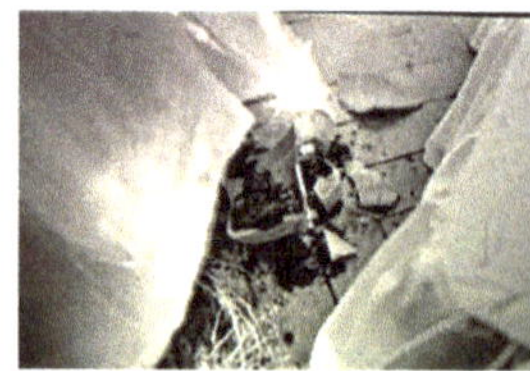

Shot 22 A curtain brushes lightly over a broken flower pot lying on the floor.

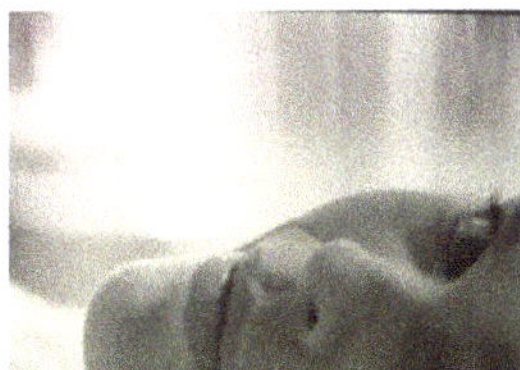

Shot 23 She slowly turns her head, this time toward her left, and smiles.

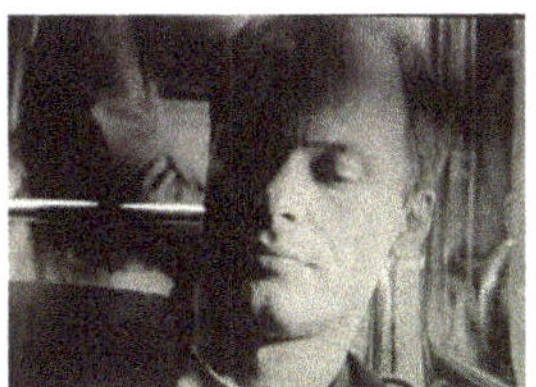

Shot 24 Back in the metro, the sleeping man awakens, very gradually gets his bearings and looks down.

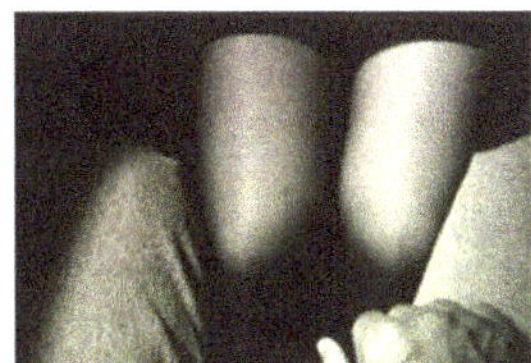

Shot 25 His p.o.v.: he sees the woman's knees nestled between his legs.

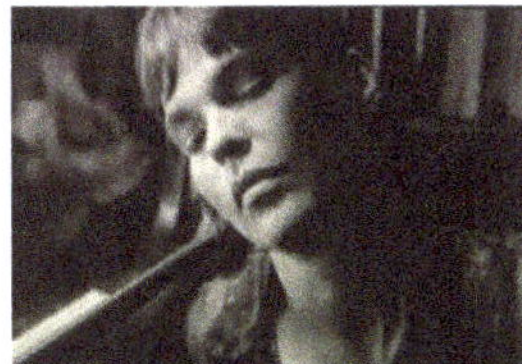

Shot 25 (cont.) He looks up at her face (the camera tilting upward). She is still asleep.

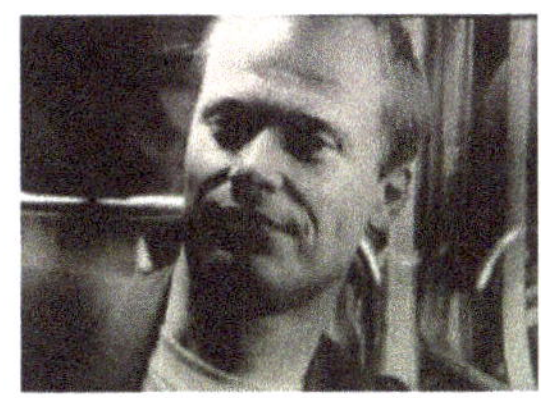

Shot 26 He smiles.

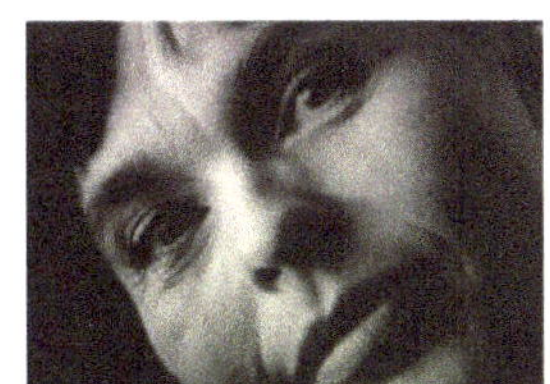

Shot 27 She slowly opens her eyes and eventually seeing him smiling at her, she smiles back at him, then looks away, lost in thought.

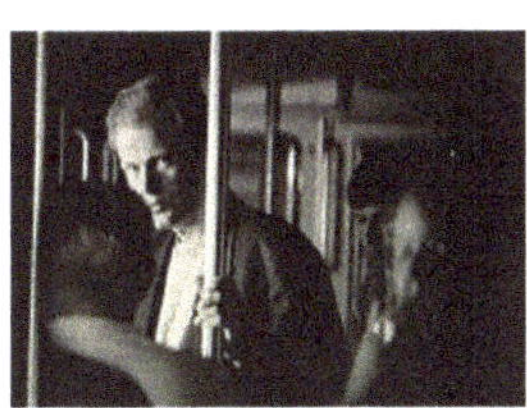

Shot 28 Now leaving the subway car, he looks back at her.

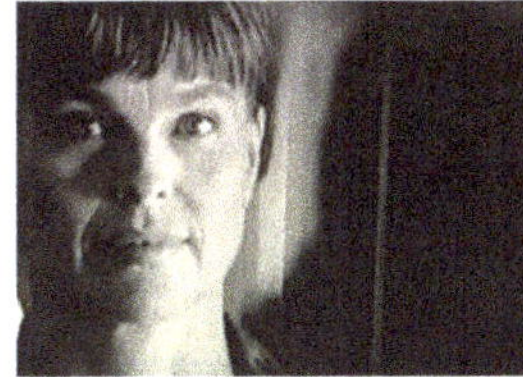

Shot 29 She is now standing as well, looking at him.

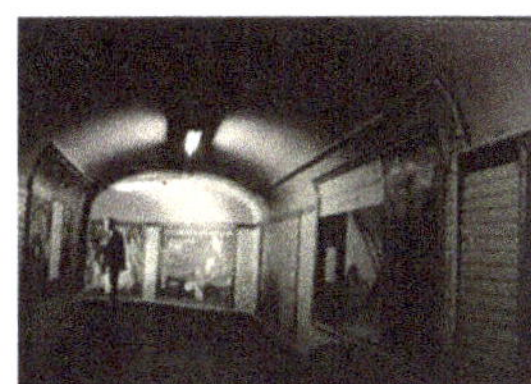

Shot 30 Walking toward the exit, he stops to look back presumably at her one last time, then disappears from view. We then hear resonant footsteps in the same passageway, without seeing to whom they belong.

YIN OF OMISSION

At least four forms of *omission* contribute to a predominantly *yin* profile for this film, with a *yin of interpretability*, saved in part for the end of the film, clinching the matter.

1. omission of dialogue

When complimented on *Derailment*'s ability to bring the viewer inside the characters, Unni Straume mentioned wordless storytelling as a possible factor:

> I guess that in a film with no words, it is easier to come inside a person. It sounds strange, but often words produce confusion and are too culturally based. When you are forced to read all communication through the way the characters move and look at each other, it may be easier for anyone to identify with them (Raskin 2003: 48).

And one commentator suggested that the absence of dialogue helps "intensify the dreamlike atmosphere" which permeates the film as a whole (Frandsen 2003: 78).

2. omission of colour

The director explained her choice to omit colour by saying:

> this film is basically close-ups of faces and I think black-and-white gives so much to portraits in general... Black-and-white also gives a certain abstraction and takes us away from the trivial world for a while" (Raskin 2003: 48).

3. omission of shots of love-making

Though this film is filled with erotic tension and a sense of sexual intimacy rarely seen in a short film, there are no shots of passionate love-making. Edvin Kau pointed out that the post-coital moments of the dream sequence don't even include a two-shot (2003: 95) – in fact, the actor and actress who appear to be looking at each other while in bed together were not even both present at the same time when those shots were filmed (Hjorth 2003: 53). When I asked Unni Straume about the omission, she replied:

> Of course this is very personal, and being a shy person in this respect, I feel it embarrassing when they show me too much on the screen. I just follow my own sensibility when shooting scenes like that, hoping that this is also that of the audience – at least of my audience (Raskin 2003: 49).

4. shots omitted in exceptionally elliptical editing

In Shot 27, the two main characters are seated across from one another in the metro train. In the very next shot, the man is already standing, ready to get off the train and looking at the woman from some distance. And in Shot 29, she is also standing, looking at him. There are no shots of them rising from their seats, or of him walking toward the door of the metro car. In Shot 30, we are no longer on a train, but now at a metro station, again with no shots first showing the train pulling in or passengers getting off.

YIN OF INTERPRETABILITY

In Shot 30, only the man is visible, seen by us presumably through the woman's p.o.v. He looks at her, we assume, one last time before rounding a corner and disappearing. We hear someone's footsteps, but there is no shot of that person at this decisive moment. Unni Straume explains:

> There are footsteps, yes, but are they hers? I wanted an open end. Up to each of us to interpret. Does she follow him or not? As we do not know either if the meeting is a dream or not (Straume 2022).

Even the status of what we saw in Shots 17 to 23 is open to interpretation, and may or may not have been a dream. If we think she follows the man at the end, that would mean even more uncertainty lying ahead. As Brian Dunnigan wrote:

> If she follows him, she risks much more than he does. She doesn't know this man.... Anything could happen... Is she walking toward life or death? (2003: 65)

And if she follows the man, might this chosen *vulnerability* lead to the "derailment" to which the title refers, with an outcome of disaster? Or has a derailment already occurred, in the sense that there may have been a sudden and unforeseen deviation from whatever plans she originally had? When I asked the filmmaker about the logic of the title, she replied with cryptic charm: "It's the logic of non-logic. Poetry, I guess" (Raskin 2003: 47).

YANG OF DOING and YANG OF MECHANIZED POWER

Counterbalancing all this *yin* – this uncertainty and holding back, primarily in the form of *omissions* – there are two forms of power. One is expressed in the surprising nerve shown in Shot 6, when in seating herself, in order to make room for her own legs, she inserts her knees between those of the sleeping man, prying his legs open in the process. This is pure *yang of doing.*

Then there are also the trains which permeate the film with their *yang of mechanized power*, experienced largely through the sounds they make. Claire Thomson describes "the cacophony of horns and pneumatic hisses that accompany the opening and closing carriage doors in Shot 2" and "the soundtrack's constant variations on the sound of metal on metal and air forced through narrow tunnel spaces…" (2011: 247), and Michael Rabiger refers to the "*'musique concrète'* of subway sounds treated to produce cathedral-choir sonorities" and to the "high squeal of the train's brakes" (2011: 235-236).

In characterizing *Derailment* as a whole, Rabiger deftly identifies the *yin* at the heart of the film, though without using that term, and describes the accompanying active role the filmmaker enables the viewer to play in decoding the film's possible meanings – what I would have called the film's *interpretability.* Rabiger writes:

> *Derailment* does what cinema does best, and owes mercifully little to theatre or literature. Aspiring screenwriters, directors and actors should see it daily, since it demonstrates what cinema can accomplish when it shuns dialogue and artificial conclusions and gives proper attention to the riddle of human behavior. Such a cinema makes us work enjoyably to create the characters' motivations and inner lives – just as we do on the subway (2011: 237).

SHORT FILM 6

Wind / Szél

Marcell Iványi, Hungary, 1996, 6 min., b/w

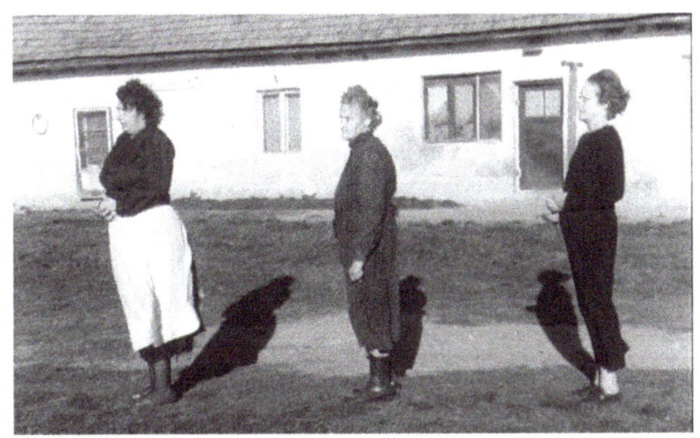

Director and Screenplay	Marcell Iványi
Director of Photography	Zsolt Haraszti
Sound Design	Peter Connelly
Assistant Director	Imre Juhász
Technical Coordinator	György Kivés
Camera Assistant	Ádám Kliegl
Costumes	Péter Kincs
Production Company	Pioneer Productions
Producer	György Durst

Link to the film: vimeo.com/kraatsfilm/szel

Palme d'Or for Best Short Film at Cannes in 1996.

Synopsis

A caption for a photo appears on a black screen: "Three Women (Audincourt, France 1951) by Lucien Hervé."

Three women look toward our left at something off-camera. The camera pans right, away from the object of their gaze in what will be a circular trajectory. Some peasants in archaic garb soon fill the frame and walk toward the left as the camera continues to pan right. Some spectators now appear, wearing the same outdated peasant costumes, looking at something off-camera. In the distance, a man has been hanged from a post and other hanged men soon appear in view. We finally see that the spectators are looking at a man being prepared for hanging. A sack is placed over his head and the hangman – in the same outmoded garb as is everyone else – awaits a signal. Someone in charge nods and the hangman kicks the stool out from under the feet of the victim, whose body twitches after he falls. The spectators watch as the camera continues its circular motion, panning right. Eventually the three women seen at the start of the film reappear, the camera having panned full circle. We are now back to where we started, only now we know what the three women were looking at. They turn away and return to their homes. Fade to white.

The photo that was captioned at the start of the film is now faded in.

Schematic breakdown of *Wind*

Wind consists of what appears to be a single, continuous, six minute shot, with a circular trajectory, framed by a photo caption on a black screen at the start of the film and by the photo itself at the film's conclusion. What follows is merely a schematic outline of the film.

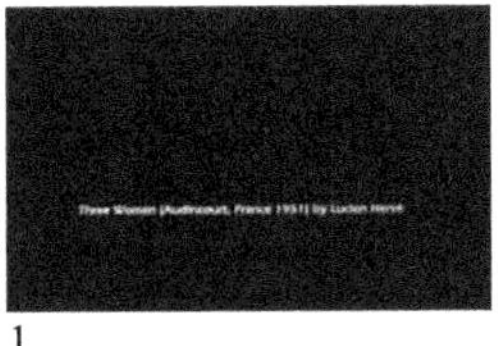

1

Caption for a photo the viewer will see at the end of the film: "Three Women (Audincourt, France 1951) by Lucien Hervé."

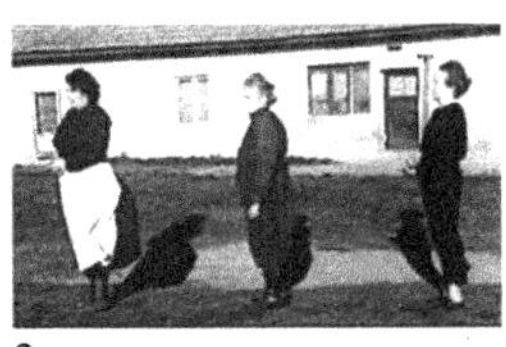

2

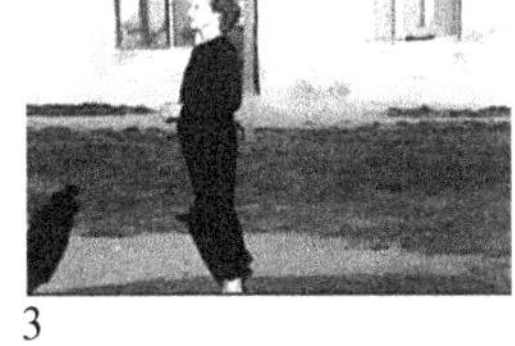

3

Three women are looking at something off camera. The camera pans right, away from the object of their gaze, while tracking forward.

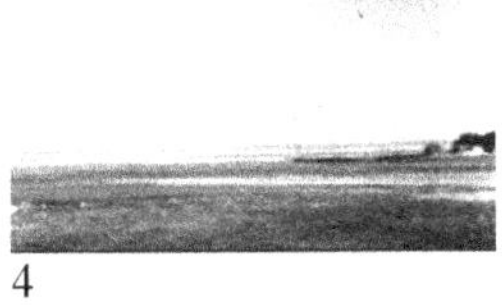

4

The camera pans past the house and birds fill the air.

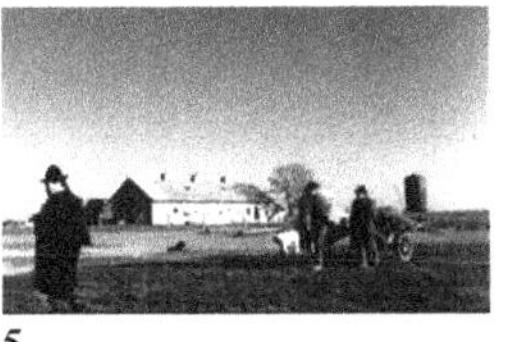

5

6

A number of farmers appear within frame and walk to the left, as the camera continues to pan right across the empty landscape, with some buildings in the distance.

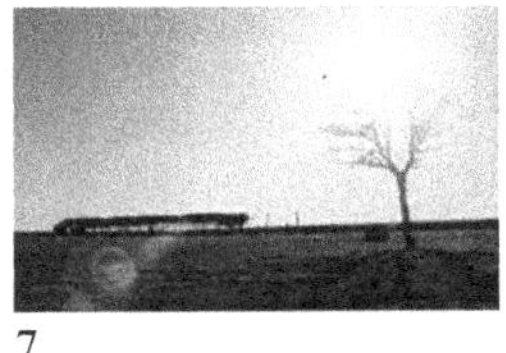

7

8

As the camera continues to pan right, a lonely tree appears, with the sun harshly shining through its branches and directly into the lens of the camera.

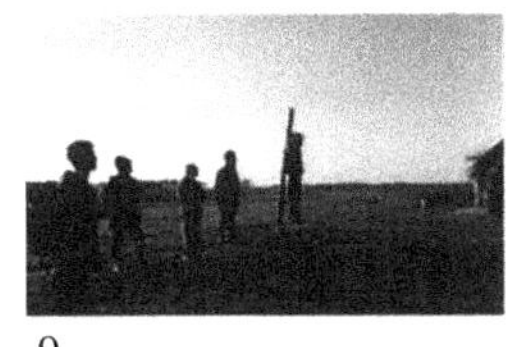

9

Spectators now appear, looking at something off camera. A man appears to be hanging from a nearby post.

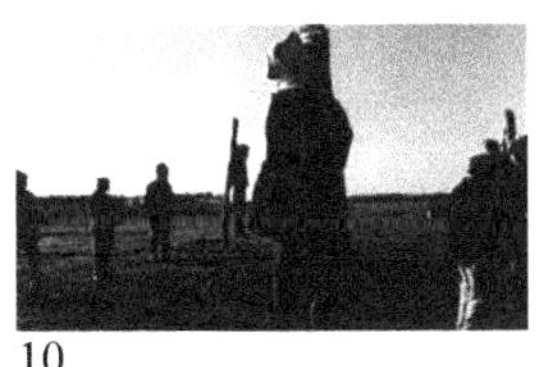

10

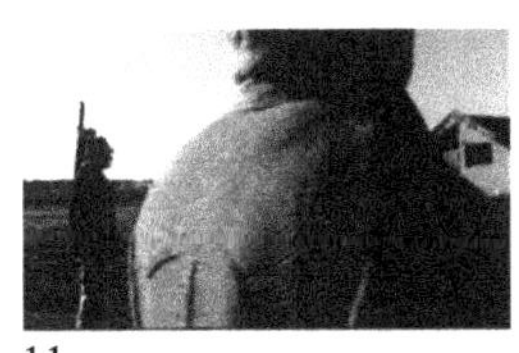

11

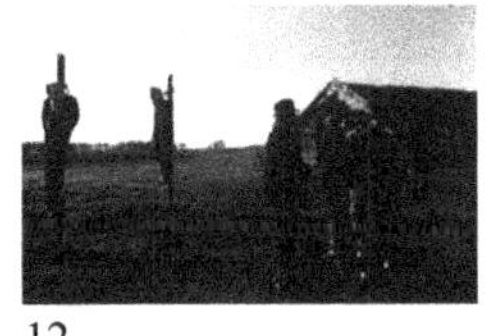

12

Other hanged men appear. We still can't see what the spectators are looking at.

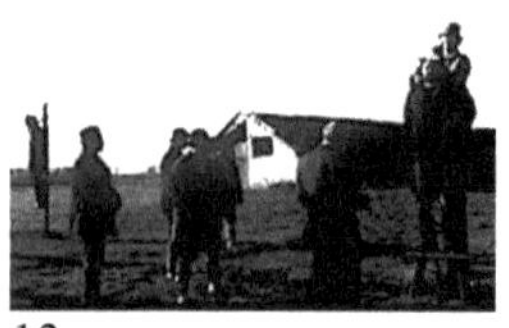
13

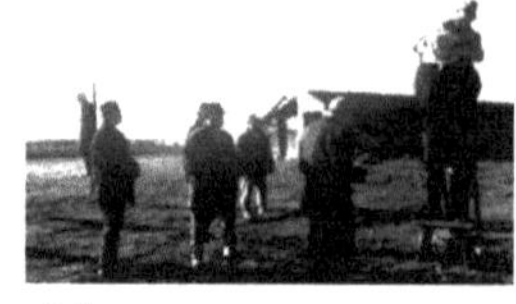
14

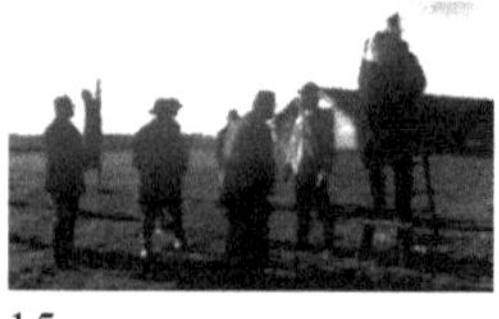
15

Now we finally see what the spectators – including the three women from the start of the shot – have been looking at: a man, whose arms are tied, is being prepared for hanging. A sack is placed over his head. Then the hangman awaits a signal.

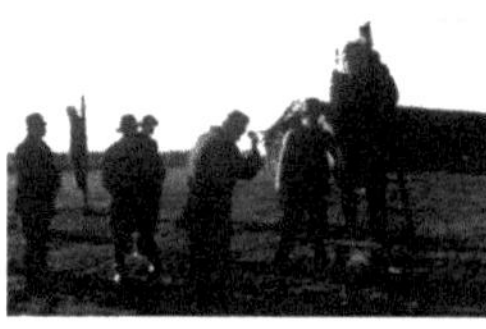
16

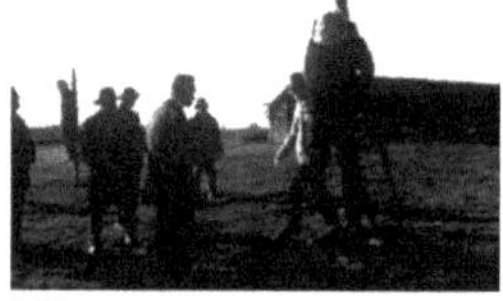
17

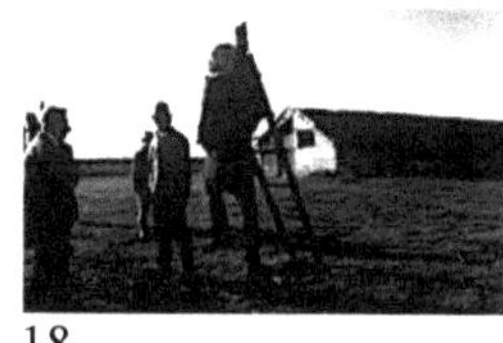
18

Someone nods his head and crosses himself, then the hangman kicks the stool out from under the feet of the victim, whose body twitches spasmodically as he dies. The camera continues panning.

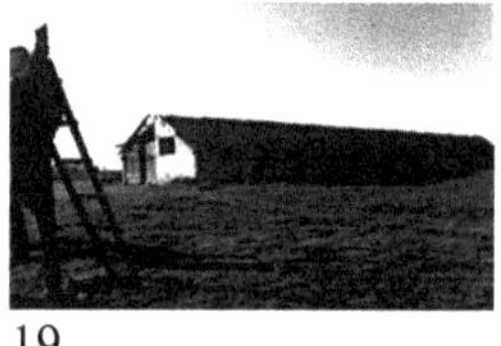
19

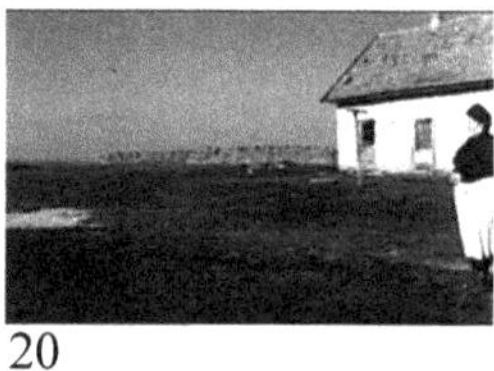
20

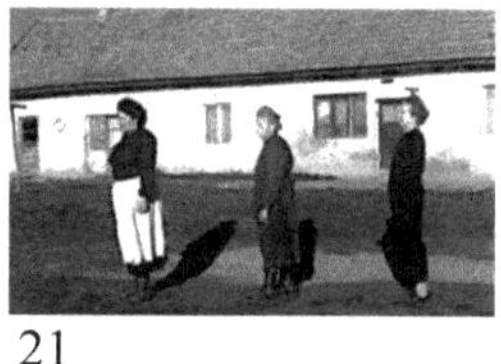
21

A dog barks. The sound of a song can be heard faintly and will continue throughout the remainder of the film. As the camera continues panning right, the three women we saw at the beginning of the film reappear in frame.

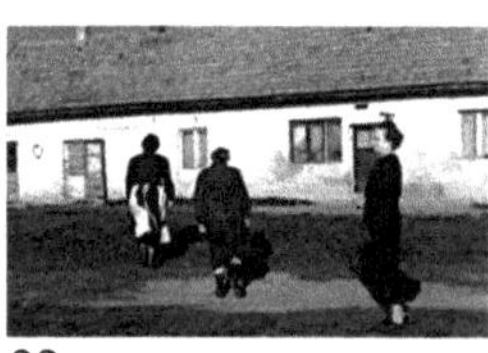
22

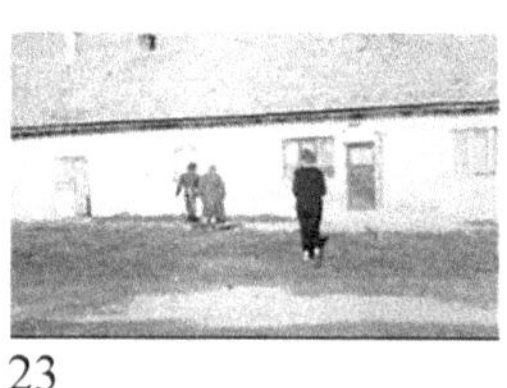
23

The first two women turn away and return to their house. Then the third woman also turns away and returns home, the image fading to white as she approaches the house.

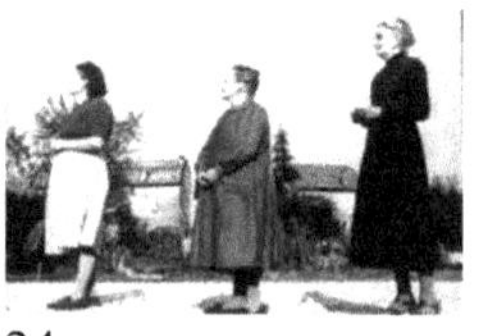
24

The Lucien Hervé photo from 1951, captioned at the start of the film, is now faded in.

Although this film won the Palme d'Or for Best Short Film at Cannes in 1996, its origins were humble: the script was written as an exercise in a screenwriting master class in 1994. The students were given three hours by their teacher, Yvette Biró, to write a script inspired by a photograph called "*Les trois femmes*" by Lucien Hervé. The photo itself can be seen in Frame 24, while its caption appears on a black background at the start of the film.

Marcell Iványi conceived of the film as a single, unbroken circular shot in which the camera panned a full 360 degrees, finally returning to its initial position. And he knew exactly what story he wished to tell:

> My story was about a group of men, about fifteen or twenty men, just riding around in the countryside, and because there's chaos everywhere, they can do whatever they want. They can just take the people's belongings whenever they want to, and if they arrive at a farm like this one, and if there are some men resisting them, the easiest and the fastest thing would be just to kill them that way. Because it looks like an execution, and it looks like something prescribed by the law, but of course it's a violation of the law. So this has been going on for maybe months now. And they've been seeing people dying before their very eyes and are just not sensitive to that any more. Just as when we watch CNN every day, and we are not sensitive any more (Raskin 1998: 18-19).

If viewers were able to understand the film exactly as intended, it would undoubtedly still have been successful. But I believe that uncertainties as to how to make sense of the story – its *yin of interpretability* – contribute greatly to the richness of this modern classic, and that those uncertainties are counterbalanced by regularities in the extraordinary camera work and closural strategies, comprising a *yang of structure*.

YIN OF INTERPRETABILITY

How are we to understand the executions shown in this film? Is it one ethnic group killing off another? Is it an oppressive authority snuffing out the leaders of a rebellion? Do we know whose side we are on? Are the victims heroes or criminals? And are we invited to connect what we see on screen to any given historical situation, past or present?

The filmmaker provides no cues whatsoever, no emblems reminiscent of political or national movements, nothing that could guide our understanding of the values embodied by either the victims or the executioners, no hints of any kind as to who is executing whom and why.

Other questions arise as well concerning the bystanders or witnesses, both those who are spread out amid the gallows and those, like the three women, who stand near their homes, as we see in Frames 22 and 23, where they don't show any reaction of horror at what they see. What are we to think of their holding back? That they are helpless, have no choice in the matter and should not be judged? That their passivity makes them complicit in war crimes and is deplorable?

The *yin* properties of the film leave us with many uncertainties, and in this case, our efforts to connect the dots are not likely to result in any revelations.

YANG OF STRUCTURE

The uncertainties just described can be counterbalanced by such *yang* processes as:

- the inexorable, unstoppable 360 degree panning movement of the camera, eventually coming full circle, returning to its point of departure;
- the symmetry of showing the same three women at the film's beginning (Frame 2) and ending (Frame 22), still looking at something off-camera only now we know what it is they are seeing;
- the closural signal of having those three women exit from the scene, before and during a fade to white, turning their backs to the camera and moving away from it;
- finally connecting the caption of the film's opening image to the photo it describes in the film's final image, thereby closing yet another circle.

While these *yang* processes do nothing to clear up the uncertainties of the film's *yin*, their potency in bringing structure to the viewer's experience helps make the viewer feel, as the film ends, that it is in balance and complete.

SHORT FILM 7

The War Is Over / La Guerra è finita

Italy, 1997, 7 min., colour

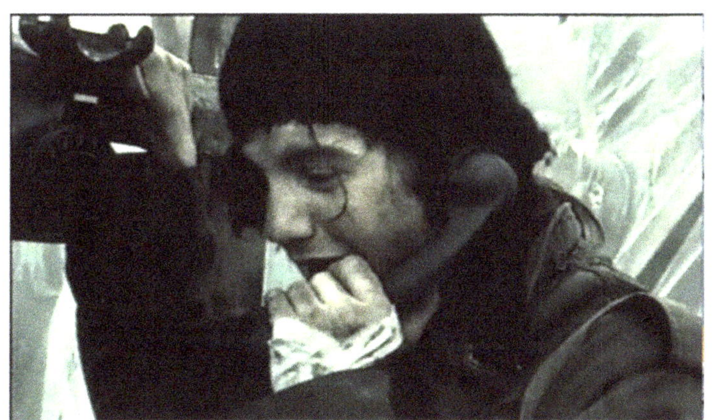

Production Credits

Writer and director	Nina Mimica
Director of photography	Mauro Faloni
Editor	Marina Vatteroni
Music	Giuseppe Napoli
Sound recording	Filippo Porcari
Costumes	Elena Del Guerra
Production	Federico Falsini, Alessandra Lentini
Distribution	Marco Gallo, Maurizio Aprea

Cast

Vincenzo Crivello
Ivana Gallo
Gillian Webster
Elena Cotta
Enzo Decaro
Ettore Belmondo
Valentina Chichi

Link to the film: https://www.youtube.com/watch?v=euqZrtagiqM

Golden Mikeldi for fiction and the Doctors Without Borders Award at the 40th International Festival of the Documentary and Short Film, Bilbao, 1998.

Synopsis

After a dream-like prelude in which a bare-chested soldier (who will turn out to be the main character) performs a euphoric dance, we see someone working on telephone lines in an open field, followed by a close shot of Marco in an improvised phone booth made of wooden beams and plastic sheets. He dials repeatedly, finally gets a connection and speaks to his family members, letting them know that he is alive and that the war is over. He speaks briefly to his grandmother, his little sister, his nearly hysterical mother who warns him not to travel at night, and finally at greater length to his father. He is surrounded by other soldiers, eagerly awaiting their turn to use the phone, and who several times urge Marco to finish his call. One soldier closest to him holds a crutch. Marco's family can't wait for him to come home. When Marco asks his father if he may bring home with him a friend who had lost a leg, there is a shot of the soldier holding a crutch. The father explains that it would be better to wait in order not to upset the mother who still has serious anxiety attacks. Marco agrees and says goodbye. The soldier who had been holding a crutch moves light-footedly and with his hands free as he takes over the phone. As Marco walks away alone in the final shot with his back to the camera, the framing eventually reveals that he is on crutches and that he is the one who has lost a leg.

Shot-by-shot breakdown of *The War Is Over*

What follows is merely a schematic outline of the film, making it possible to refer to specific shots by number.

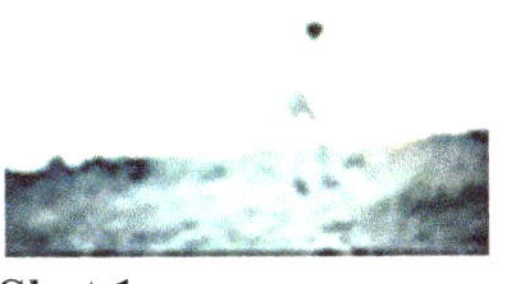

Shot 1

Shot 2

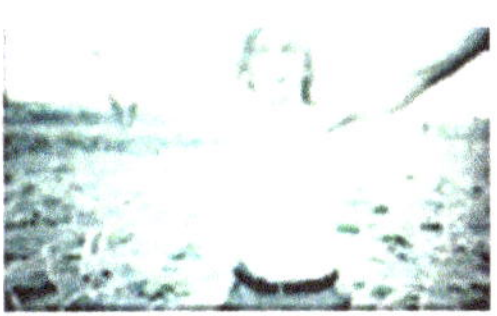

Shot 3

A euphoric dance is performed by the man who will turn out to be the main character. The image is distorted at first, then becomes clearer and is finally overexposed.

Shot 4

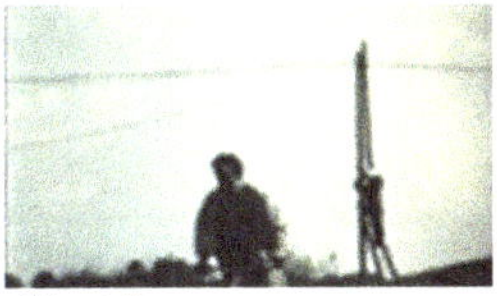

Shot 5

In the background, someone is working on telephone lines. The title is superimposed.

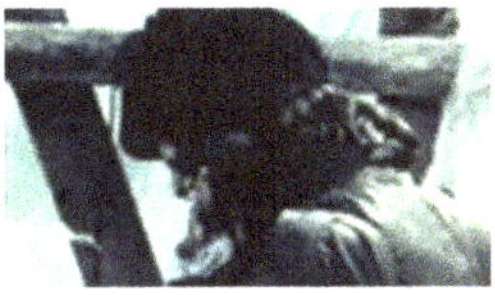

Shot 6

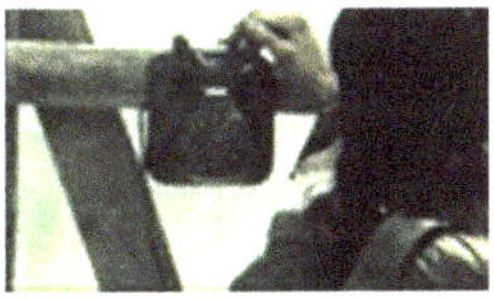

Shot 7

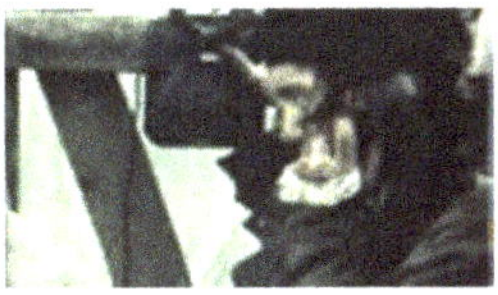

Shot 8

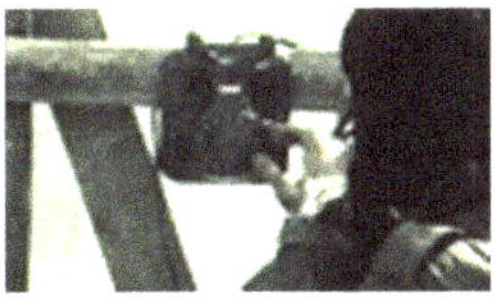

Shot 9

Marco dials and redials a number he knows by heart, without getting a connection.

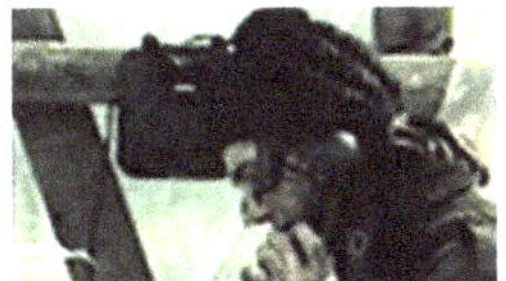

Shot 10

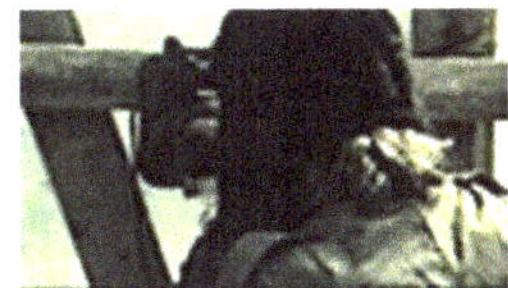

Shot 11

Marco dials yet again.

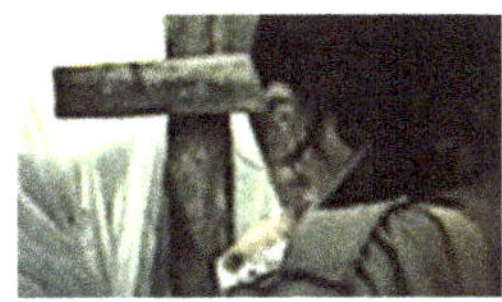

Shot 12

The connection is finally made.

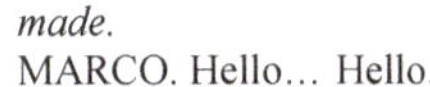

MARCO. Hello… Hello.

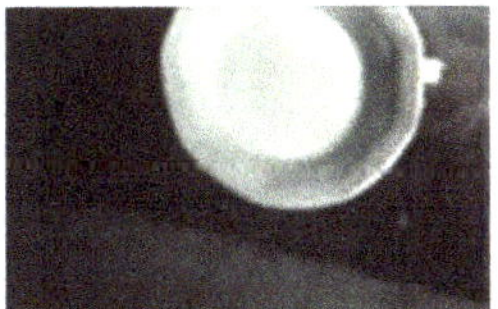

Shot 13

Dishes fall and break on the floor.

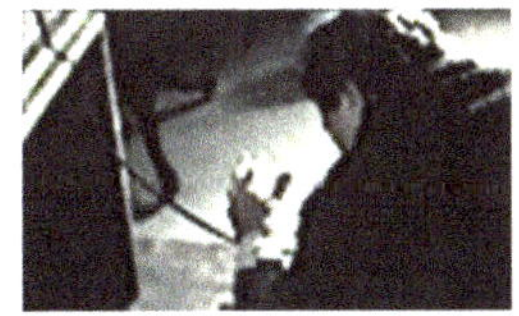

Shot 14

GRANDMA. My little…

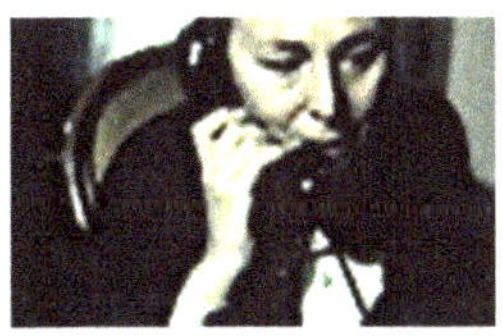

Shot 15

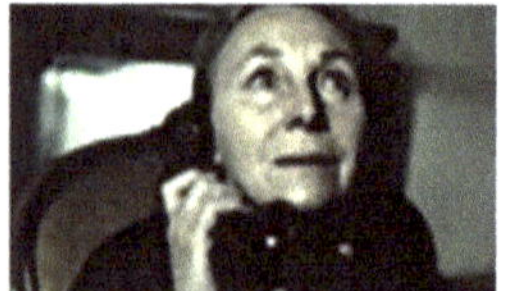

Shot 16

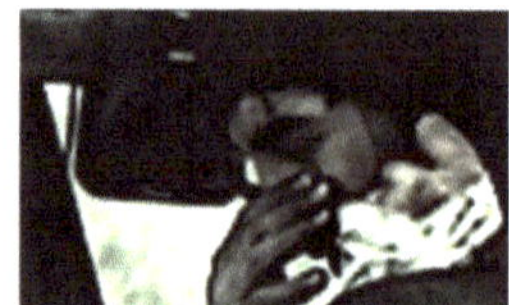

Shot 17
Marco wipes away a tear.
GRANDMA *(off)*. …my little boy.

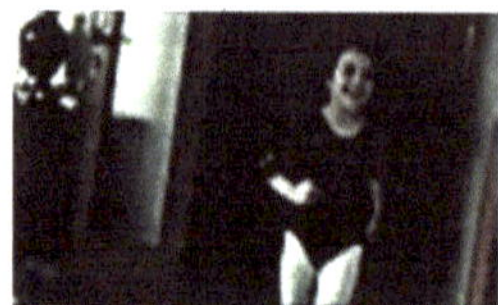

Shot 18
Marco's little sister comes running toward the phone.

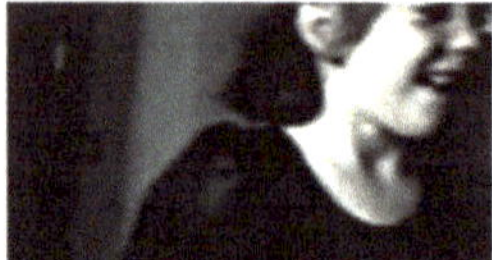

Shot 19
LITTLE SISTER. Marco!

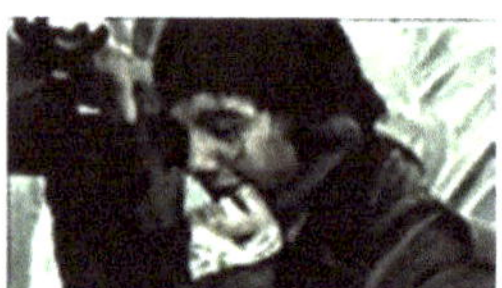

Shot 20
MARCO. Anna, little rascal... …in a village up north. … it's all over.

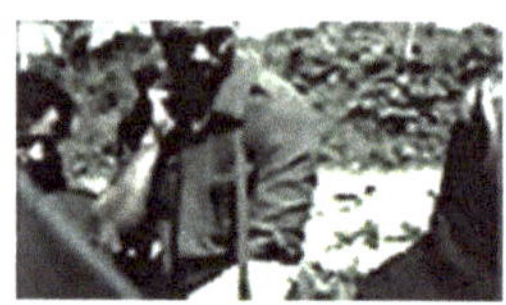

Shot 21
MARCO. ...don't worry, silly… I'm alive!

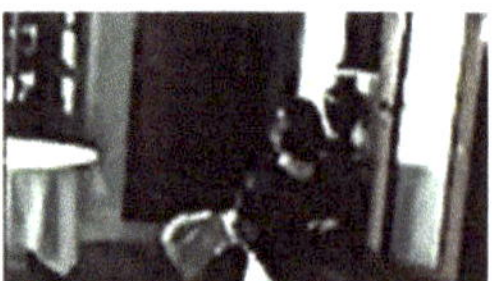

Shot 22
MARCO. Yes!
FATHER. Marco!
GRANDMA. When is he coming back?

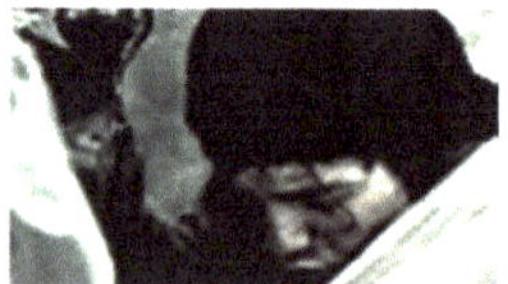

Shot 23
MARCO. I hoped some–body would tell you. We were up in the mountains…

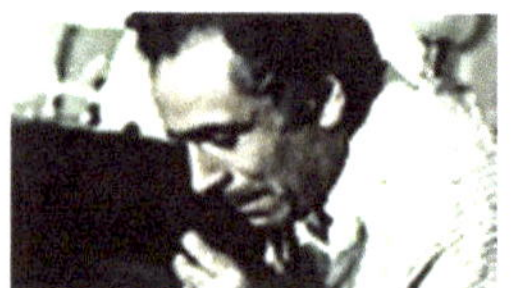

Shot 24

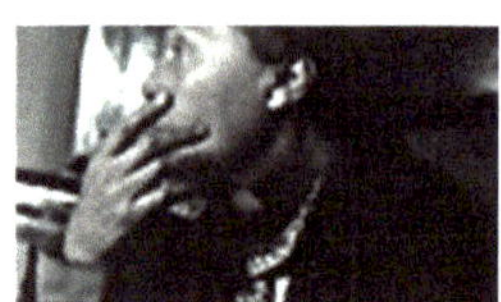

Shot 25
FATHER (*off*). You're alive, only that matters!

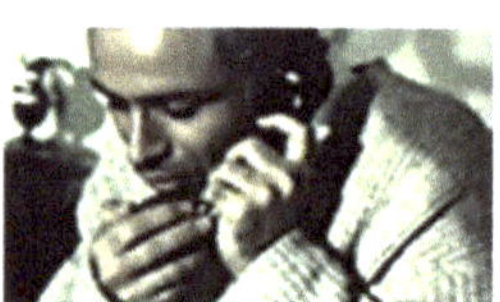

Shot 26
FATHER. They'll open up the roads.

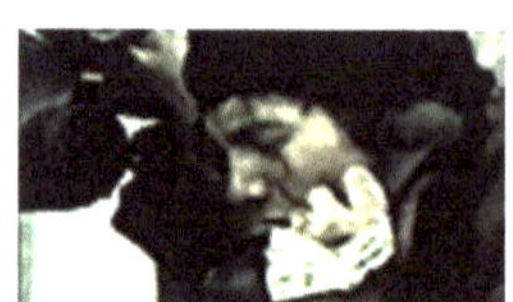

Shot 27
MARCO. How's Mum?

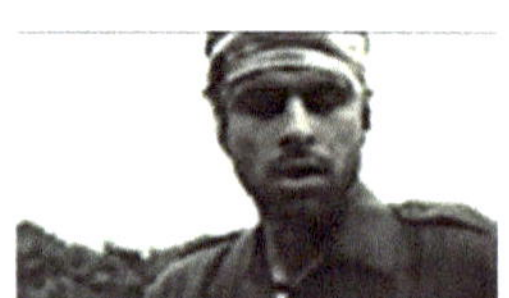

Shot 28
MARCO (*off*). And you?

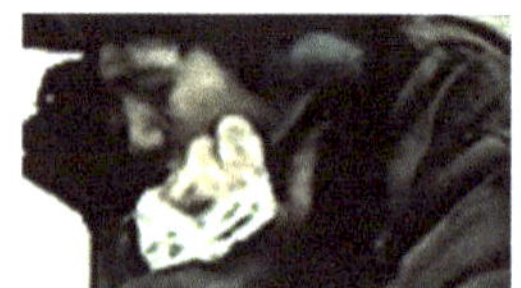

Shot 29
MARCO. I can't hear you!
FATHER (*to Marco*): Hello. (*to Little Sister*) Be a good girl.

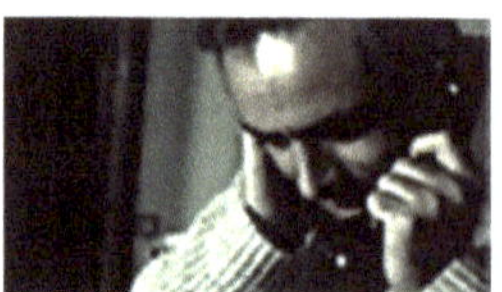

Shot 30
FATHER. Are you still there?

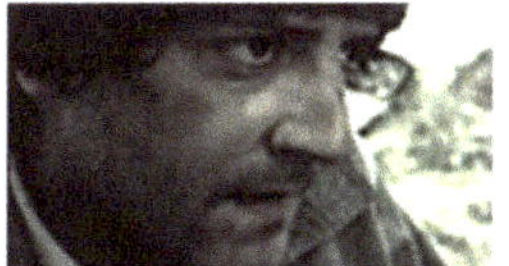

Shot 31
FATHER. We can't wait to see you.
MARCO. Hello?
FATHER. Your room's as you left it.
MARCO. I can't hear you!
FATHER. ...all your things.

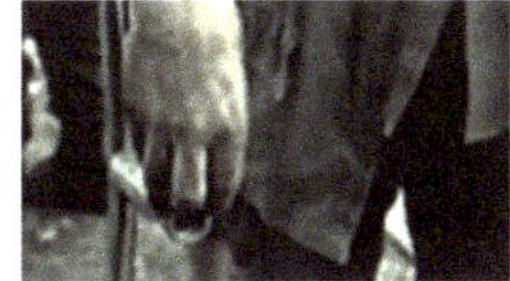

Shot 32
MARCO. What did you say?

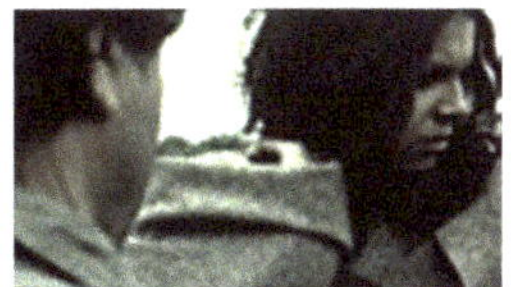

Shot 33
FATHER. Your desk too.

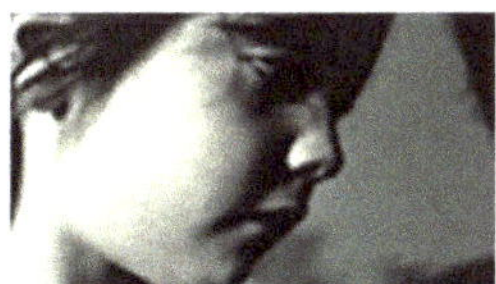

Shot 34
FATHER. There was no wood to keep warm...

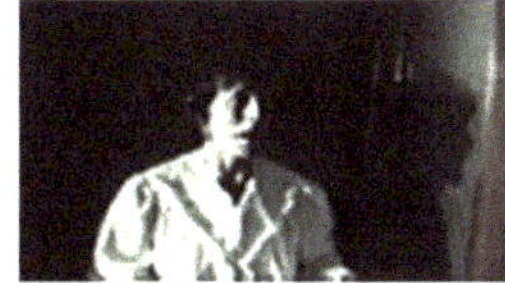

Shot 35
FATHER. But Mum said "Marco's things are not to be touched."
MOTHER *(approaching)*. Marco!

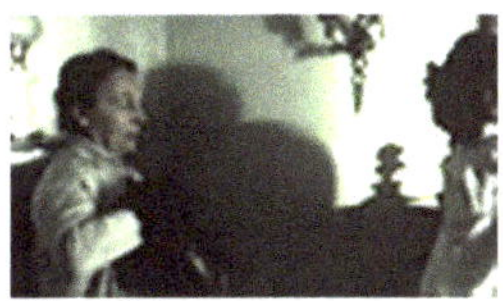

Shot 36
MOTHER. Marco!

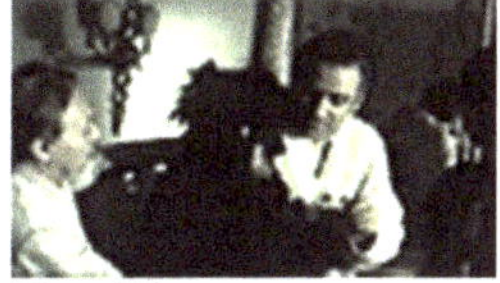

Shot 37
MOTHER: Marco!

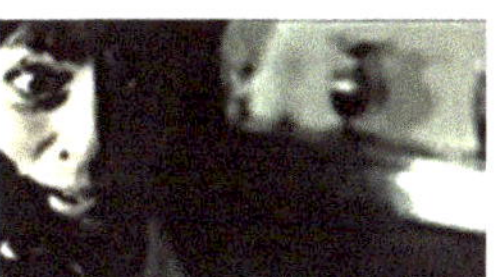

Shot 38
MOTHER *(hysterically, asthmatic)*. You hear me, Marco? Marco, don't travel at night. No.

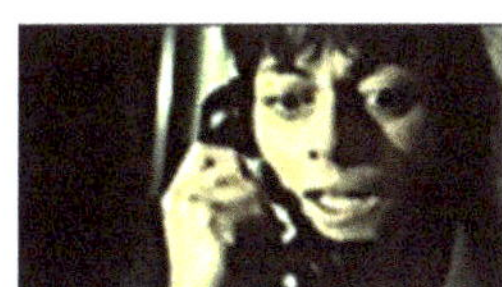

Shot 39
MOTHER. It's not safe yet.

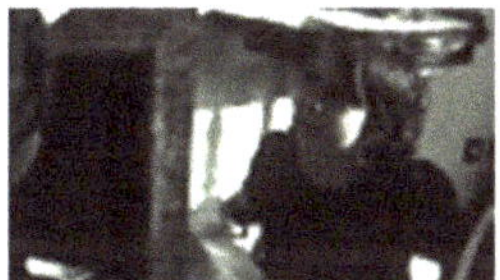

Shot 40
MOTHER. Marco!

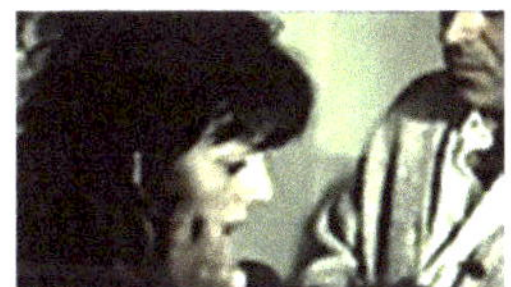

Shot 41

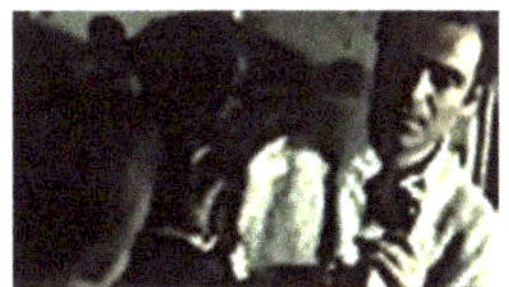

Shot 42

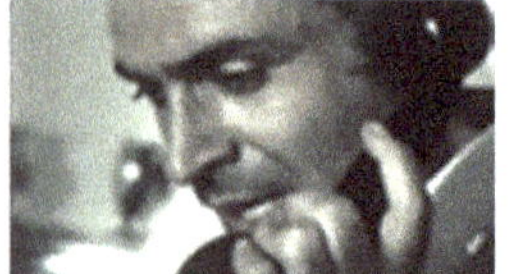

Shot 43

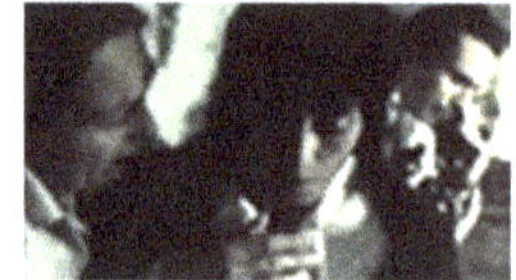

Shot 44
GRANDMA *(escorting the mother away)*. Our boy'll be back safe and sound.
FATHER. Marco.

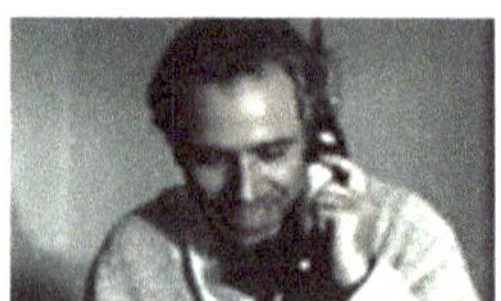

Shot 45
FATHER. Marco, could you hear her!? In two years she never had such strength!

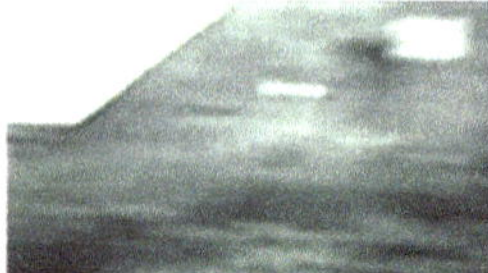

Shot 46

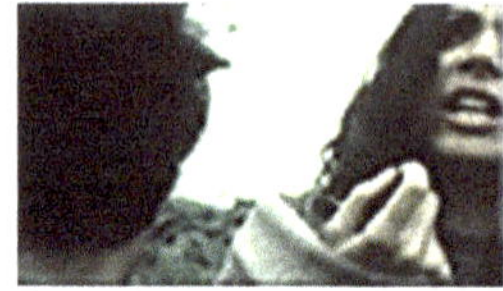

Shot 47
A GIRL. Hey! The war's over for us, as well!

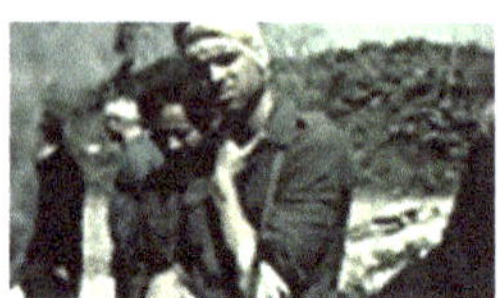

Shot 48

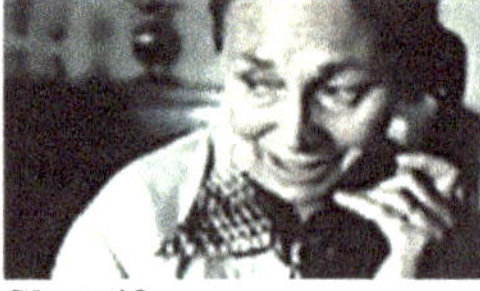

Shot 49
GRANDMA. Your friends went to the beach, Marco.

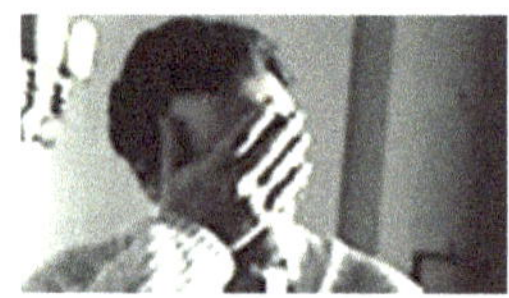

Shot 50
GRANDMA. You can join them now if you hurry!
LITTLE SISTER. Daddy! I want to listen too.

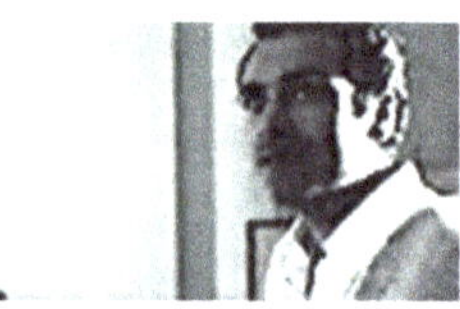

Shot 51
GRANDMA. Two years. Nothing has changed, Marco...

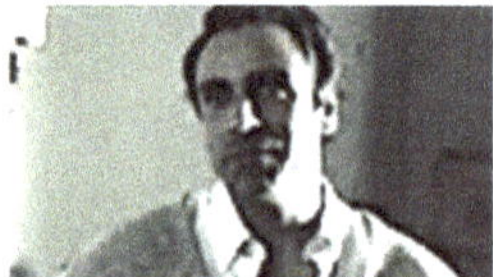

Shot 52
FATHER. We'll have a hot coffee together!
LITTLE SISTER. Marco...

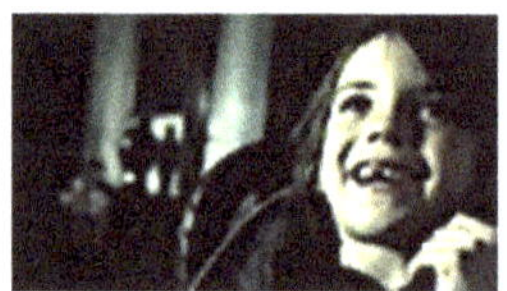

Shot 53
LITTLE SISTER: I lost a tooth, you see?

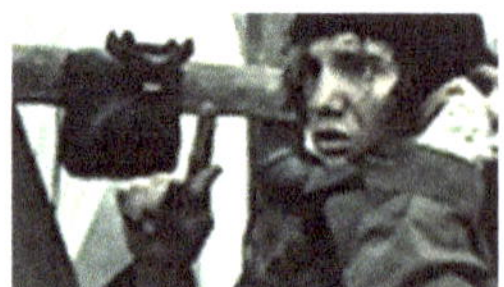

Shot 54

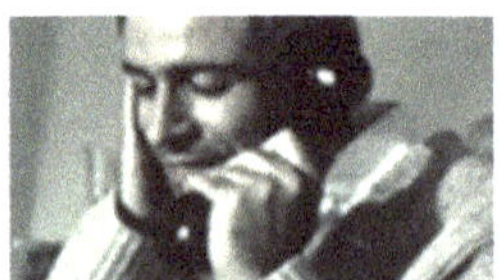

Shot 55
FATHER. We're all waiting for you!

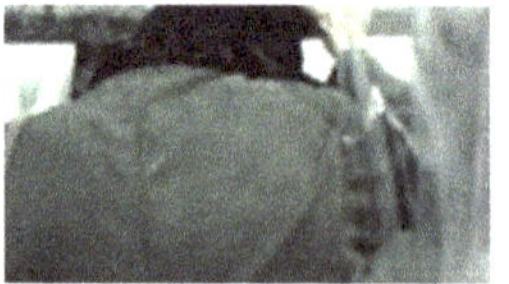

Shot 56

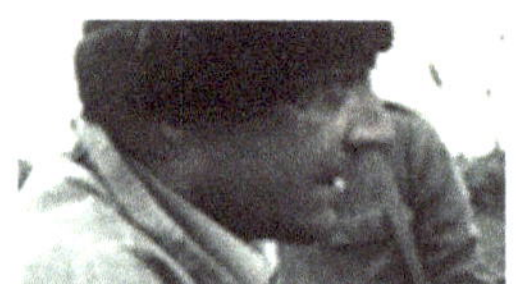

Shot 57
A SOLDIER. Hey! There are people waiting...

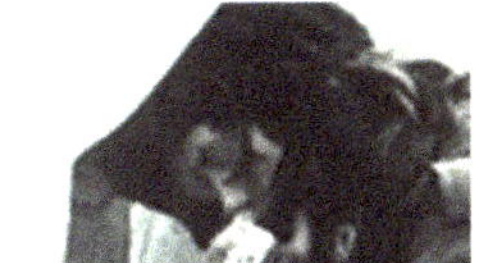
Shot 58

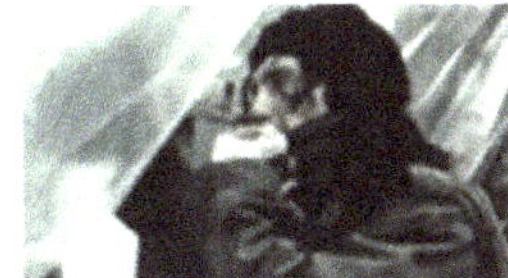
Shot 59
MARCO. Dad! Can you hear me?

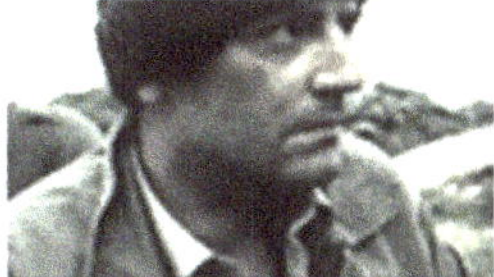
Shot 60
MARCO *(off)*. I have a friend with me.

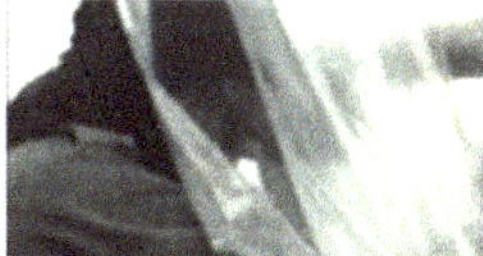
Shot 61
MARCO. We fought together…

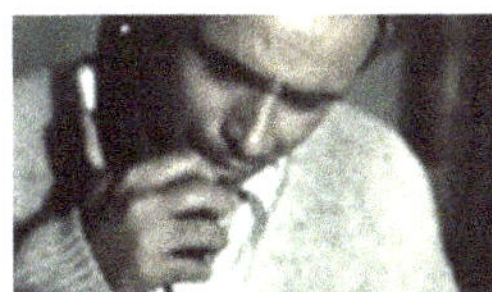
Shot 62
FATHER. Speak louder!

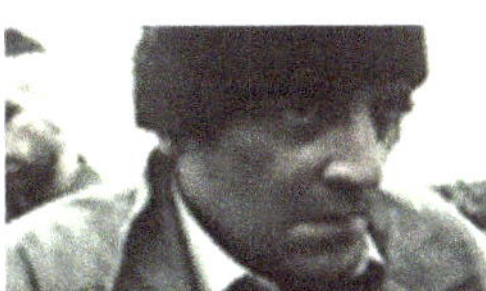
Shot 63
MARCO. I'd like to bring him with me...

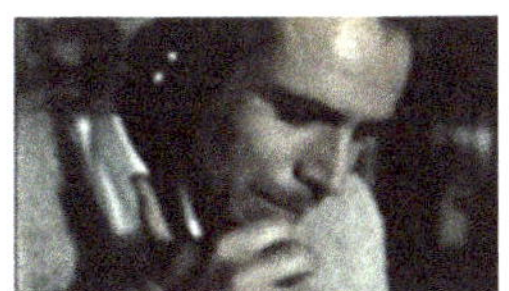
Shot 64
FATHER. You don't even have to ask!

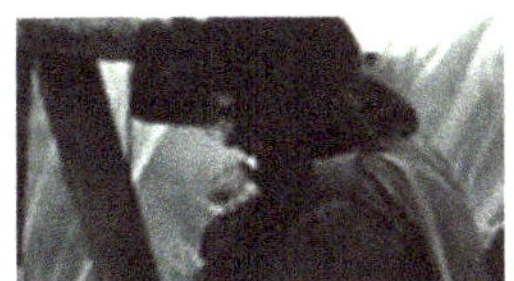
Shot 65
MARCO. Listen, Dad. He lost a leg.

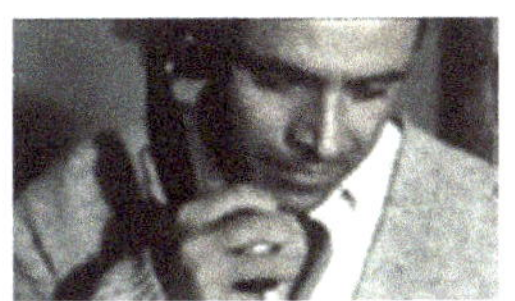
Shot 66

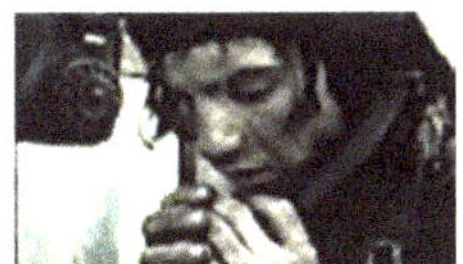
Shot 67

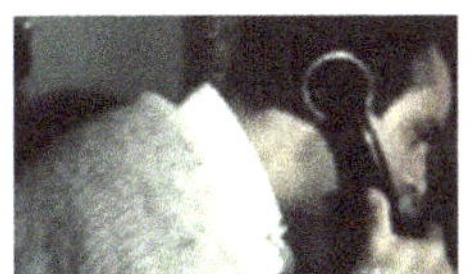
Shot 68
FATHER. Well, you know. Your mother's not so well.

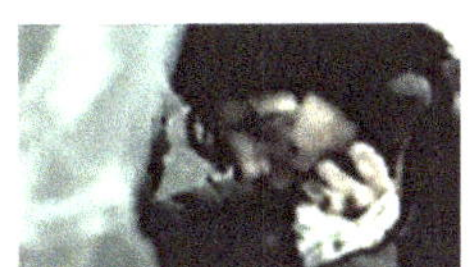
Shot 69
FATHER (*off*). She shouldn't get anxious.

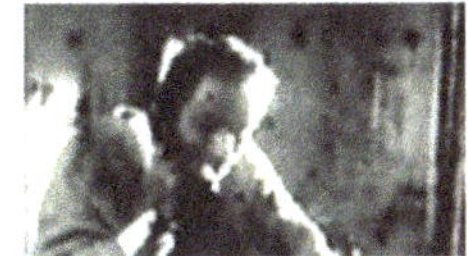
Shot 70
FATHER. Her last episodes were quite strong. I know…

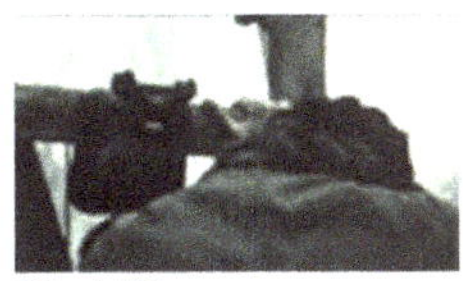
Shot 71
FATHER (*off*). …what a buddy from the front means.

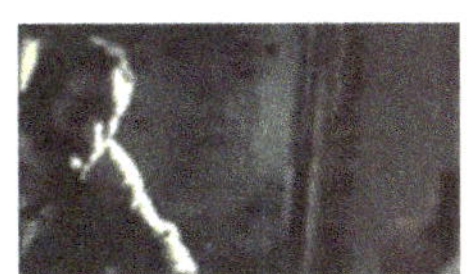
Shot 72
FATHER. Maybe later on.

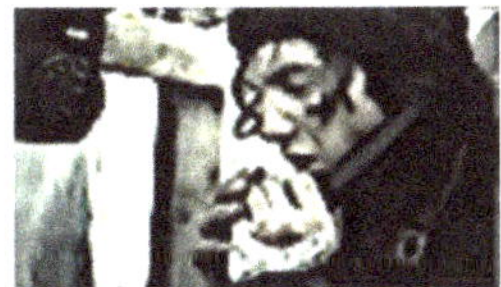
Shot 73
MARCO. Yes, maybe later.

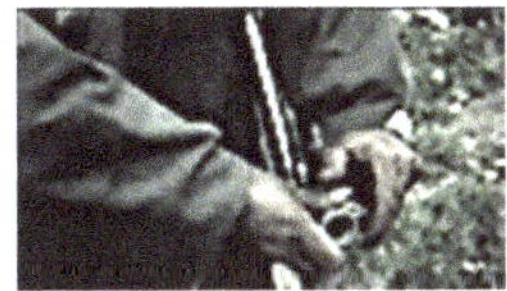
Shot 74
FATHER (*off*). We must help her to forget…

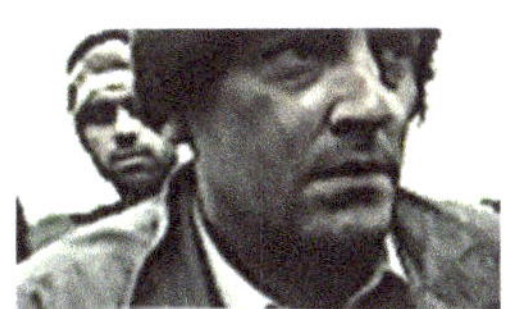
Shot 75
FATHER (*off*). ...what we all went through.

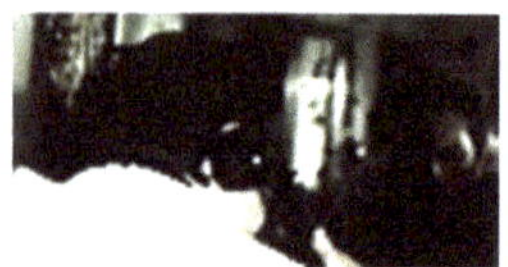

Shot 76
FATHER. As soon as she sees you she'll get better!

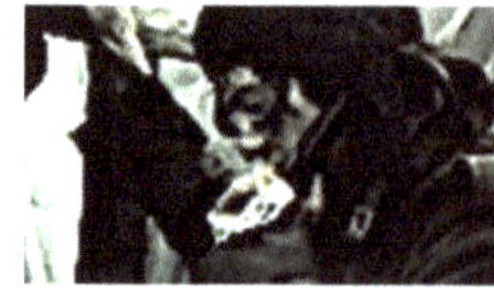

Shot 77
MARCO. Sure! Don't worry. As soon as I can! Ok, Dad. I have to hang up now. Give everybody a hug!

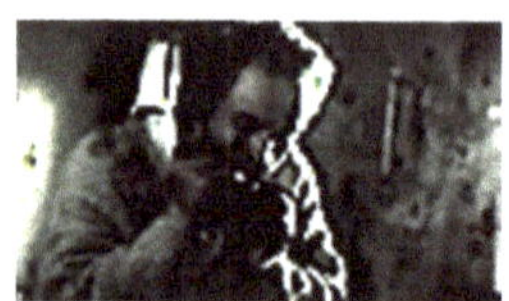

Shot 78
FATHER. Come home, son. Come back soon!

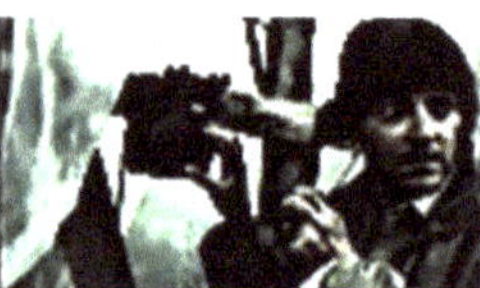

Shot 79
The soldier who had been holding a crutch, now takes over the phone. He is perfectly mobile and his hands are free.

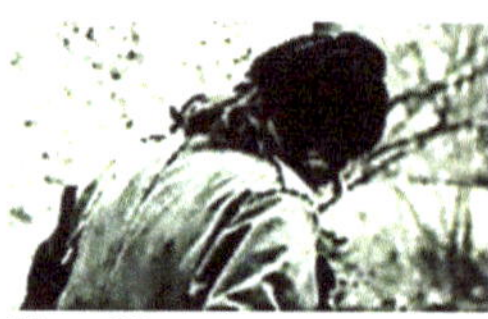

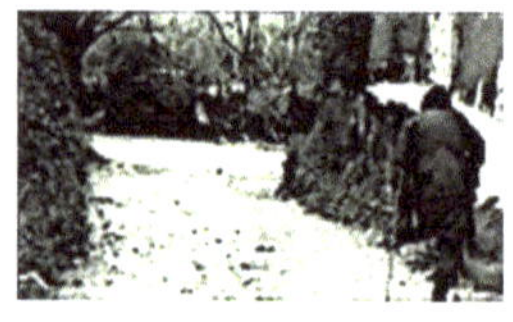

Shot 80
Beginning as a close shot of Marco and evolving into a total shot of him as he walks further away from the camera on his crutches, this final shot eventually reveals that it is Marco who has lost a leg.

YIN OF INTERPRETABILITY

Once again, we are dealing with a short film that leaves a great deal to the viewer to figure out by using his or her interpretive skills.

The most important issue in this context is understanding Marco's reason for making the phone call, and having used this film in my classes for many years, I know from experience that not everybody 'gets' it at first. If all the dots are connected, including the father's key statement about Marco's mother, "We must help her to forget what we all went through" (Shots 74–75), we can work out the underlying story:

> When the war ended, Marco had to decide whether or not he could return to his family. Having lost a leg, he suspected that his disability would be a constant reminder of the war to his mother and feared that that might worsen her already unstable mental condition. He needed to find out from his father whether his suspicions were correct but couldn't just tell him the truth and expect an honest answer. So he made up the story of a friend he would like to bring home with him. Marco's father unknowingly confirms his son's worst suspicions, without realizing that he was preventing his son from returning home.

That's a substantial amount of complex subtext for the viewer to work out on the basis of the cues. But there is also another interpretive question viewers have to deal with in one way or another.

Once we have seen the ending of *The War Is Over*, and realize that Marco has lost a leg, the opening sequence in which he dances euphorically to celebrate the end of the war (Shots 1–4) doesn't make sense in any ordinary way. Even the actor who played Marco was confused when asked to do that sequence, and replied: "I dance? Nina, I've only got one leg!" When I asked Nina Mimica about this apparent defiance of logic, she replied:

> Actually, this sequence was not in the screenplay, which began with the phone call. But just before the end of the two-day shoot, on the second day, I had an intuition that something essential was missing: a counterpart to the soldier. Even in war, beauty coexists with what might be called raw reality. Maybe it's something of the marvellous and terrible that go together.
>
> Again and again, it happens that I dream parts of a story, if not practically the entire story, and experience has taught me that those parts should never be changed; so I leave them as they appear to me in those little revelations. I know that everything else can be changed, all the things I thought up consciously could be developed and improved, but the things I dream, and which come to me as a necessity without my understanding why, I have learned simply to do them and not to ask myself why (Raskin 2011: 23).

Nina Mimica makes a sharp distinction between conscious script development and the "little revelations" that come to her in dreams – between a *yang* process under her control and subject to improvement, and a letting go of that process in a *yin* perspective in which there is only compliance and no asking why. In this respect, dream plays for her a role similar to that played by chance for Jørgen Leth.

But how might viewers make sense of the opening sequence? One possibility would be to view the initial dance sequence and the long final shot (Shot 80, running 29 seconds) of a disabled soldier walking alone into an uncertain future, as framing pieces, showing first how euphoric the end of the war *should* or is *imagined* to be, and finally the grim reality that the war never ends. That doesn't resolve the riddle of the anatomic inconsistency but it does make the very divergence of the two portrayals of Marco meaningful in its own way.

YANG OF BEING IN CHARGE

The *yang* that counterbalances the *yin of interpretability* just discussed, is Marco's power in shaping his own story. Though it is retrospectively that we understand what he is doing, we see him carrying out a strategy he had conceived for finding out what he needs to know. *Being in charge* of one's own story is the ultimate power to which any character can aspire.

SHORT FILM 8

Below the Belt / Under bæltestedet

Alexander Kølpin, Denmark, 2006, 10 min., colour

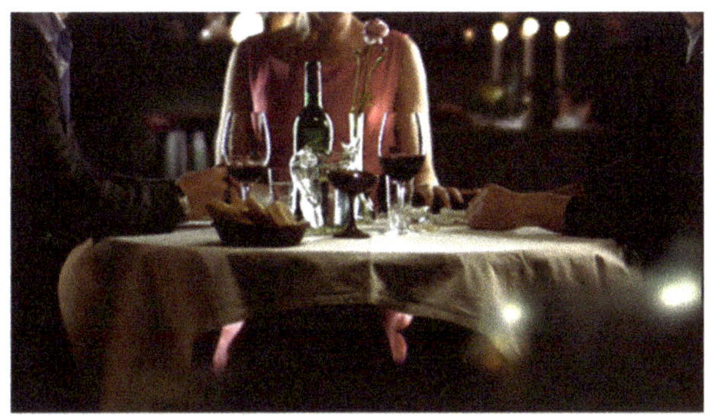

Director	Alexander Kølpin
Cinematographer	Mads Thomsen
Editor	My Thordal
Screenwriters	Ine Urheim, Lars Andreas Pedersen, Alexander Kølpin
Production	Fridthjof Film
Producer	Emilie Brandt
Sound	Thomas Jæger, Jason Luke
Composer	Jesper Mechlenburg
Scenographer	Mia Stensgaard

Cast

Trine Dyrholm	Naja
Troels Lyby	Søren
Lars Brygmann	Mikkel

Link to the film: https://www.youtube.com/watch?v=fica53Ydn4Q (unfortunately without English subtitles)

Given the limits established by the director for the camera's framing of the three characters, this film sets a bold challenge for itself. I know of no other short film that could compete with it in that respect.

Synopsis

Glimpses of Naja alone, removing her gloves, opening her jacket. Elsewhere, Søren and Mikkel are seated at a small round table in a restaurant. Mikkel had previously confided in Søren that he has erection difficulties, and Søren now asks Mikkel how that potency problem is going. When Mikkel's answer shows he is resigned to be among the 30% who suffer from the problem, Søren berates him for being passive and urges him to do something about it. Søren then tells about a girl he has met and is crazy about. As Søren and Mikkel talk about her, Naja approaches the table where the two men stand to greet her. Søren, amazed to see her unexpectedly, reaches out to kiss her but she deftly turns their contact into a handshake. Søren tells her she is beautiful and asks if she wouldn't like to sit down. She says she can't because she is meeting a girlfriend. He jokes about not having anything else he can do for her and they both laugh. He introduces her to Mikkel, but Naja and Mikkel already know each other, having been at school together. Mikkel slips his hand around her waist and she accepts his kiss on the cheek. Søren says they should all stay now for five minutes. Naja takes her jacket off and sits down. Asked by Mikkel if she still eats like a horse, Naja says she still enjoys food. Søren proposes some champagne. But touching her hand, Mikkel asks whether she wouldn't rather have red wine, which she would. They order a bottle of Bourgogne. Søren asks Naja if she isn't working as a consultant and she says yes, and has twelve people working under her. Her business is doing well. Under the table, we see Naja's stockinged legs – she has taken off one of her high heeled shoes – and Søren's and Mikkel's feet with their shoes on, Søren nervously jiggling one foot. Back to the table top, Søren is nervously jiggling something in one hand as Naja tells a story moving her arms and playing with a delicate necklace she is wearing. Mikkel reaches out and pulls a perhaps imaginary speck or hair from her bare shoulder. Søren compliments Naja on her beautiful dress. Conversation then turns to preparing food and Mikkel tells how much he enjoys working with quality ingredients when cooking. Annoyed by Naja's and Mikkel's interest in one another, Søren almost audibly scoffs as Mikkel speaks. Naja crosses her legs, bringing them close to Mikkel's as we see under the table. Trying to break the little spell developing between Naja and Mikkel, Søren says he hears that it's 30% – Naja asks of what? that are vegetarian, Søren answers, and offers to make Naja a really delicious meal some day. He wants to pour more wine in her glass but she stops him. Under the table we see that Mikkel is caressing Naja's leg with one shoe. She smiles and runs her fingers up and down one arm. Her respiration becomes more sensual as she and Mikkel continue playing footsies under the table. Søren proposes coffee but Mikkel says no, they can all go to his place for coffee, to which Søren complains that Mikkel doesn't even drink coffee. Søren accidentally drops a spoon on the floor and when he bends down to pick it up, he can see what has been going on under the table. He then starts picking on Mikkel and threatening to tell about his little problem. Søren knocks over a glass of wine and Mikkel gets up and walks away. Søren tells him not to forget his potency in the cloakroom. Then Naja gets up and leaves. Søren is now alone at the table. The waiter hands him the check.

Shot-by-shot breakdown of *Below the Belt*

What follows is merely a schematic outline, making it possible to refer to specific shots by number. At no point are the actors' faces fully visible. My translations from the Danish.

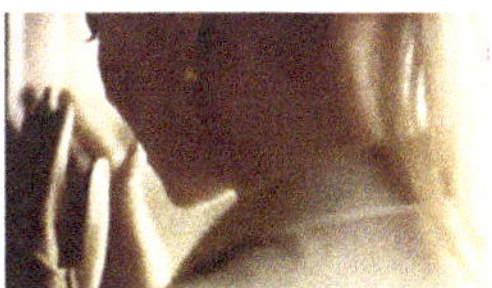

Shot 1
Naja removes her gloves.

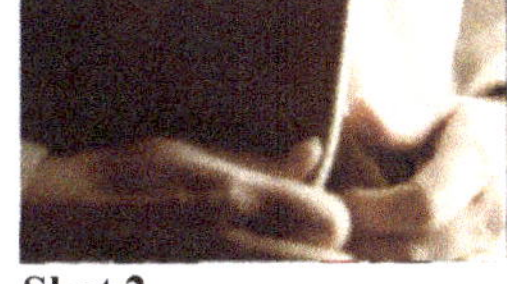

Shot 2
She opens her jacket.

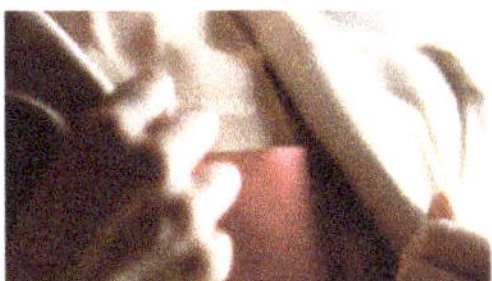

Shot 3

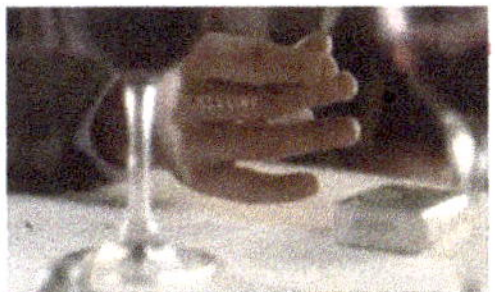

Shot 4

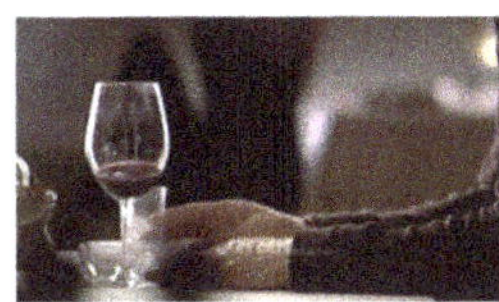

Shot 5

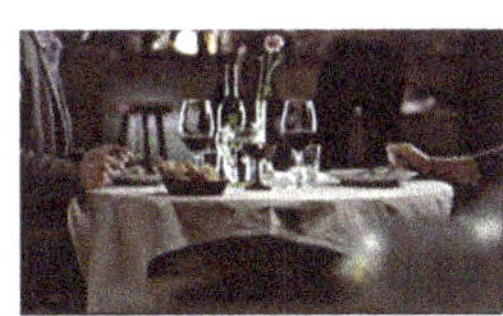

Shot 6
SØREN: Man, this tastes terrific and I'll bet it's good for potency.
MIKKEL: Really? I've got to have a taste. Wow, that is good. It's what I should have ordered.

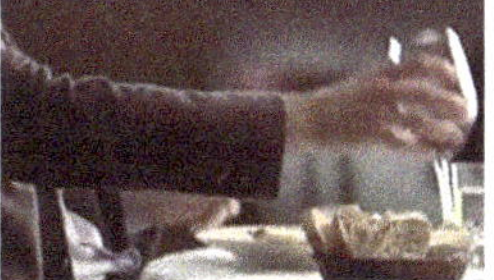

Shot 7

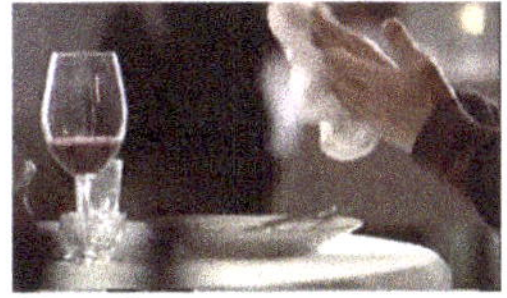

Shot 8

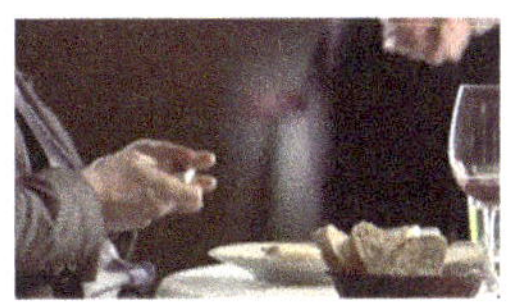

Shot 9
WAITER: I hope you liked it.
SØREN: It was delicious. Very good.

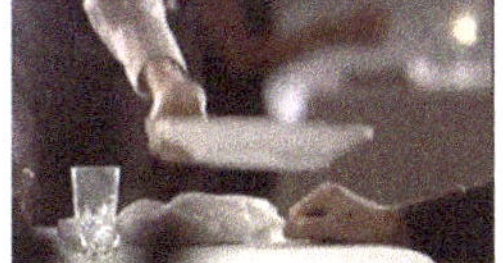

Shot 10

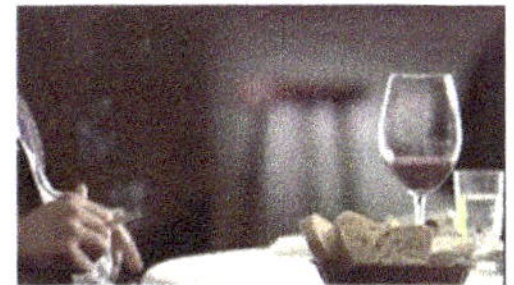

Shot 11
SØREN: How are things going with…

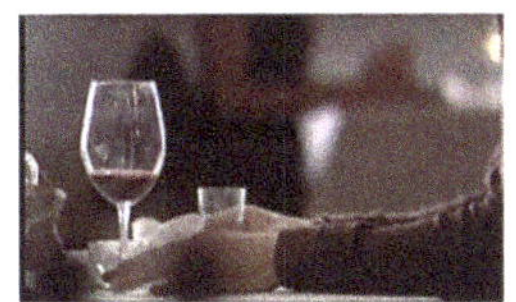

Shot 12
MIKKEL: Yes, it went the way things like that go.

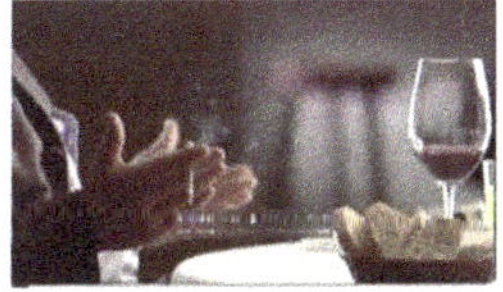

Shot 13
SØREN: You should be taking something for it, shouldn't you? Can't you take some Viagra?

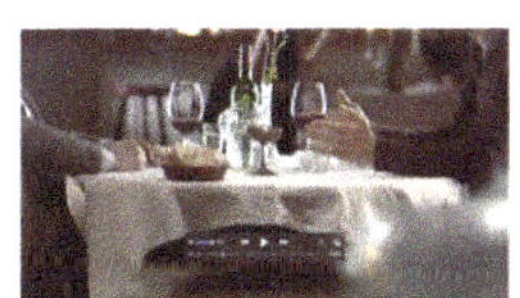

Shot 14
MIKKEL: It's not a problem. It happens to 30%.
SØREN: 30%?

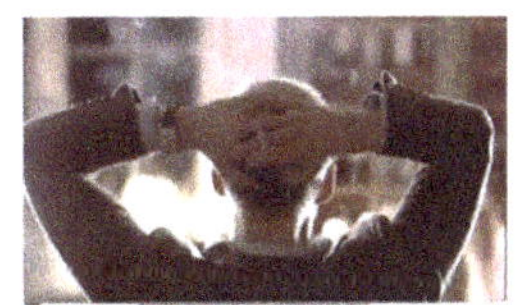

Shot 15
SØREN: Damn it, you shouldn't be so passive, right?

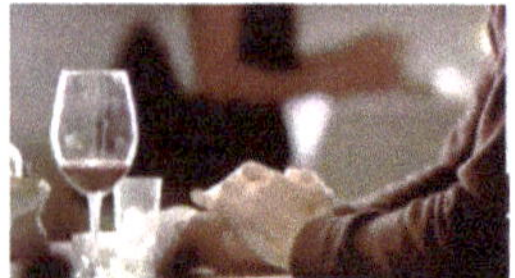

Shot 16
SØREN: Just get back into the battle.

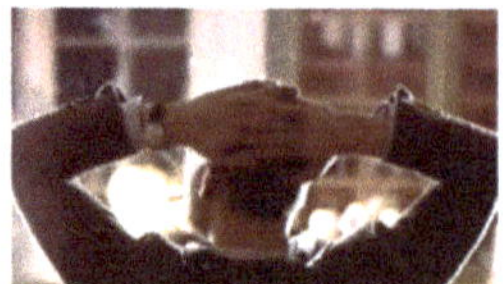

Shot 17
SØREN: And when the right one comes along, you'll know that for sure.

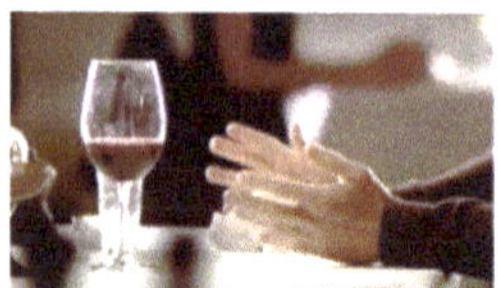

Shot 18
MIKKEL: Yeah, and in the meantime, I don't get any pussy.

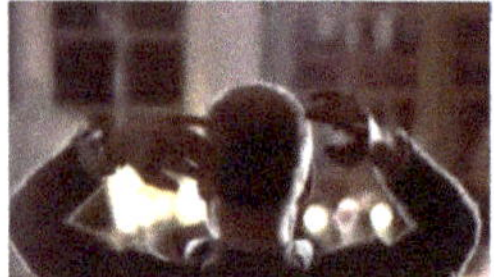

Shot 19

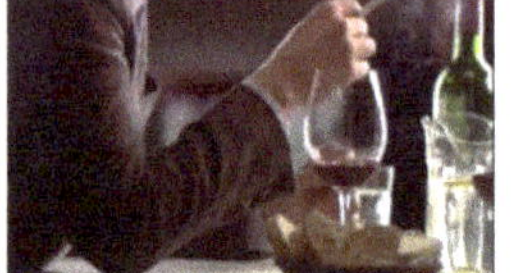

Shot 20
SØREN: I met a girl last week, at that meeting. She was very pretty…

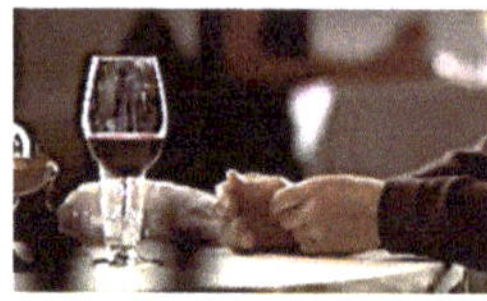

Shot 21
SØREN: and a really sharp consultant.

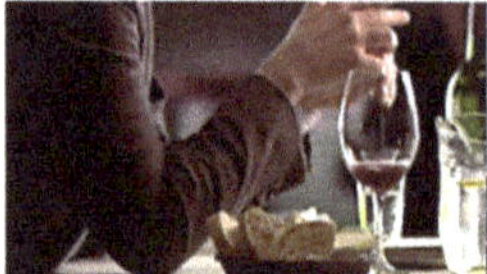

Shot 22
SØREN: She's smart as a whip and gorgeous.

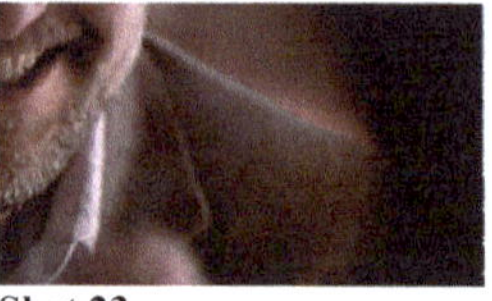

Shot 23
MIKKEL (*off*): I haven't heard you talk like that for years.

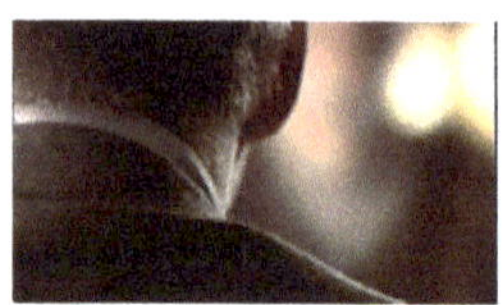

Shot 24

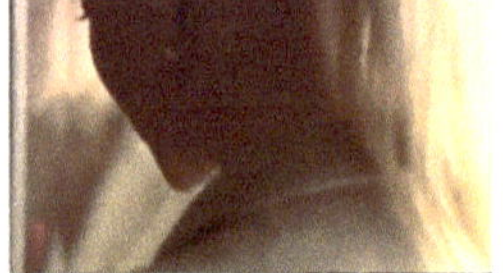

Shot 25

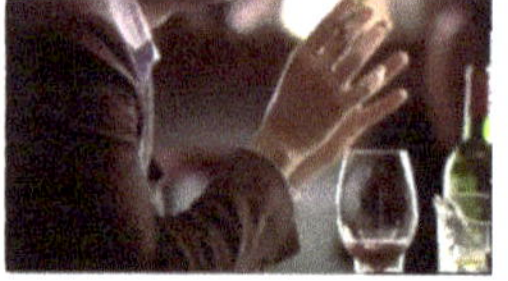

Shot 26

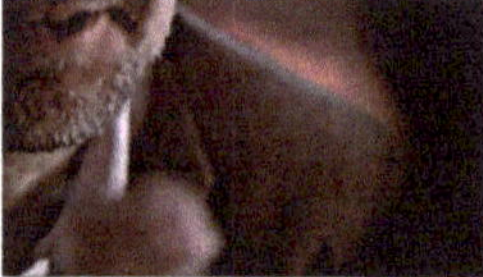

Shot 27

SØREN: She is…. I've never seen anyone like her. She's simply fantastic. She's sweet. And there's something other…

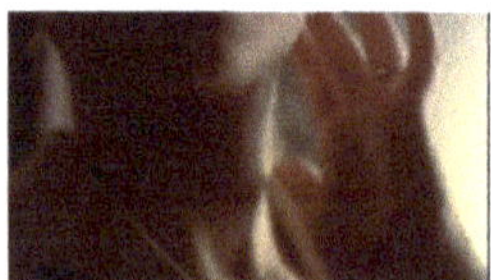

Shot 28

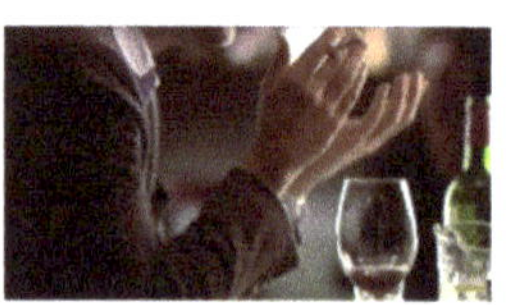

Shot 29

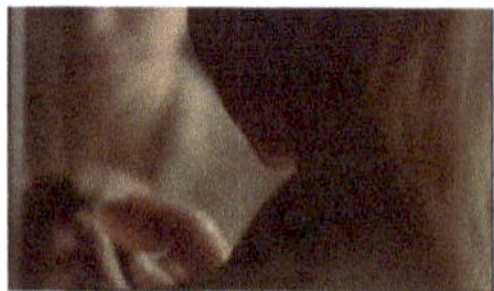

Shot 30

SØREN: that she does. Just the way she looked with those big blue eyes. But it's also her body language.

Naja fixes her hair and puts on lipstick. She may be able to hear what Søren and Mikkel are saying.

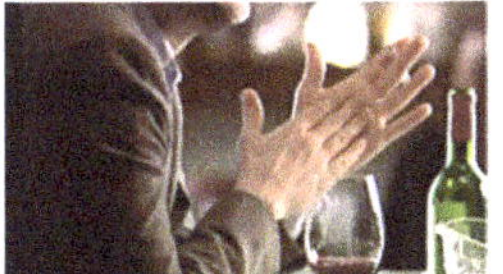

Shot 31

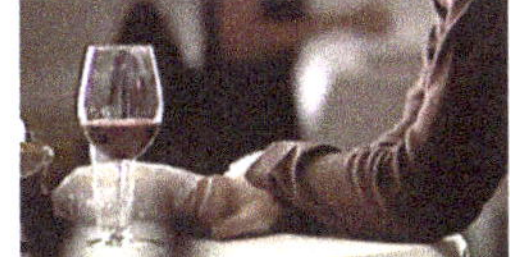

Shot 32

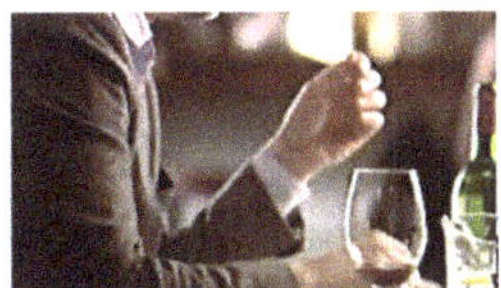

Shot 33
SØREN: It's too soon to say anything.

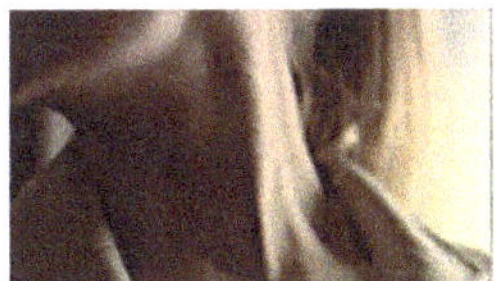

Shot 34
SØREN: What the hell, I'm not 30 any more.
MIKKEL (*off*): Yeah but Søren, that's great! That's wonderful.

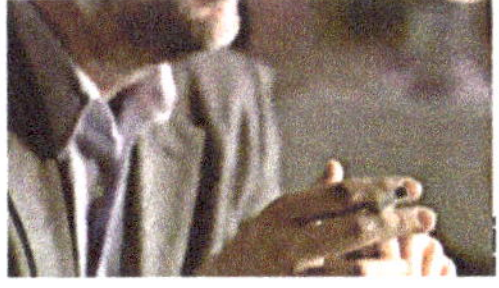

Shot 35
SØREN (whispering): This is fucking insane, man. She just walked in the door.

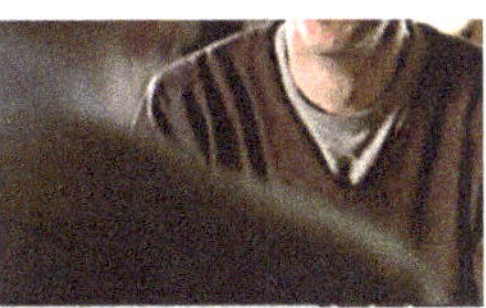

Shot 36
MIKKEL: That's fantastic!

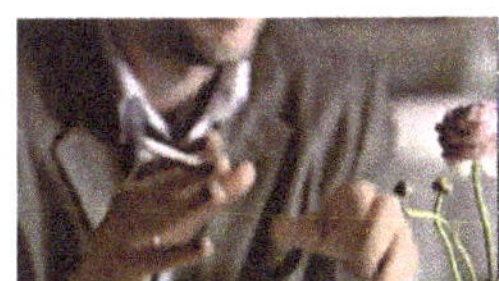

Shot 37

Shot 38

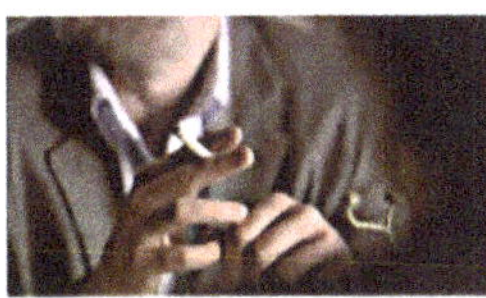

Shot 39

SØREN: Don't look. Take it easy, take it easy, take it easy. It's a sign.

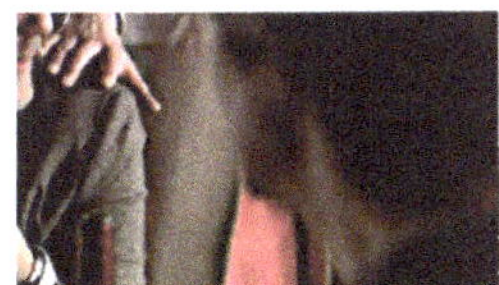

Shot 40
NAJA: Hey, Søren!

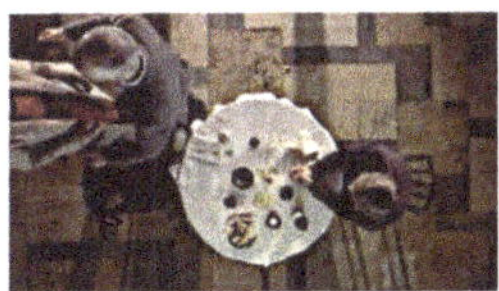

Shot 41a

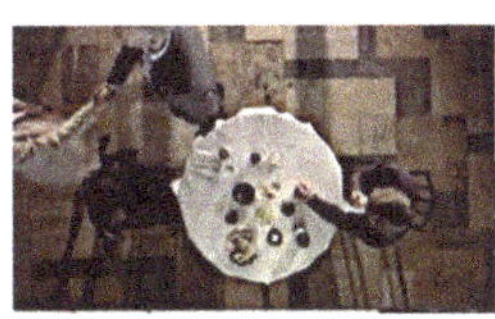

Shot 41b

SØREN: My God, hello! This is funny.
NAJA: Thanks for the last time we were together.
SØREN: Thank you.

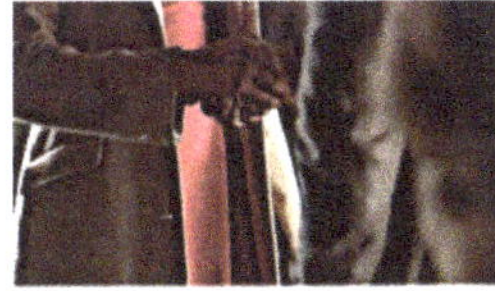

Shot 42
SØREN: How nice to see you again. It's always good to see you.

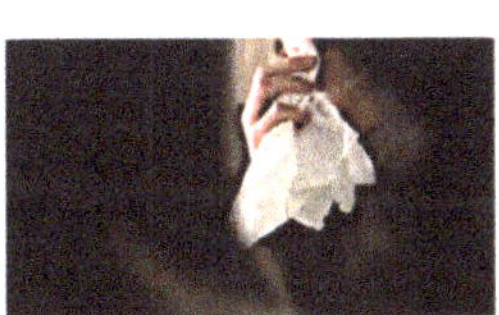

Shot 43
SØREN: You look terrific!
NAJA: Thanks.

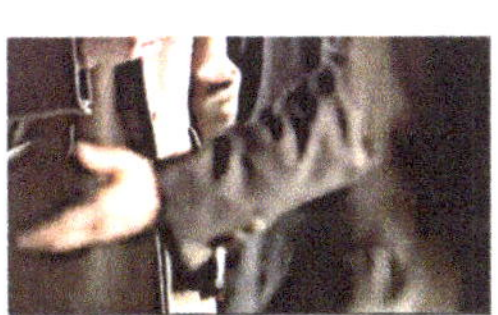

Shot 44
SØREN: Wouldn't you like to sit down?

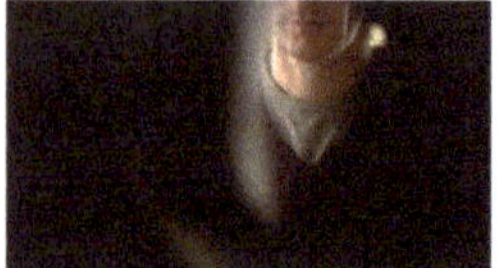

Shot 45
NAJA: No I'm meeting a girlfriend.

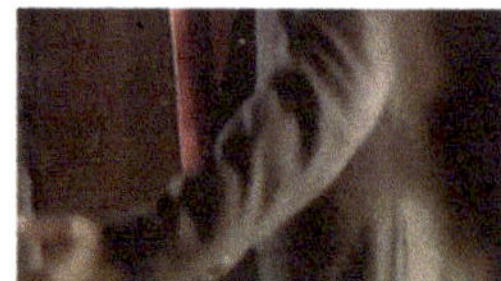

Shot 46
SØREN: Okay. What else can I do for you?
NAJA: Not so much. (*They laugh.*)

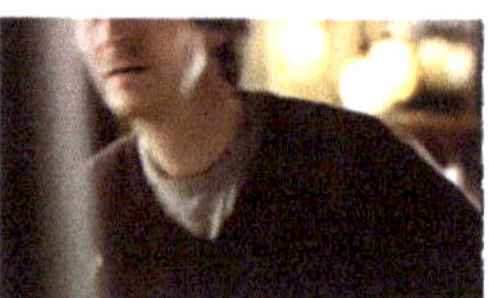

Shot 47
SØREN: You can say hello to my friend, Mikkel.
NAJA: Mikkel Hvid?

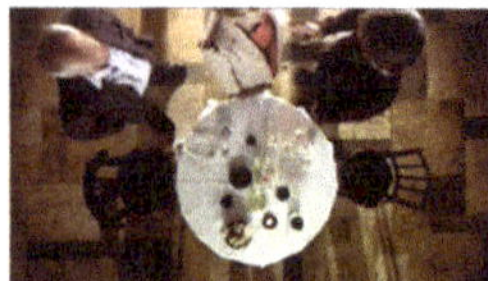

Shot 48
MIKKEL: That's right. Naja Tholstrup?

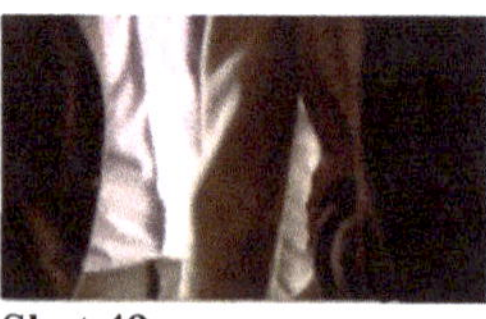

Shot 49
NAJA: Hi.

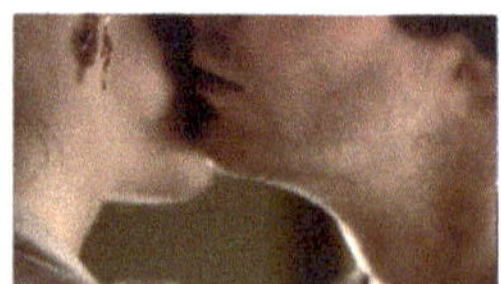

Shot 50

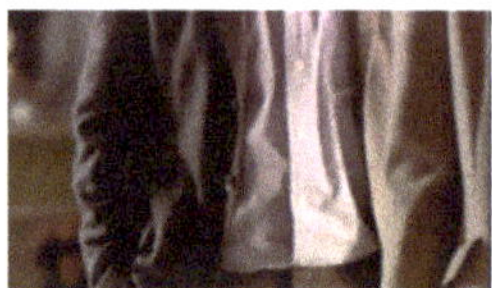

Shot 51
SØREN: How do you know each other already?

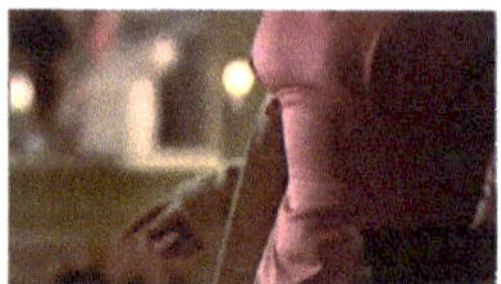

Shot 52
NAJA: We were at school together.
SØREN: You know what? You're just going to have to stay here for five minutes.

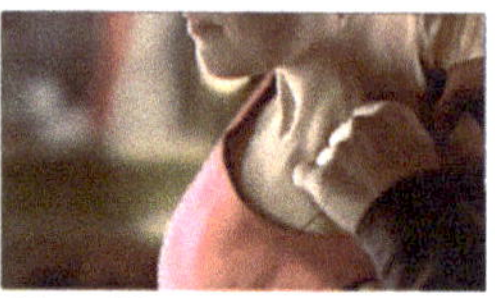

Shot 53
MIKKEL (*adjusting her necklace*): I'll just take this. Uh oh, now there's trouble.
NAJA: You're funny.

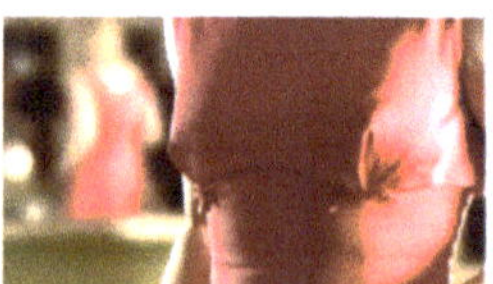

Shot 54

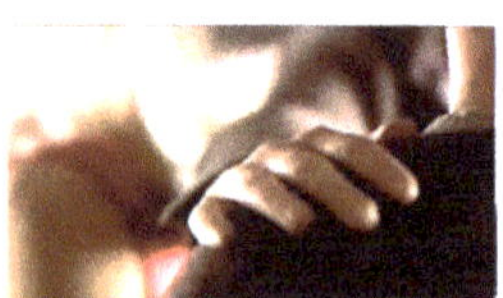

Shot 55
SØREN (*to Mikkel*): Please take the jacket?

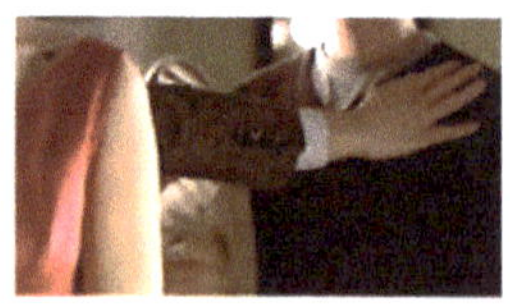

Shot 56
SØREN: I'll just find a chair for you.

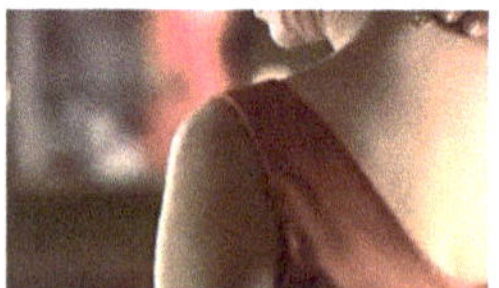

Shot 57

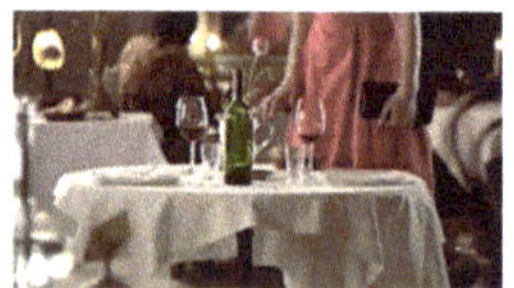

Shot 58a

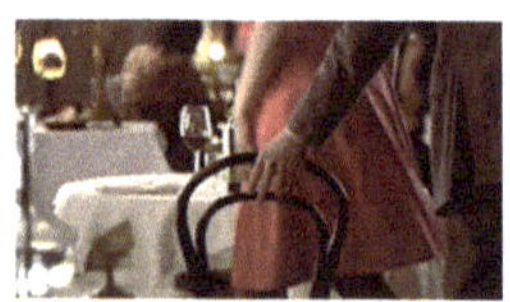

Shot 58b

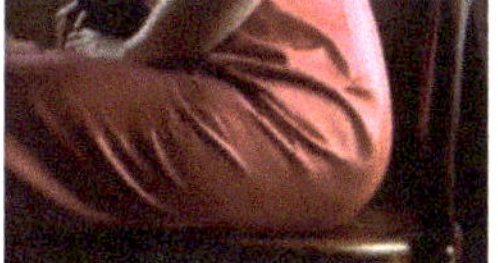
Shot 59

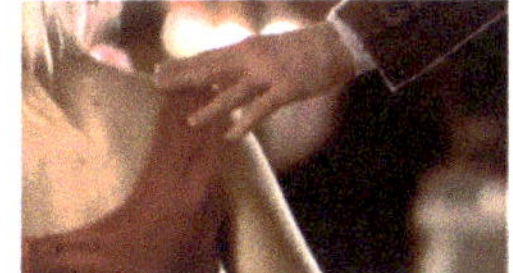
Shot 60

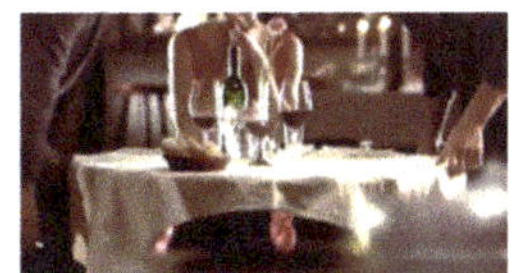
Shot 61
MIKKEL: Do you still eat like a horse?
NAJA: Yes, I actually do.

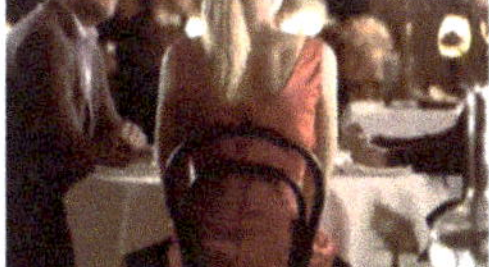
Shot 62
NAJA: I still enjoy food.

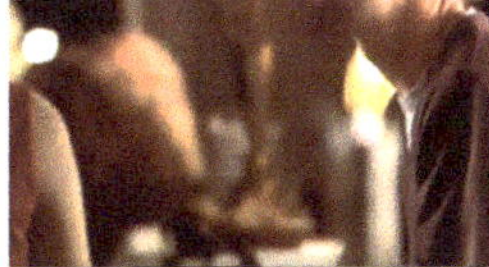
Shot 63
WAITER: Would you like something to drink?
SØREN (*to Naja*): A glass of Champagne for you?

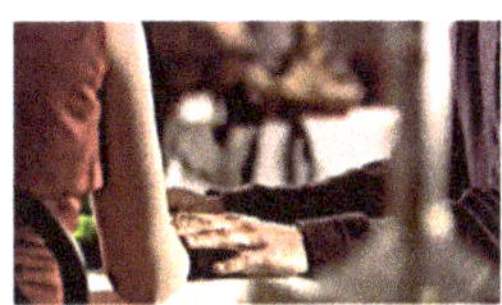
Shot 64
MIKKEL (*to Naja*): Or are you more into red wine?
NAJA: Yes, how did you know?

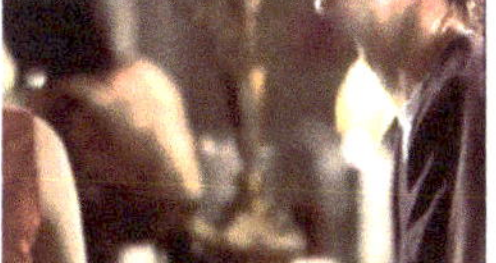
Shot 65
MIKKEL (*to waiter*): A bottle of good Burgogne.

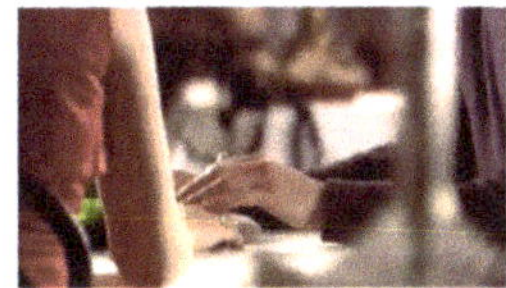
Shot 66

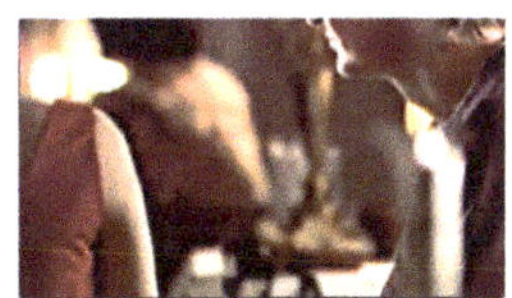
Shot 67

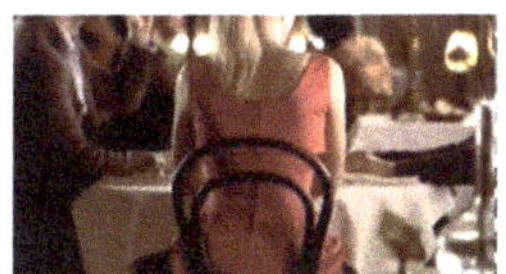
Shot 68

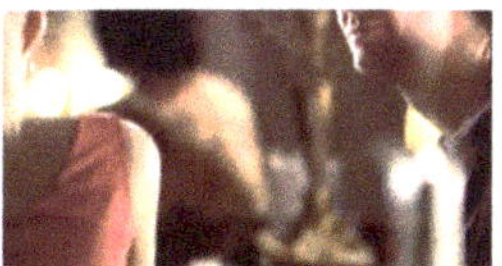
Shot 69
MIKKEL: Tell me, Naja. Weren't you going to be a consultant?
NAJA: Yes, and I am. I actually have twelve employees now and business is going well.

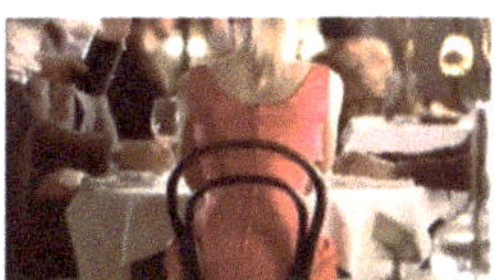
Shot 70
WAITER: Who would like to taste the wine?

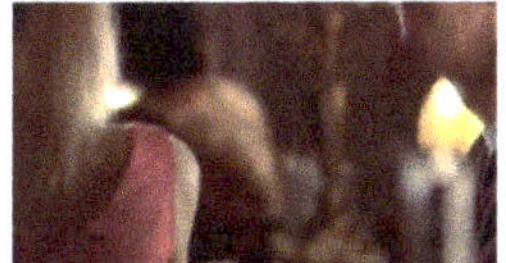
Shot 71

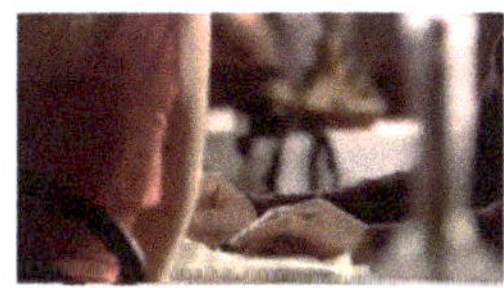
Shot 72

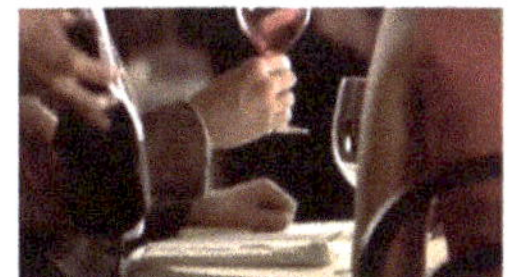
Shot 73
SØREN: Beautiful color.

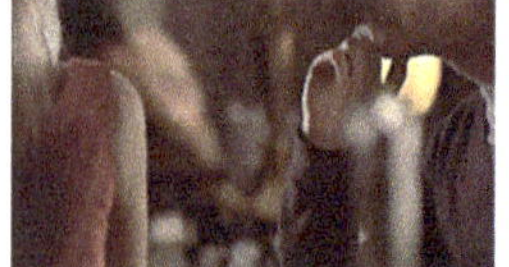
Shot 74

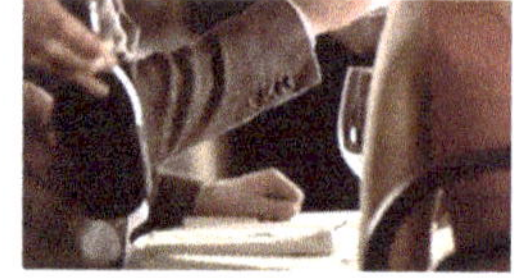
Shot 75
SØREN: Mmmm.

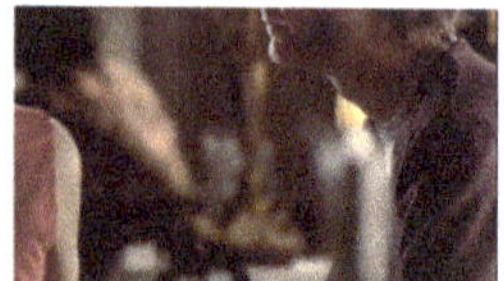
Shot 76
SØREN: Mmm, mmm, mmm, mmm. It's very good. It's delicious. Perfect. Just like you, Naja. We'll take it.

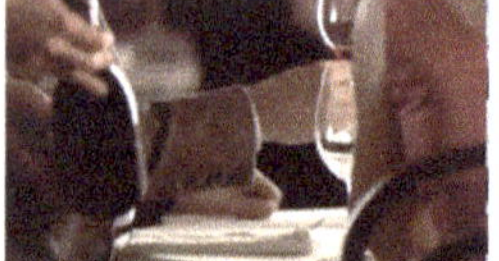
Shot 77

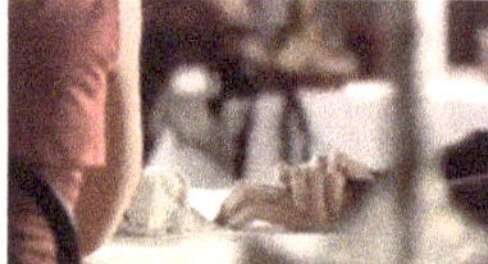
Shot 78

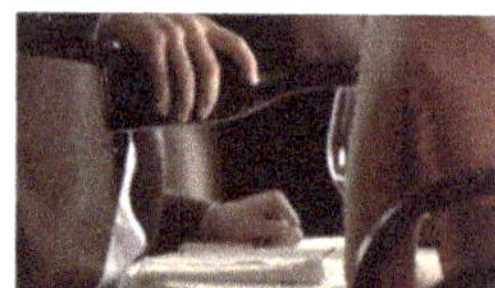
Shot 79

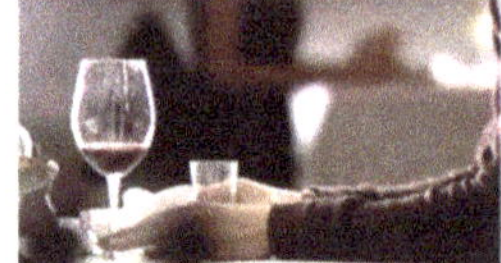
Shot 80

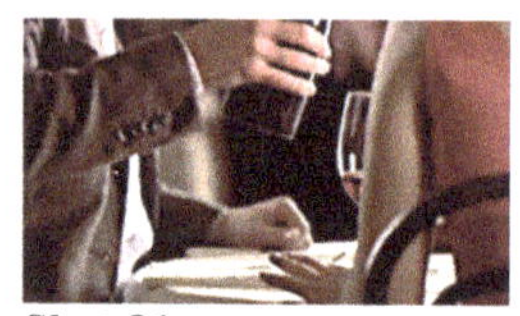
Shot 81

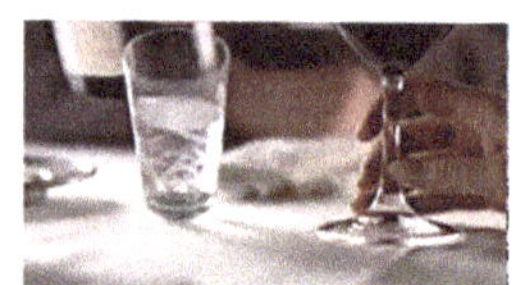
Shot 82
Søren knocks over a glass of water.

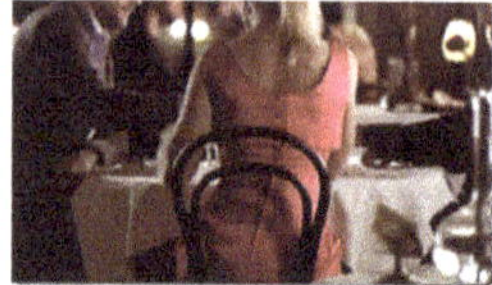
Shot 83
SØREN: Oh, great!

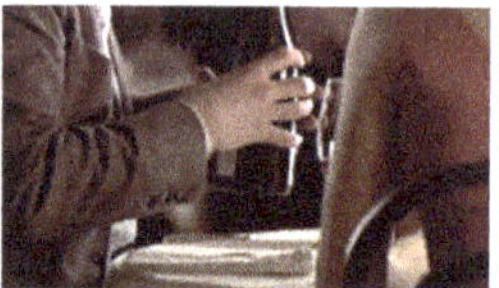
Shot 84
MIKKEL (*to Søren*): You shouldn't have any more to drink, right?

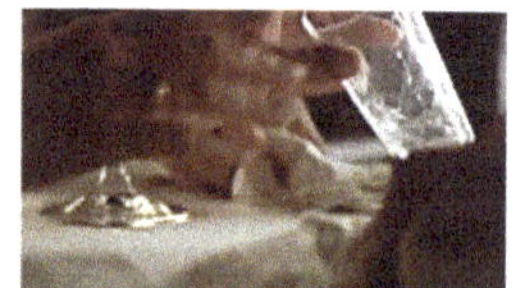
Shot 85

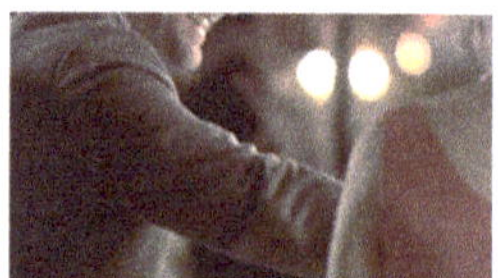
Shot 86

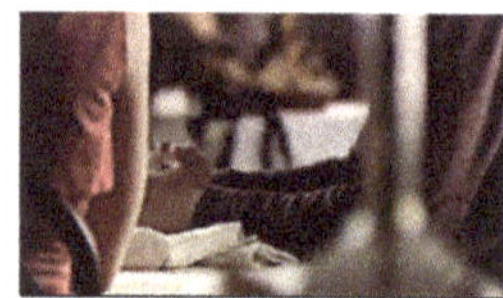
Shot 87

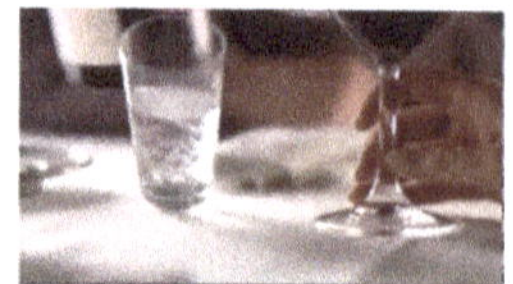
Shot 88

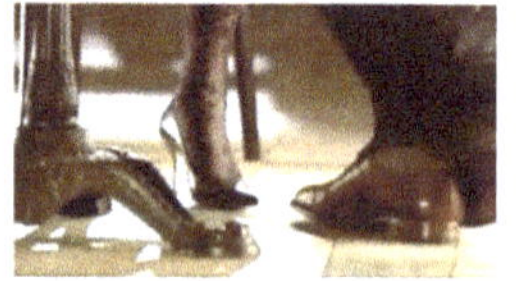
Shot 89

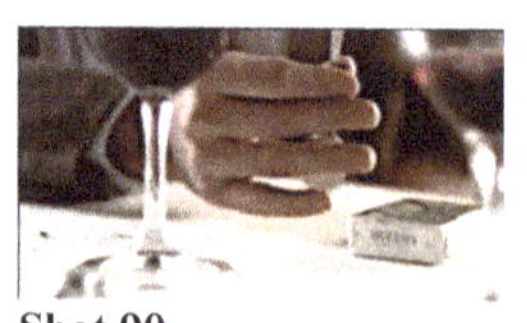
Shot 90

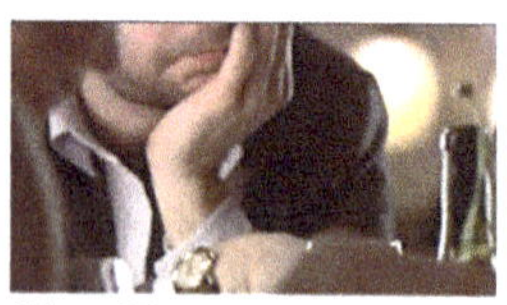
Shot 91

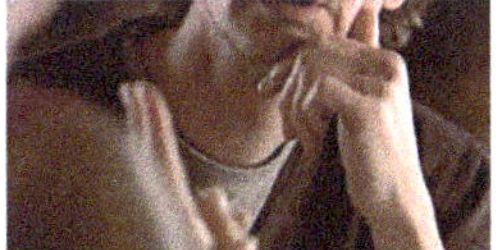
Shot 92

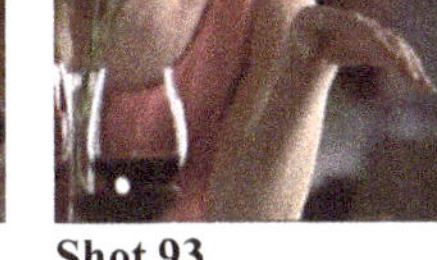
Shot 93

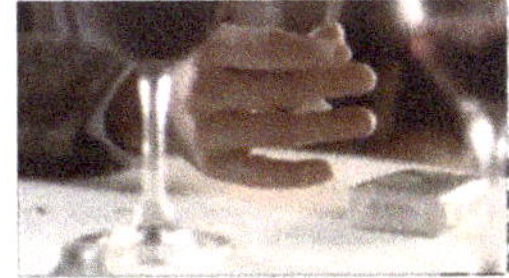
Shot 94

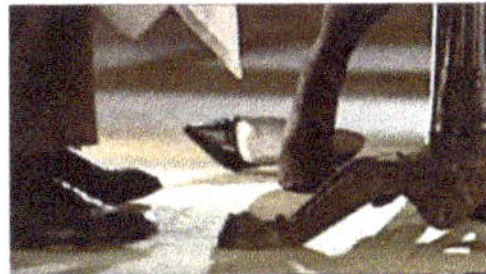
Shot 95

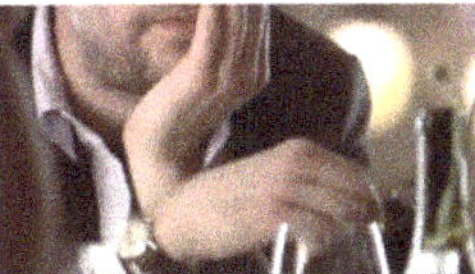
Shot 96

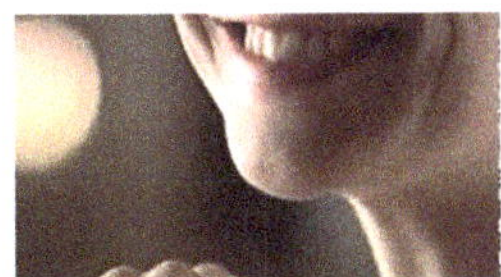
Shot 97
MIKKEL: So you never got there?

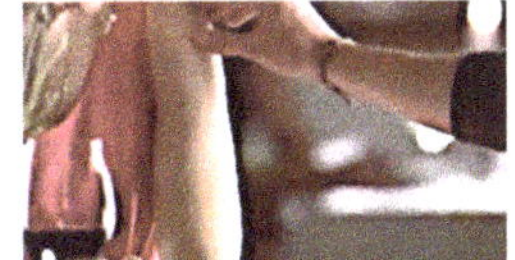
Shot 98
NAJA: No.

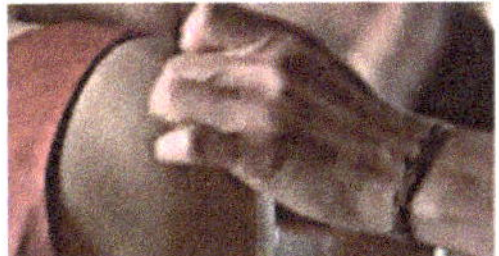
Shot 99

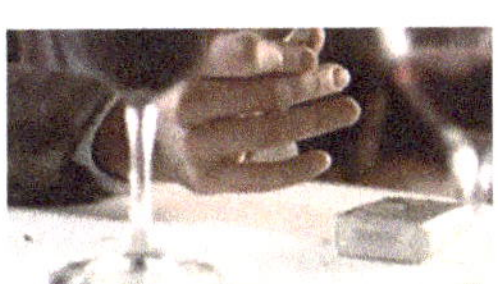
Shot 100

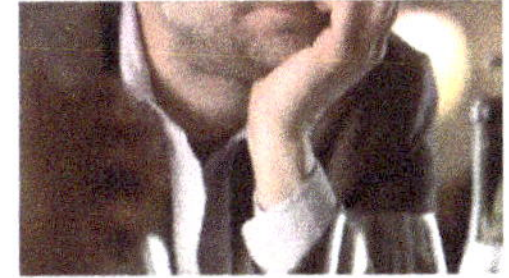
Shot 101
SØREN: You have cake on your fingers. That's a shame for your beautiful dress.

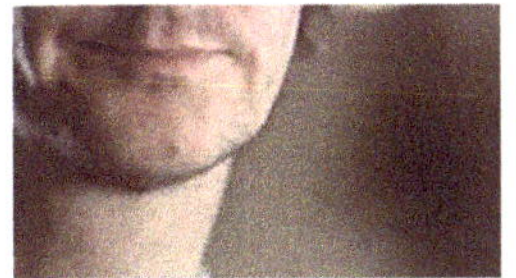
Shot 102

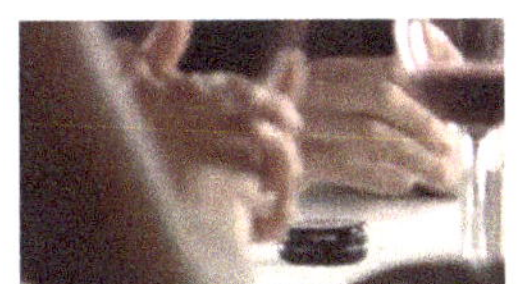
Shot 103
NAJA: No, that doesn't matter. I love to cook, right?

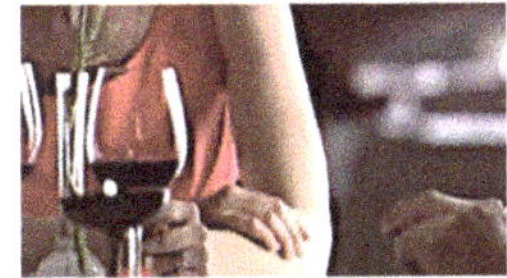
Shot 104
MIKKEL: There's nothing better.

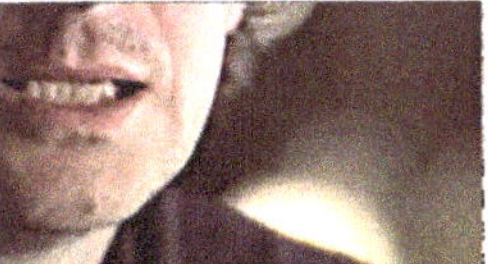
Shot 105
MIKKEL: I have to admit that I'm also something of a food lover.

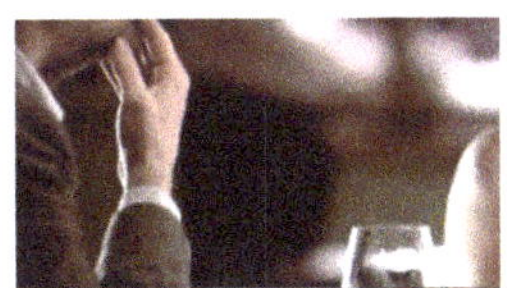
Shot 106
MIKKEL: Now it's said.

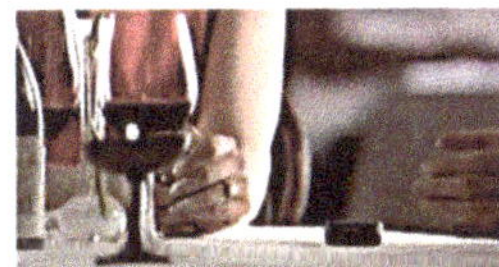
Shot 107

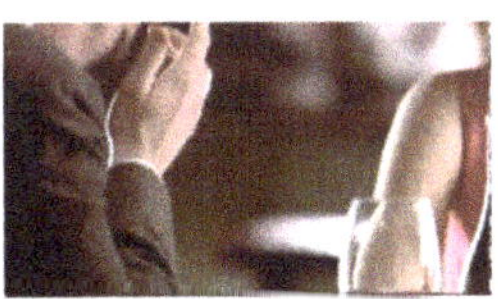
Shot 108

MIKKEL: I love cooking. (*Søren sighs demonstrably.*) Standing in the kitchen and having bought the coolest ingredients. The best meat. (*Søren sighs again.*) The best fish.

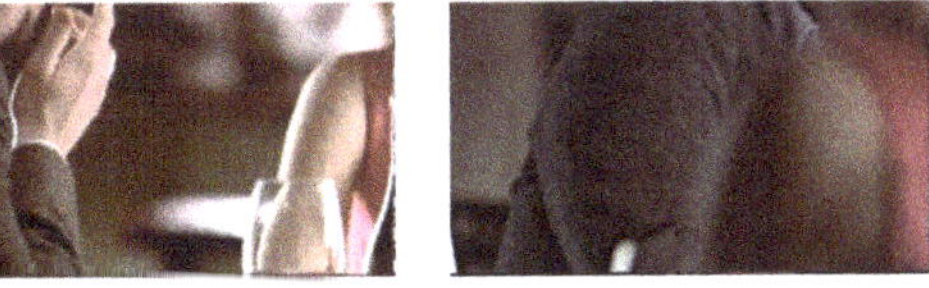
Shot 109
MIKKEL: And we'll give a damn about cook books and all those refined feelings. Just what can the food be.

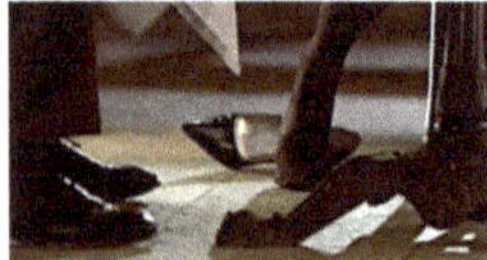

Shot 110
NAJA: Have you tasted Kobe beef?
MIKKEL: Yes, and I'll never forget.

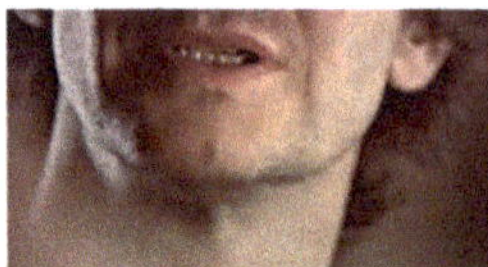

Shot 111
MIKKEL: Great, great experience.

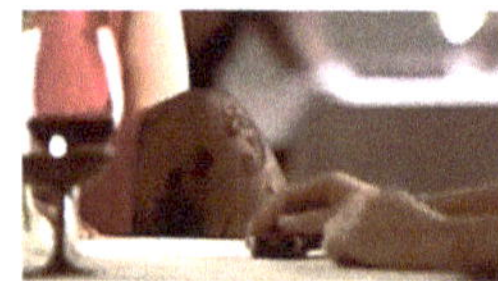

Shot 112
NAJA: Fantastic.

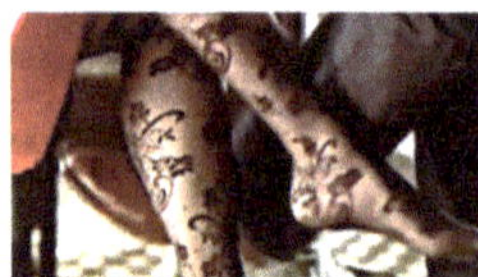

Shot 113
Mikkel caresses Naja's leg with his shoe.

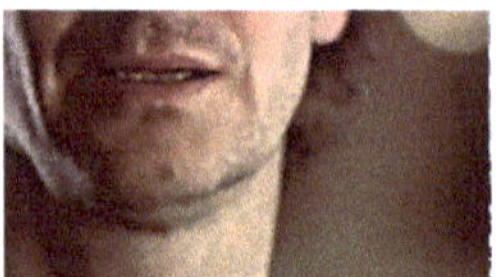

Shot 114

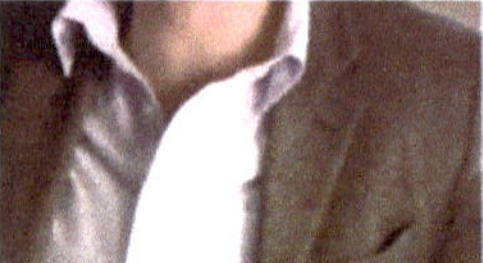

Shot 115
SØREN: You know, I hear it's 30%.

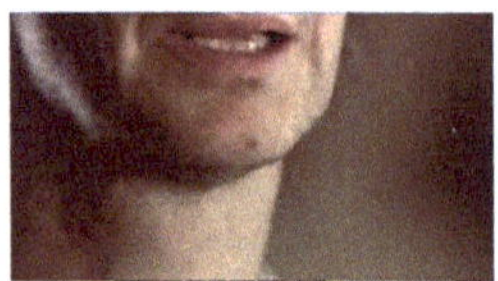

Shot 116
NAJA (off): 30% of what?

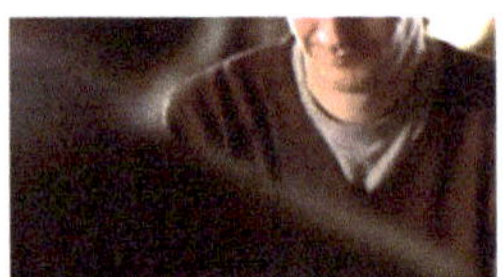

Shot 117
SØREN: That are vegetarians.

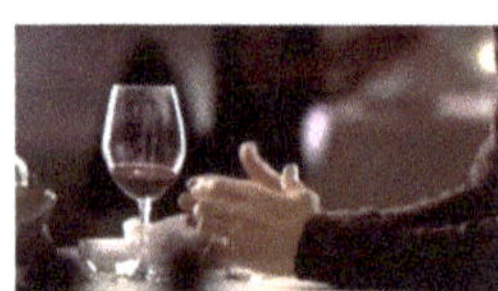

Shot 118
SØREN: Just think what a shame it is.

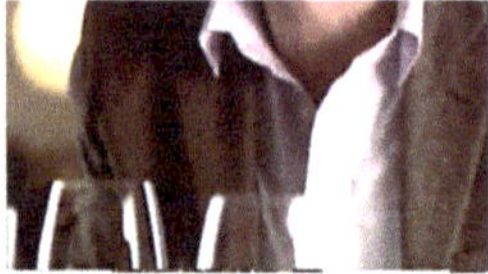

Shot 119

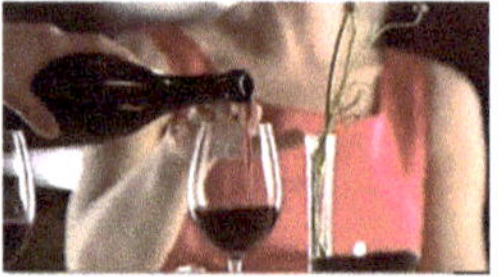

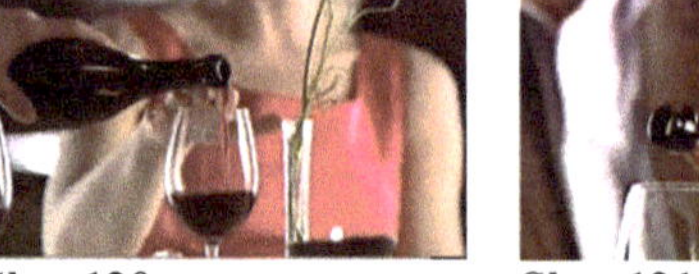

Shot 120
SØREN: Naja, if you like, I would love to prepare a really delicious meal for you some time.

Shot 121
NAJA: No thanks, that's enough Søren.

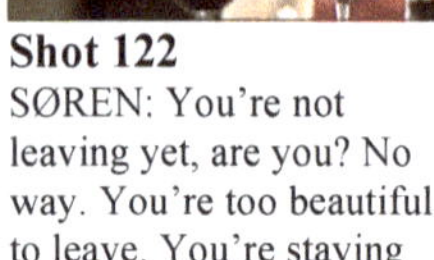

Shot 122
SØREN: You're not leaving yet, are you? No way. You're too beautiful to leave. You're staying here.

Shot 123
SØREN: It looks as though your girlfriend may have stood you up. But we could make some of that meat. What was it called, that Kobe beef?

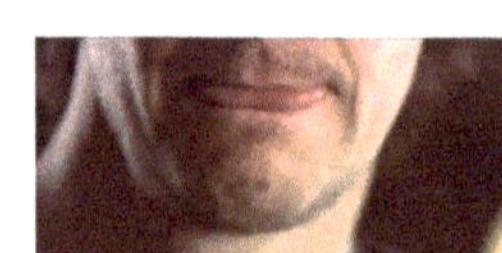

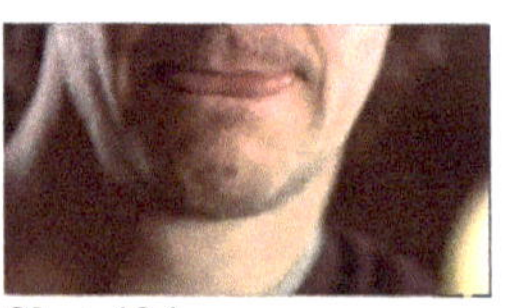

Shot 124
SØREN (*off*): And we could fry some broccoli in a wok with ginger.

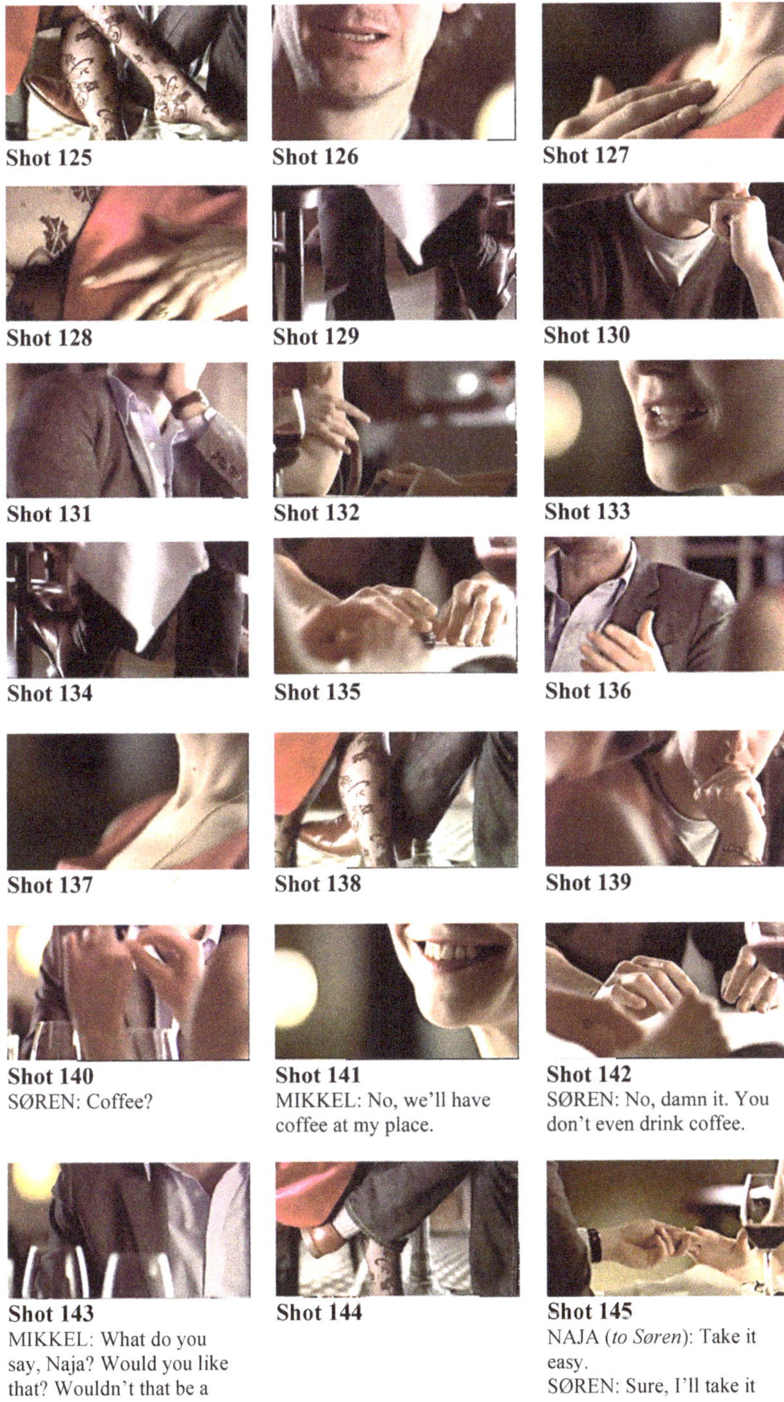

Shot 125

Shot 126

Shot 127

Shot 128

Shot 129

Shot 130

Shot 131

Shot 132

Shot 133

Shot 134

Shot 135

Shot 136

Shot 137

Shot 138

Shot 139

Shot 140
SØREN: Coffee?

Shot 141
MIKKEL: No, we'll have coffee at my place.

Shot 142
SØREN: No, damn it. You don't even drink coffee.

Shot 143
MIKKEL: What do you say, Naja? Would you like that? Wouldn't that be a little cozier?

Shot 144

Shot 145
NAJA (*to Søren*): Take it easy.
SØREN: Sure, I'll take it easy.

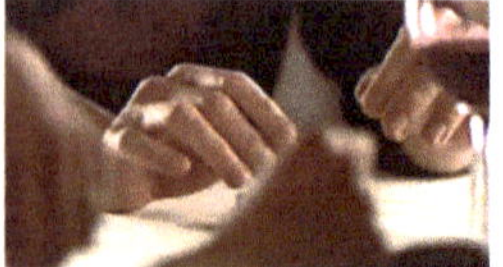

Shot 146

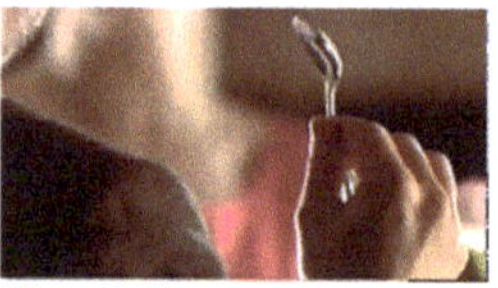

Shot 147

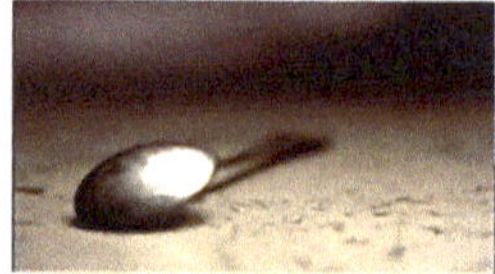

Shot 148

SØREN: It's just a little difficult when you are sitting there looking so incredibly lovely.
A spoon falls to the floor.

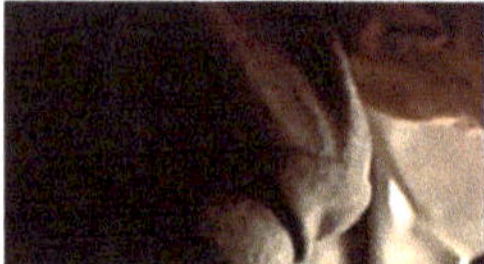

Shot 149

Shot 150

Søren leans down to pick up the spoon and sees what's going on under the table.

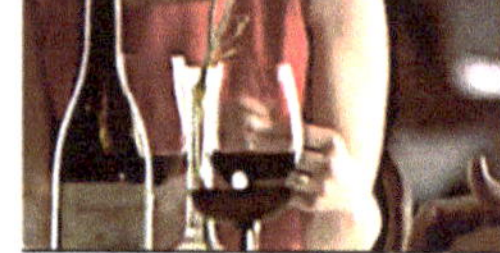

Shot 151

NAJA: I don't quite get it.

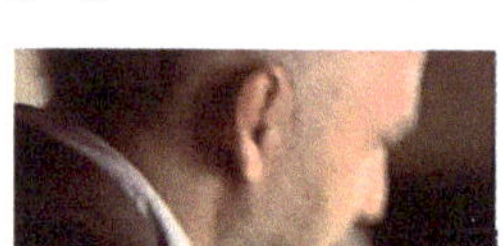

Shot 152

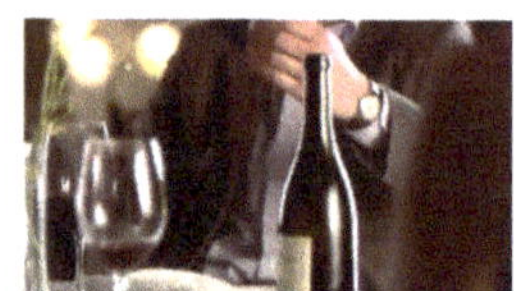

Shot 153

SØREN: No, I apparently don't get it either.
NAJA: What do you mean?

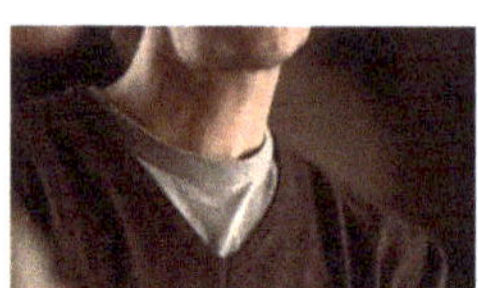

Shot 154

SØREN: Take for example my friend Mikkel, here. It's funny how you've always managed to twist things.

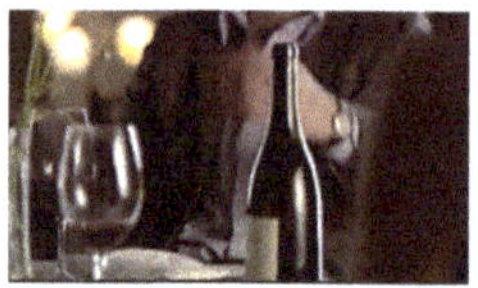

Shot 155

SØREN: You can cook and you can play music. And what the hell do I know?

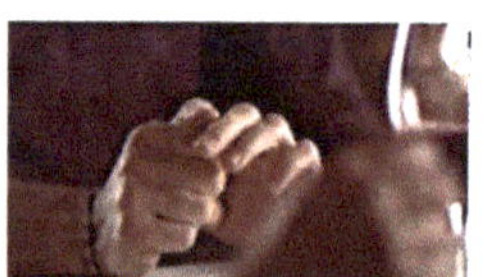

Shot 156

SØREN: And yet it's as though you are lacking in what makes the difference between the two of us.
MIKKEL: Drop it.

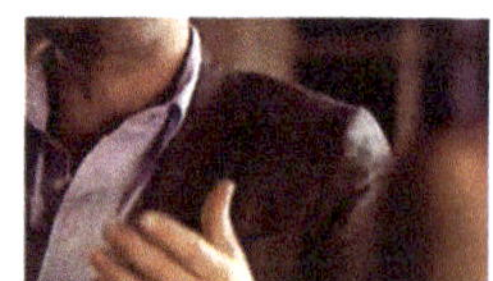

Shot 157

SØREN: Or men in general, right?

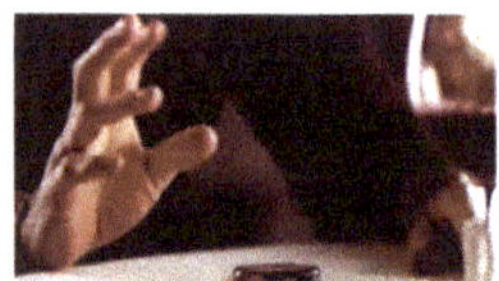

Shot 158

NAJA: What are you doing?

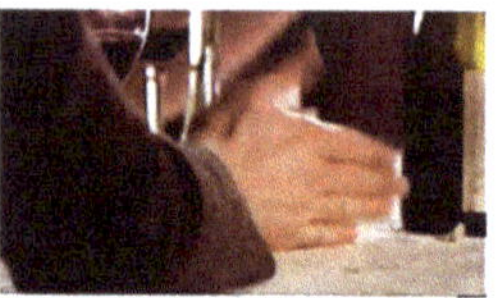

Shot 159

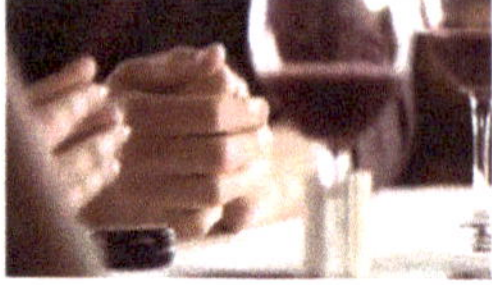

Shot 160

SØREN: What I love about Mikkel is how he can sit there and be nice and always stage things around himself.
MIKKEL: I mean it, just relax.

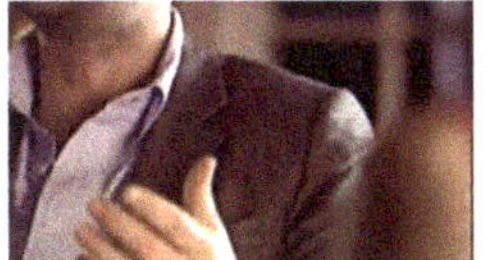

Shot 161
SØREN: Relax? That's your specialty, isn't it.

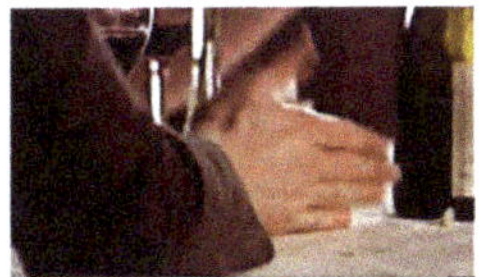

Shot 162

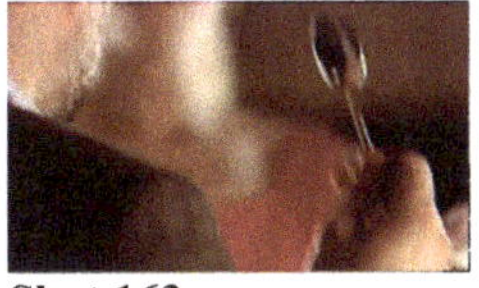

Shot 163

SØREN: So let's really relax so we can begin to talk about your little problem.

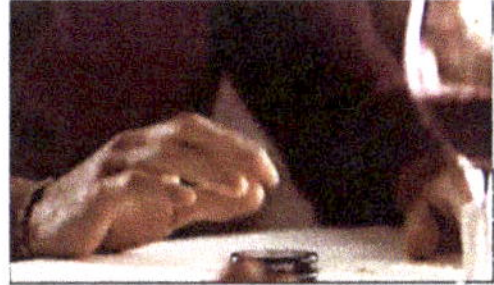

Shot 164
MIKKEL: You think, damn it, that everything is about…

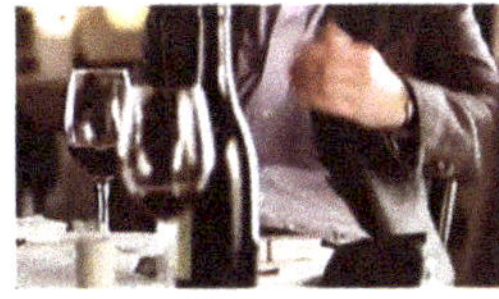

Shot 165
SØREN: Naja, what about you, do you think friends should be…

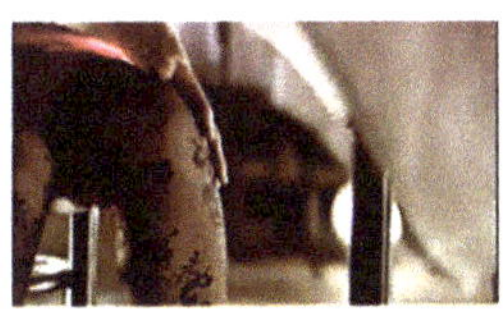

Shot 166

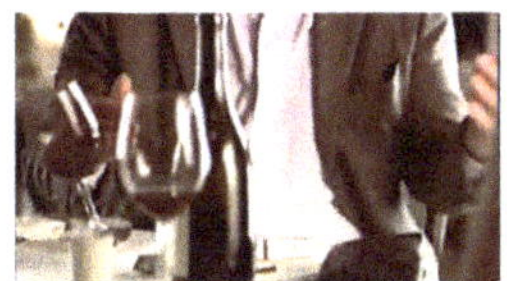

Shot 167
SØREN: honest with one another?

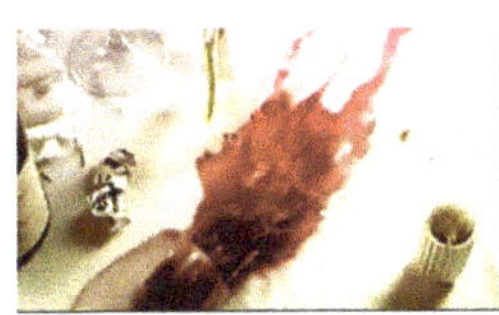

Shot 168
Søren knocks over a glass of wine.

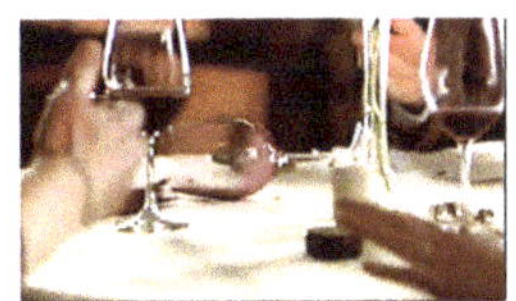

Shot 169

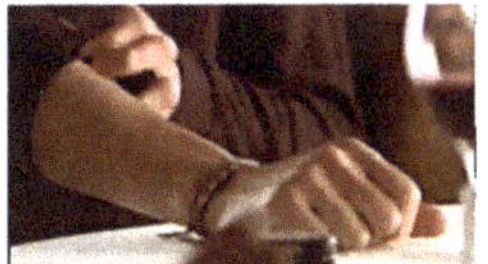

Shot 170
MIKKEL. Now you shut the fuck up. You've crossed a line.

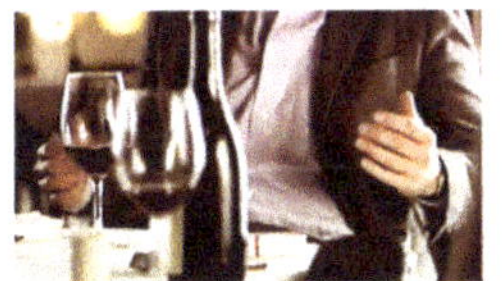

Shot 171

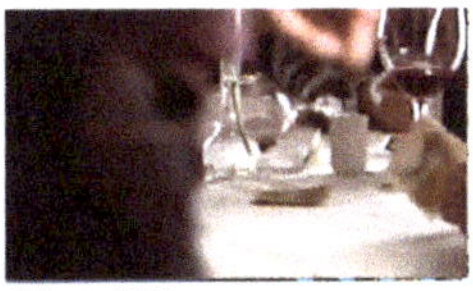

Shot 172

SØREN: Crossed a line? I'm not the one carrying on under the table. (*Mikkel gets up and leaves.*) Mikkel, you forgot the princess. And remember your potency in the cloakroom.

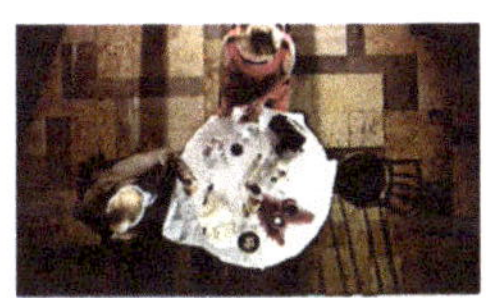

Shot 173a
Naja gets up and leaves.

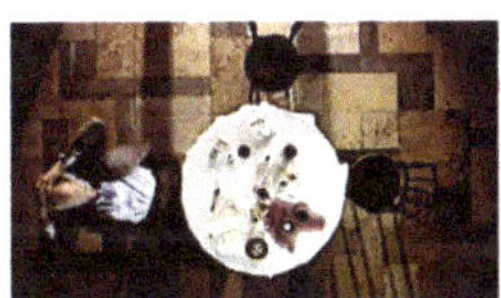

Shot 173b

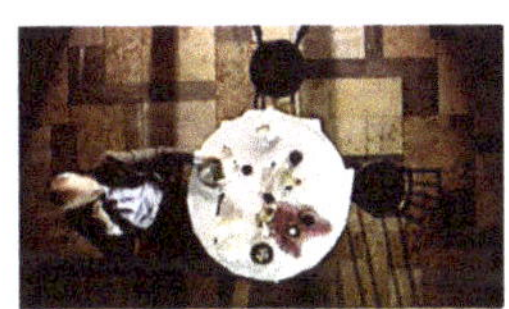

Shot 173c
The waiter gives Søren the check.

YIN OF OMISSION

Directed by ballet dancer Alexander Kølpin, this film was made with a radical *omission*: the actors' faces would at no point be fully visible. His main reason for doing this: to focus on body language, rather than faces, in relation to what characters say (Kølpin 2008). I know of no other film of any format in which this daring omission was attempted. Making *Below the Belt* unique in this respect, meant an extra challenge for the actors, who relied on their ballet-dancing director's awareness of "how the body reveals emotions" (Lyby 2021).

In most shots, the actor is filmed without his or her head within the frame.

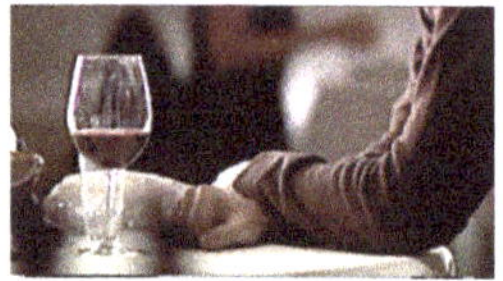
Shot 32

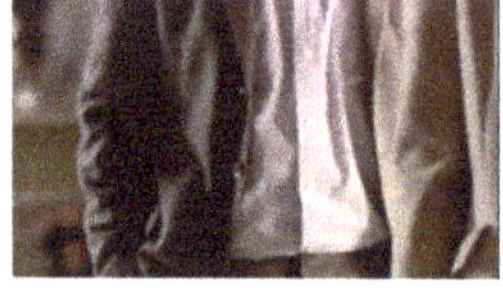
Shot 51

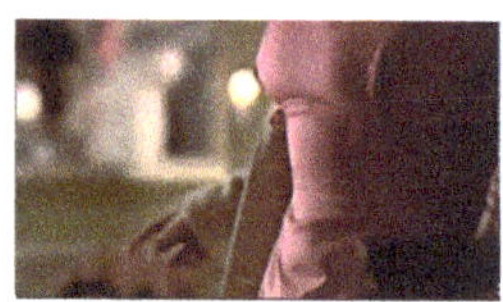
Shot 52

When portions of an actor's face are visible at all in this film, the actor is either seen from behind

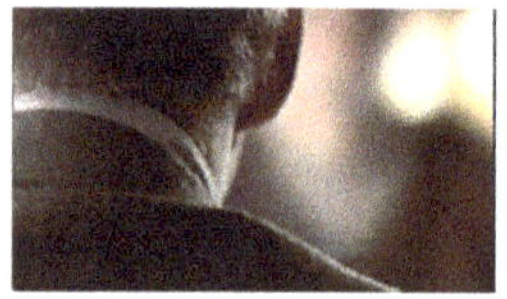
Shot 24

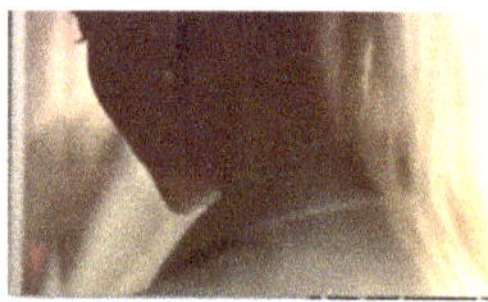
Shot 25

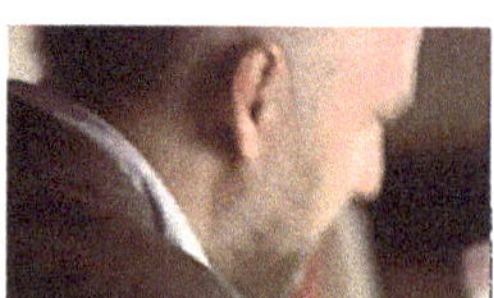
Shot 152

or with the face cut off just above the mouth

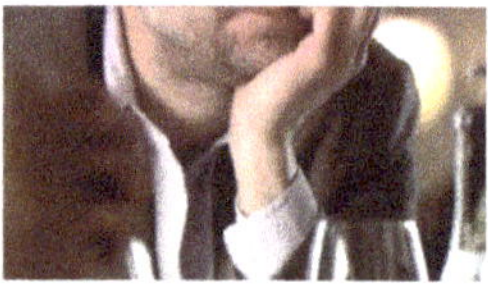
Shot 101

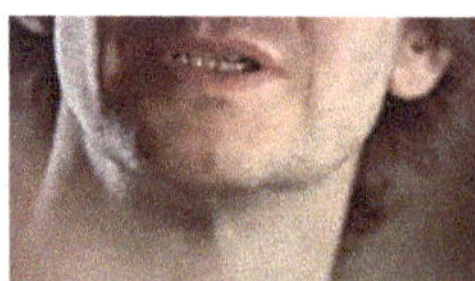
Shot 111

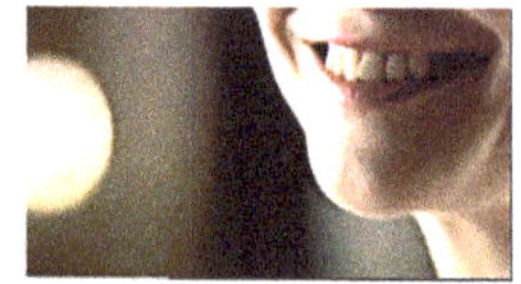
Shot 141

The actor's eyes are never visible.

Body language as YANG OF DOING

In focusing on body language, Kølpin showed characters *doing* things. Søren's most revealing gesture is the one in which he places his hands behind his head with his elbows flared. This is called "the catapult" by body language specialists, who say it might be used "before the boss begins a meeting, to show how important he is" or "in a casual encounter where someone with higher status is trying to lord it over the others" (Allen 2020).

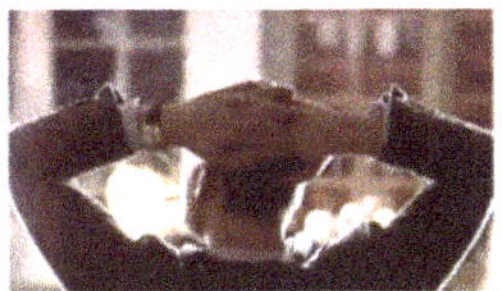
Shot 17

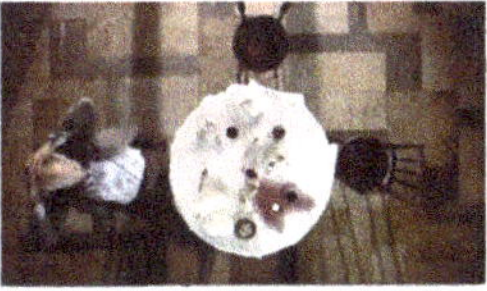
Shot 173

Naja's hands at times carry out auto-erotic functions, as when excited by the touch of Mikkel's shoe rubbing on her calf beneath the table, she touches her own heaving chest (Shot 127) or runs her fingers caressingly along her arm (Shot 132).

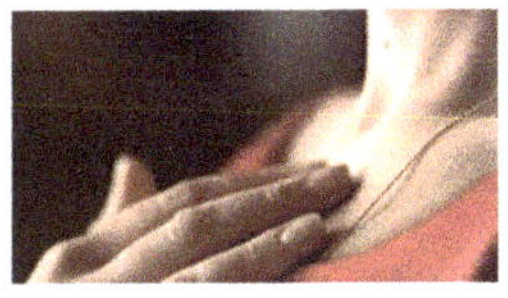
Shot 127

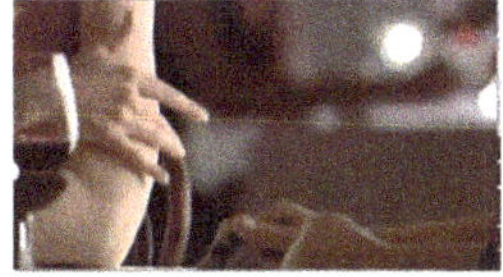
Shot 132

Other examples of the *yang* of body language are the shots in which Søren nervously jiggles something in his hand while equally nervously tapping his foot on the floor (Shots 94–95), or the fact that Søren knocks over a glass of water (Shot 22) and a glass of wine (Shot 168), or that Mikkel finds excuses to touch Naja, by disengaging her necklace from her dress (Shot 53), or touching her arm when asking her whether she isn't more into red wine than Champagne (Shots 64, 66) or by removing a possibly imaginary hair or speck from her arm (Shots 98–99). And of course, Mikkel and Naja are playing footsies under the table, starting with Shot 113 and continuing until they leave the table.

Competing for Naja as YANG OF DOING

The opening shots are devoted to Naja, preparing us to see her as a willing object of desire. That Søren is taken with her is made clear from the first times he mentions her to Mikkel, as being "very pretty" (Shot 20) and "simply fantastic... with those big blue eyes" (Shots 25–29). When she joins them at their table, he flatters her, telling how good she looks (Shots 43, 76, 122), to which she is not especially responsive, and he is perhaps unpleasantly surprised to learn that Naja and Mikkel already know each other.

Mikkel doesn't put Naja on a pedestal. He asks her for example: "Do you still eat like a horse?" and she appears comfortable with that down to earth treatment, replying "Yes, I actually do" (Shots 61–62). It soon becomes clear that Søren sees in Mikkel a rival for Naja's attention and as someone he needs to undermine. In that connection, his greatest weapon is something Mikkel has confided in him before Naja joined them: a problem with maintaining an erection, which he says "happens to 30%" of all men.

Regarding Søren's wish to undermine Mikkel, just saying "You know, I hear it's 30%" (Shot 115) is a threat, even though he answers "That are vegetarian" (117) when Naja asks "30% of what?" (Shot 116). And once he sees what is going on under the table (Shot 149), and realizes he has lost the contest for Naja, he simply wants to hurt Mikkel and refers aggressively to what Mikkel lacks (Shot 156) and to his "little problem" (Shot 162).

All of this engages us in what the late Mogens Rukov, known affectionately by some as 'the Yoda of Danish screenwriting,' would call *a natural story*, one we can all relate to. That natural story, along with the extra attention to body language, counterbalances the *yin of omission* – the absence of the actors' faces from the screen.

YIN and YANG as loci

In this film, 'below the table' might be regarded as *yin* and 'above the table' as *yang* in the sense of hidden versus overt, just as in *The Office*, the storage room with its hidden realities could be seen as *yin* while the public part of the office, as a realm of appearances, could be seen as *yang*. Here in *Below the Belt*, this adds an extra layer to the storytelling by creating the possibility of a secret complicity between two characters.

SHORT FILM 9

On Suffocation

Jenifer Malmqvist, Sweden, 2013, 7 minutes, colour

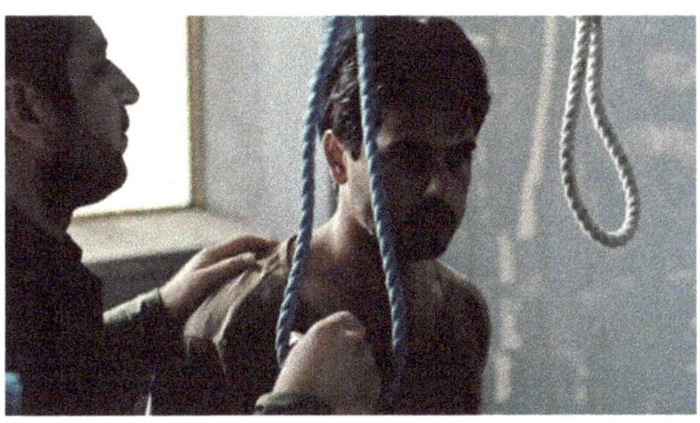

Writer/Director	Jenifer Malmqvist
Producer	China Åhlander
Director of photography	Ita Zbroniec-Zajt
Editor	Jenifer Malmqvist
Editing consultant	Petra Ahlin
Set designer	Mattias Engström
Costumes	Nicklas Östergren
Make-up	Katarina Kovacs
Sound recording	Mikael Körner
Sound mix	Claus Lynge
Production company	Anagram

Cast

Prisoners	Poyan Karimi, Pershang Rad
Guards	Ali Dawoud, Zana Penjweni, Kurdi Kara, Ako Rauf

Guldbagge Award for Best Short Film, 2014
Nordic Short Film Award, Best Film, Nordisk Panorama, 2013.

Link to the film:
http://vimeo.com/62081427 Password: Machine

Synopsis

On a beach, the bare feet of two men lying next to each other playfully and affectionately touch. Elsewhere, a young uniformed guard repeatedly pushes a button on a handheld control box. It finally begins to work, raising the height of nooses from the ground. Another guard is now readying nooses, as a prisoner about to be hanged stands there in what is apparently an empty factory building used as an execution facility. A door opens and a second prisoner is led in by an officer and another uniformed guard. The new prisoner stares intently at his mate, hits the guard who is restraining him, and rushes forward toward his lover. A scuffle ensues and ends with his being pinned to a wall by several guards as the first prisoner now stands with a noose around his neck. Prisoner two has his wrists bound behind his back and cigarette burns are visible on his bare forearms. The officer calmly lights a cigarette and nods yes and the young guard with the control box pushes the button again. At first it works, raising the height of the nooses but then it stops. The officer approaches and as he takes the box and bangs it against the wall, the second prisoner again rushes to his mate and manages to kiss him on the lips before the two men can be separated. The officer surveys the situation and signals to the guards holding the second prisoner that he is now to be readied for hanging. The two prisoners look at each other and the young guard with the controls resumes pushing the button. The prisoners' feet are seen lifted off the ground. The officer calmly looks at his watch as the two men are raised higher by the ropes. A rubber sandal drops to the floor. The young guard notices it as well as the flailing legs of the two men being hanged. He is clearly unhappy with his role in the execution. The officer, unperturbed, looks at the two bodies in the air, checks his watch again, and takes his time before signaling with a nod that they can now be lowered again. The young guard with the controls begins lowering them, as the officer hastily exits. When the bodies are on the ground, the foot of one of the dead men happens to lie on top of the foot of the other one. The young guard stands by watching as two other guards cut the ropes and remove the bodies, leaving the victims' rubber sandals scattered on the floor.

Shot-by-shot breakdown of *On Suffocation*

What follows is merely a schematic outline of the film, making it possible to refer to specific shots by number.

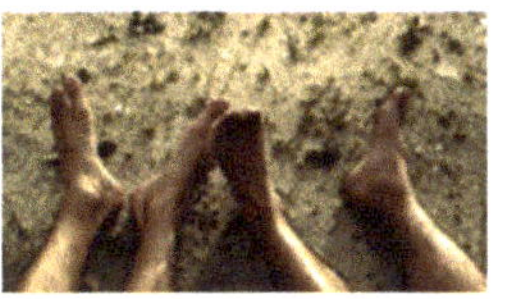

Shot 1

On a beach, the bare feet of two men lying next to each other touch playfully and affectionately.

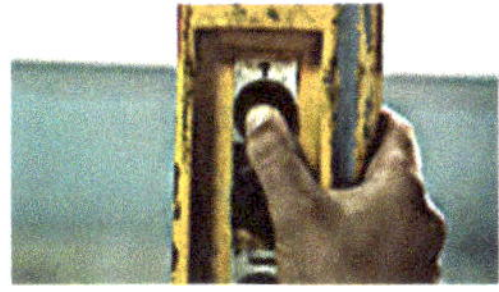

Shot 2

A young guard repeatedly pushes a button on a handheld control box.

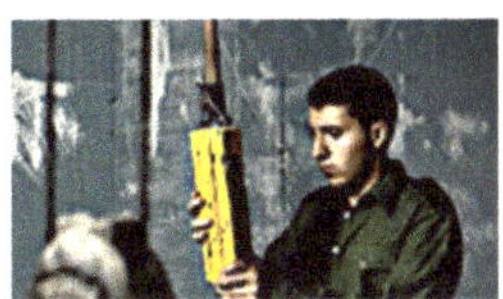

Shot 3

It finally begins to work...

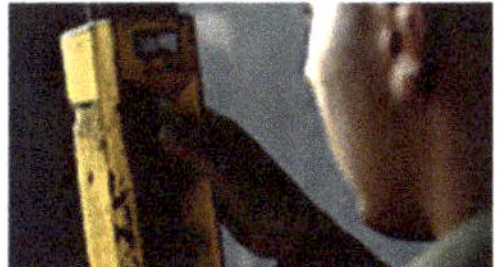

Shot 4

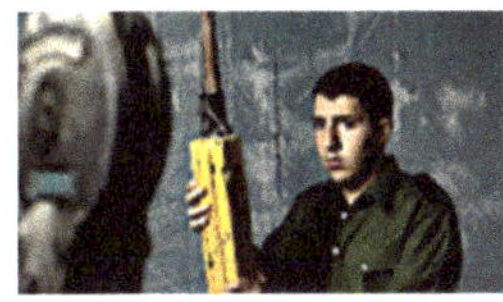

Shot 5

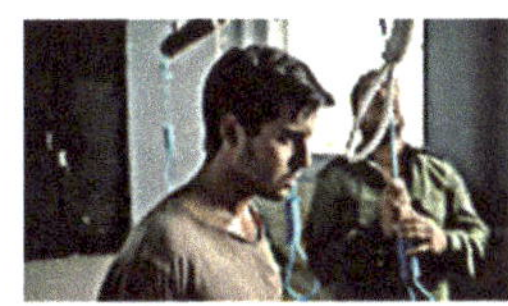

Shot 6

... elevating the nooses in an improvised gallows.

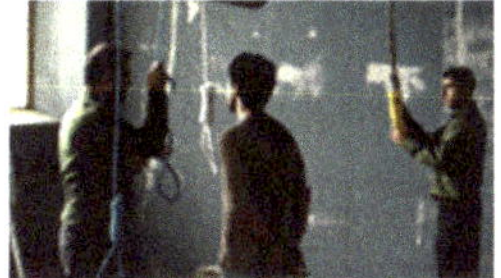

Shot 7

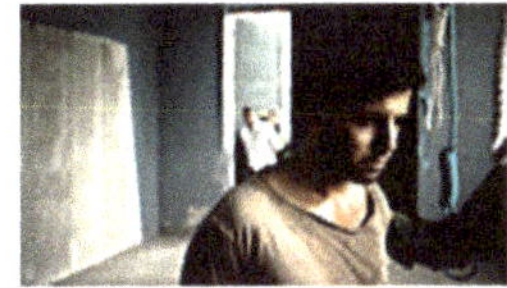

Shot 8

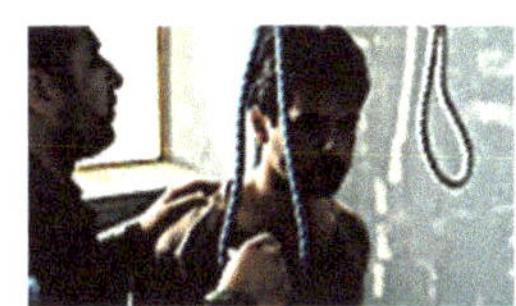

Shot 9

A guard fits a noose around a prisoner's neck.

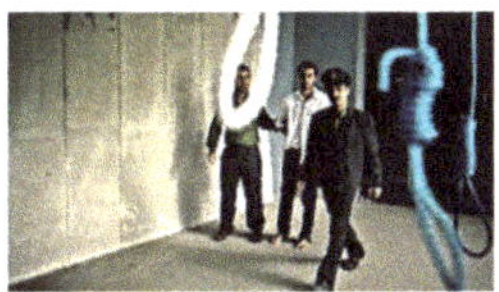

Shot 10

An officer enters with a guard and another prisoner.

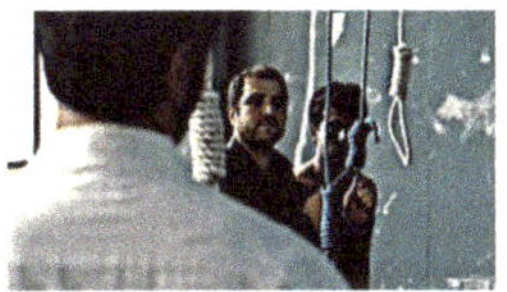

Shot 11

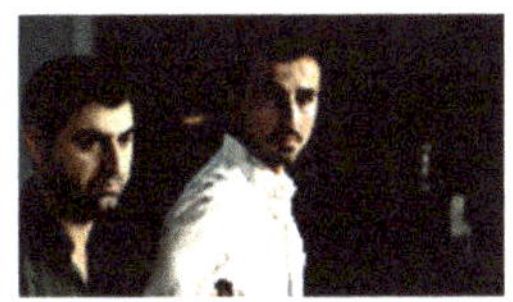

Shot 12

The new prisoner looks intently at his mate...

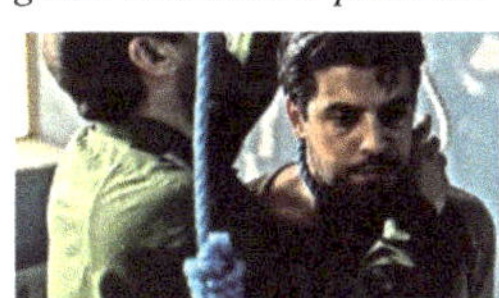

Shot 13

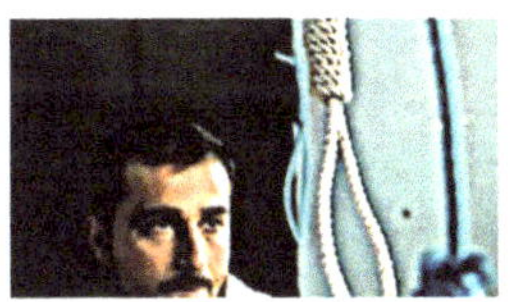

Shot 14

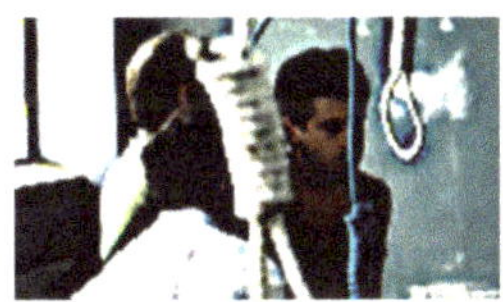

Shot 15

hits the guard holding him and rushes forward toward his lover. A scuffle ensues...

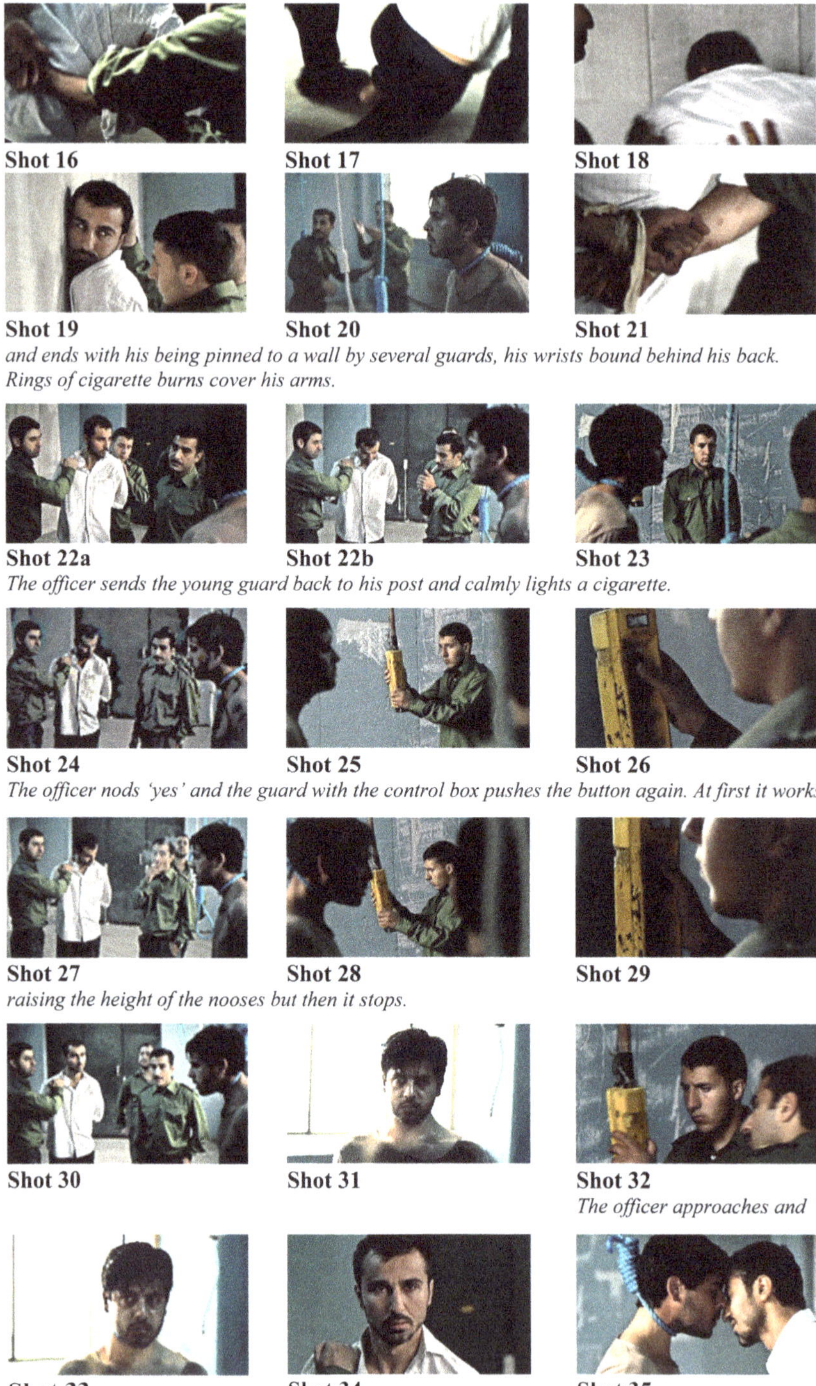

Shot 16 Shot 17 Shot 18

Shot 19 Shot 20 Shot 21

and ends with his being pinned to a wall by several guards, his wrists bound behind his back. Rings of cigarette burns cover his arms.

Shot 22a Shot 22b Shot 23

The officer sends the young guard back to his post and calmly lights a cigarette.

Shot 24 Shot 25 Shot 26

The officer nods 'yes' and the guard with the control box pushes the button again. At first it works,

Shot 27 Shot 28 Shot 29

raising the height of the nooses but then it stops.

Shot 30 Shot 31 Shot 32

The officer approaches and

Shot 33 Shot 34 Shot 35

as he takes the box and bangs it against the wall, the second prisoner again rushes to his mate…

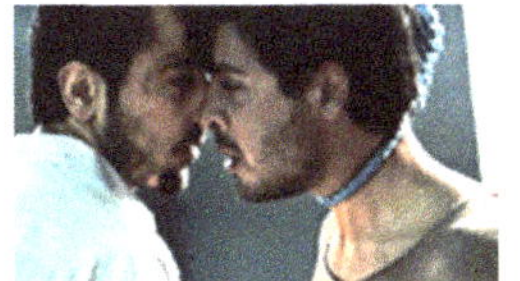
Shot 36

Shot 37

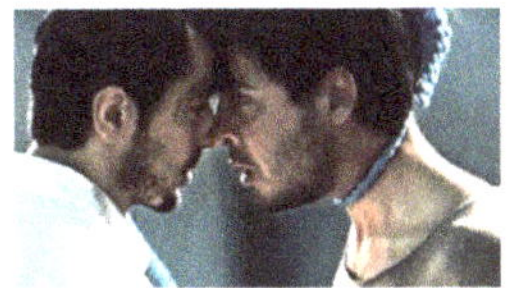
Shot 38

and manages to kiss him on the lips before guards can separate the lovers.

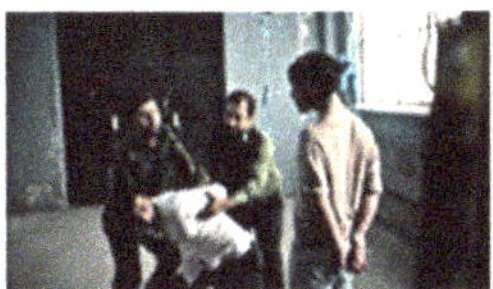
Shot 39

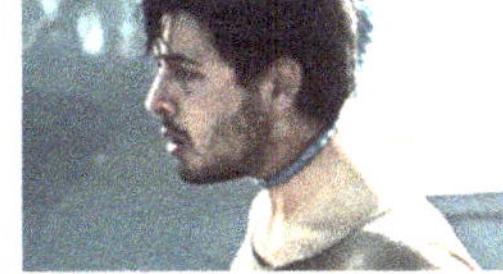
Shot 40

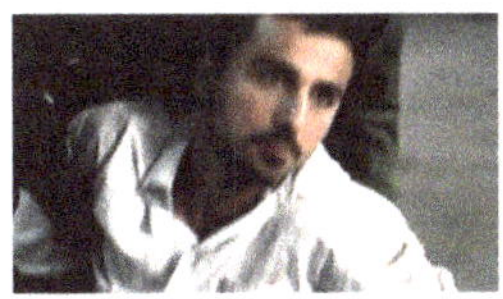
Shot 41

Shot 42

Shot 43

Shot 44

The officer surveys the situation and signals to the guards holding the second prisoner that he is now to be readied for hanging.

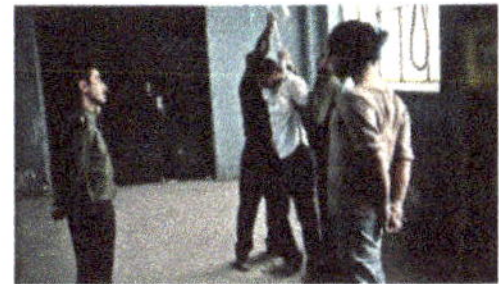
Shot 45

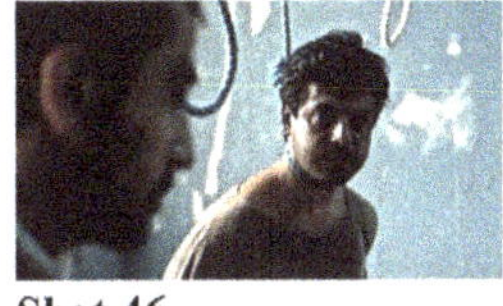
Shot 46

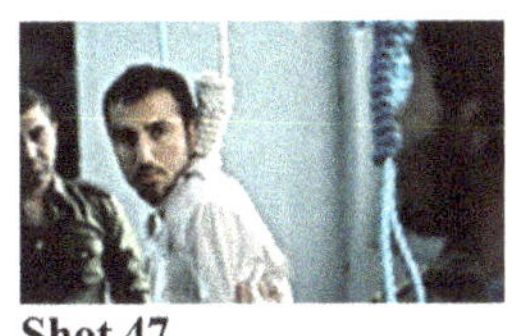
Shot 47

The two prisoners look at each other

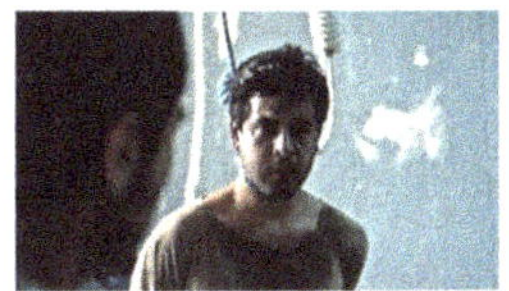
Shot 48

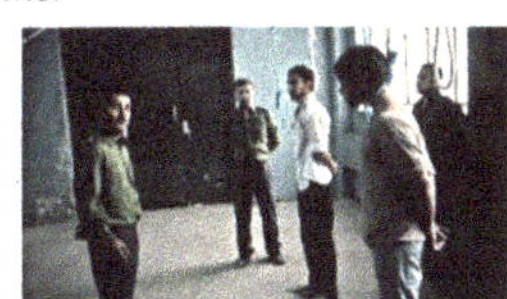
Shot 49

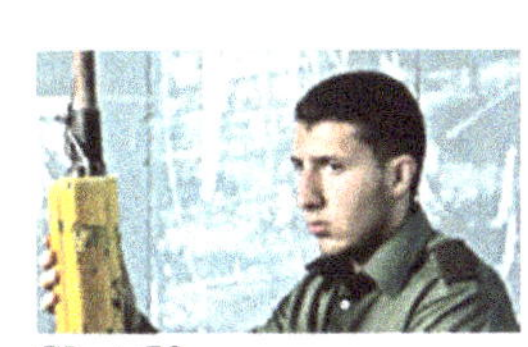
Shot 50

and on a signal from the officer, the young guard resumes pushing the button.

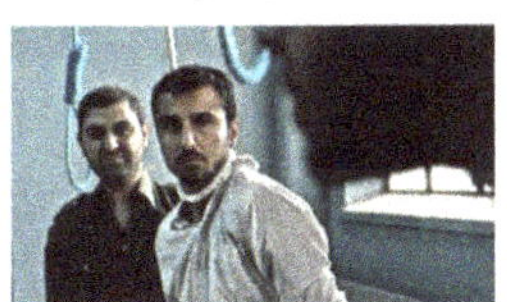
Shot 51

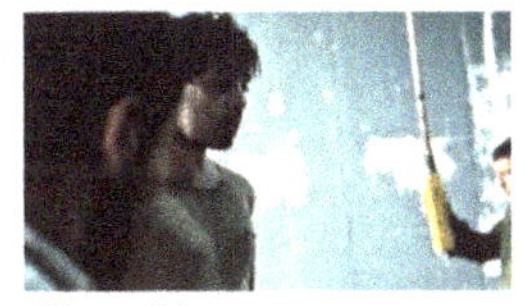
Shot 52

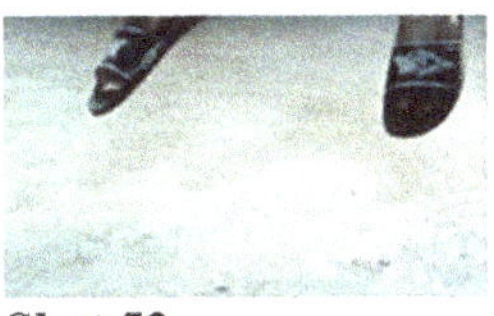
Shot 53

The nooses are mechanically raised in the air and the double hanging proceeds.

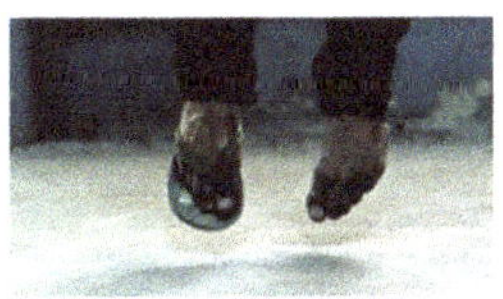
Shot 54

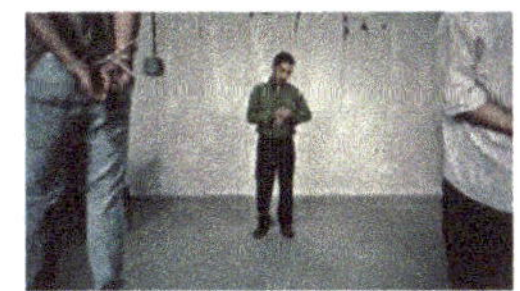
Shot 55a

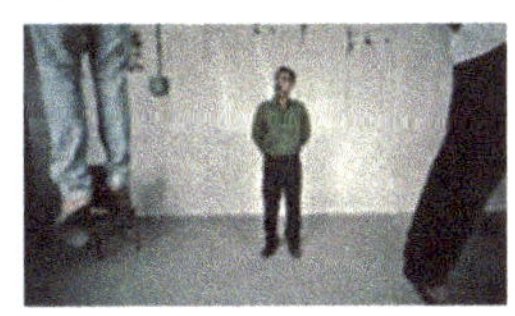
Shot 55b

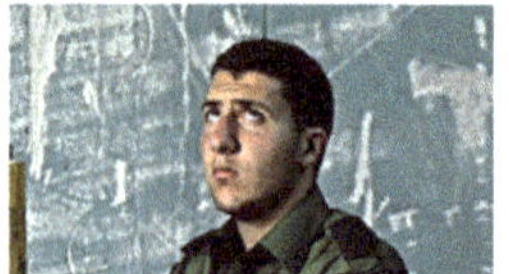

Shot 56

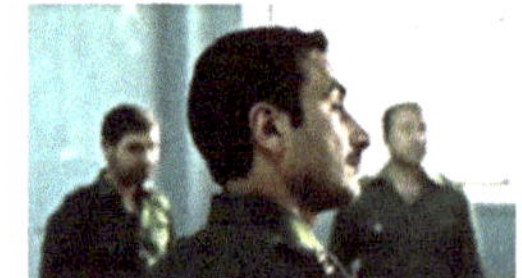

Shot 57

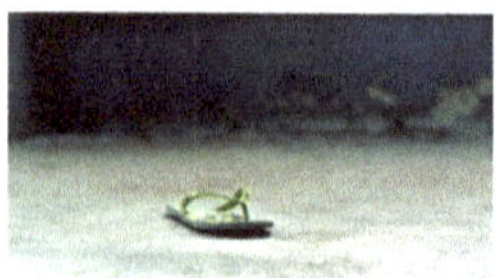

Shot 58

A rubber sandal drops to the floor.

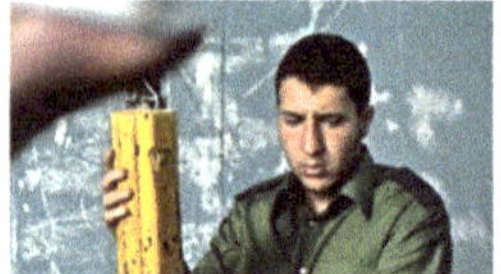

Shot 59a

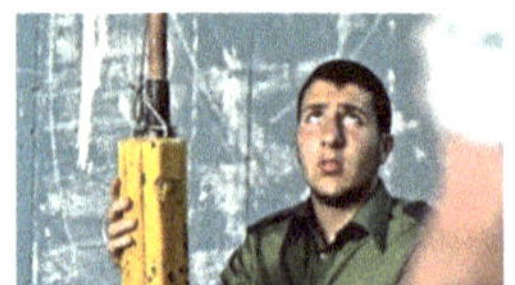

Shot 59b

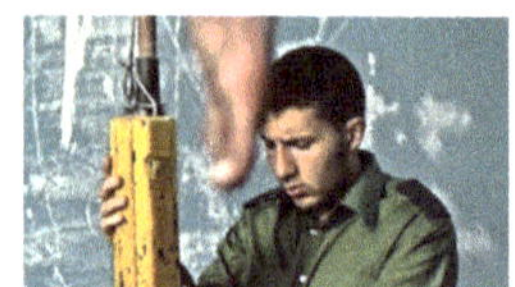

Shot 59c

The young guard operating the control box is visibly distressed.

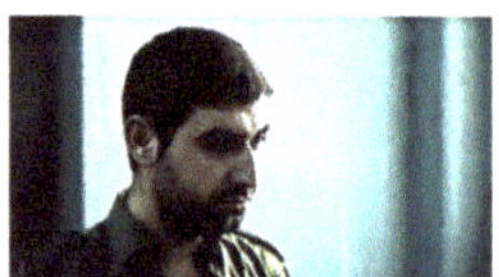

Shot 60

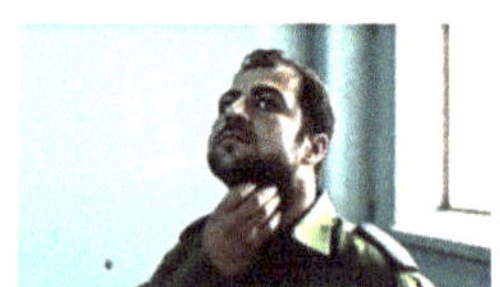

Shot 61

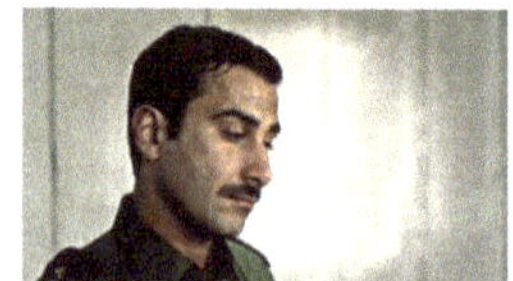

Shot 62

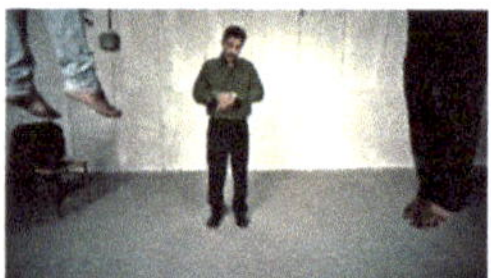

Shot 63a

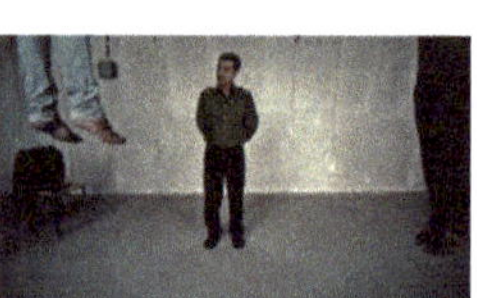

Shot 63b

The officer looks at his watch and finally signals that the bodies can now be lowered.

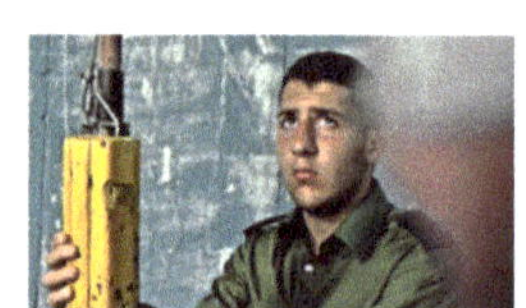

Shot 64

The young guard lowers them.

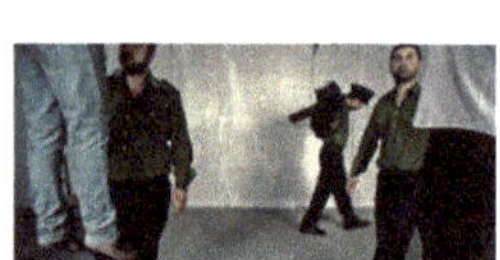

Shot 65

As the bodies descend, the officer quickly exits.

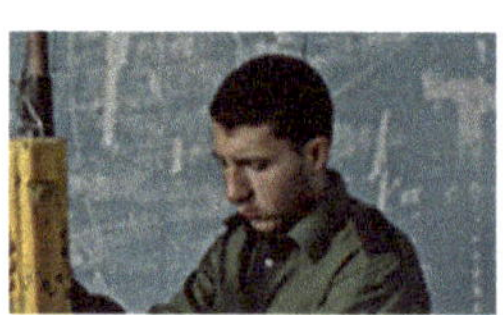

Shot 66

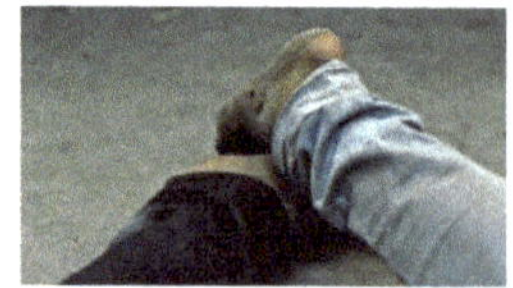

Shot 67

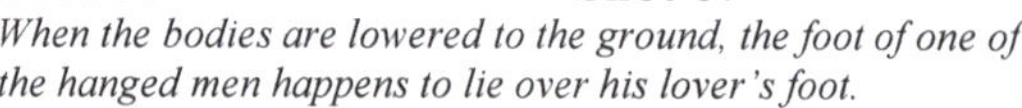

When the bodies are lowered to the ground, the foot of one of the hanged men happens to lie over his lover's foot.

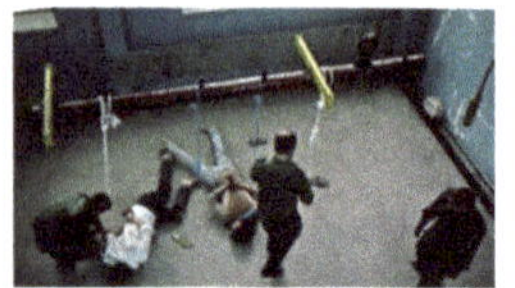

Shot 68a

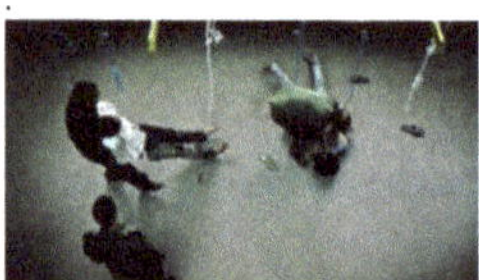

Shot 68b

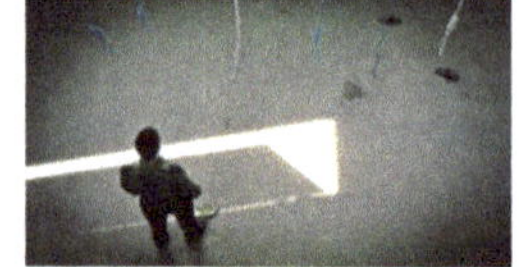

Shot 68c

Two guards cut the ropes and remove the bodies as the young guard watches. The prisoners' sandals remain on the floor.

In addition to the most obvious *yang* processes involved in the hanging of the two prisoners – such as the use of the button on the control box to trigger the *mechanized power* in play, and the officer's nods to his subordinates to move things on to the next step in the execution process – there is a noteworthy *seriality*, combined with a *symmetry* of sorts.

The film begins and almost ends with an image of the prisoners' feet touching. In the opening shot at the beach – here a *locus* of freedom – the feet touch each other with a playful and affectionate interaction. In the film's penultimate shot (Shot 67), on the floor of the improvised gallows – a *locus* of death – the feet are lifeless.

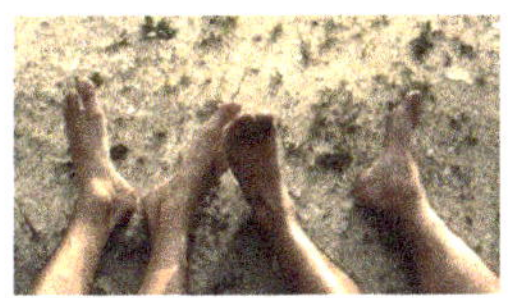

Shot 1

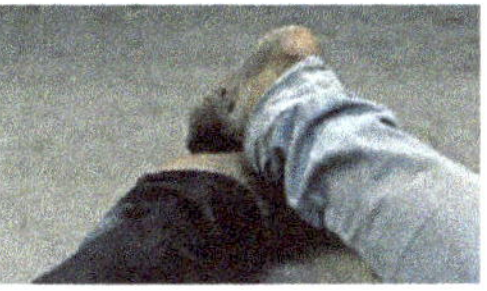

Shot 67

And in addition to this framing of the film with a striking *symmetry* of opposites, feet appear in four more shots: Shots 53 and 54, when the prisoners are first raised from the floor by the rope machine; in the foreground of Shot 59, with the young guard looking distressed in the background; and in Shot 63, when the bodies are still hanging but the prisoners are dead. This *seriality* is further enhanced by images of rubber sandals (Shot 58, when one falls to the floor and Shot 68, when four are visible on the floor in the upper right quadrant of the screen).

Similarly, in addition to the obvious *yin of vulnerability* embodied by the prisoners, there are two other forms of *yin* in play that should be mentioned now.

One is the *yin of doubt* that can be read on the young guard's face, as he is seen feeling guilty about his role in executing the two prisoners (Shots 56 and 59). This makes him unmistakably the most interesting character in the film. By my count, he gets a close shot or close-up in 16 of the film's 68 shots – far more than any other single character. When Jenifer Malmqvist was asked about him, she replied:

> The biggest interest for me with this film is his perspective. That was my "entry" to the film, the doorway. Or maybe the key, I don't know. What would you have done in his place? [...] And would you risk your own life to save someone else's, someone you don't even know? Would you? In this case I think everyone is a victim, the perpetrators as well (Raskin 2016: 94).

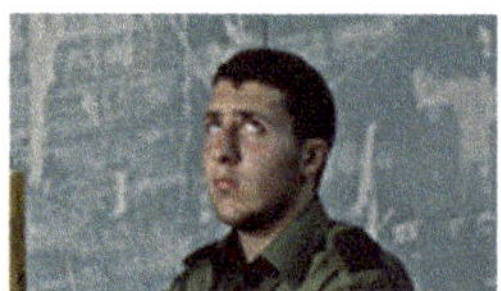
Shot 56

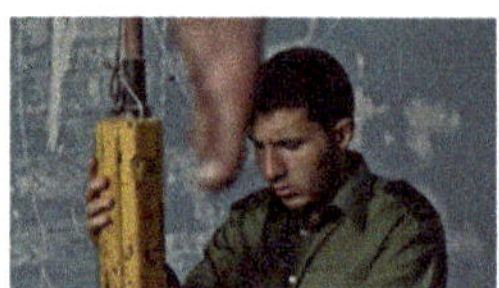
Shot 59c

The remaining form of *yin* to be mentioned is the *yin of interpretability*.

It is up to the viewer to work out that the men whose feet are seen on the beach in Shot 1 are homosexual lovers and the same two people as the prisoners; that the circular marks on the arms of the second prisoner (Shot 21) are cigarette burns used as torture; that the setting of this film is a country in which homosexuality is punishable by death; and that it is the execution of the two men that is the abomination, and not their love for one another. And the basis for connecting all of the dots is communicated wordlessly to the viewer, thanks to the filmmaker's holding back also in that regard.

SHORT FILM 10

Witness / Témoin

Ali Asgari, France/Iran, 2020, 15 min., colour

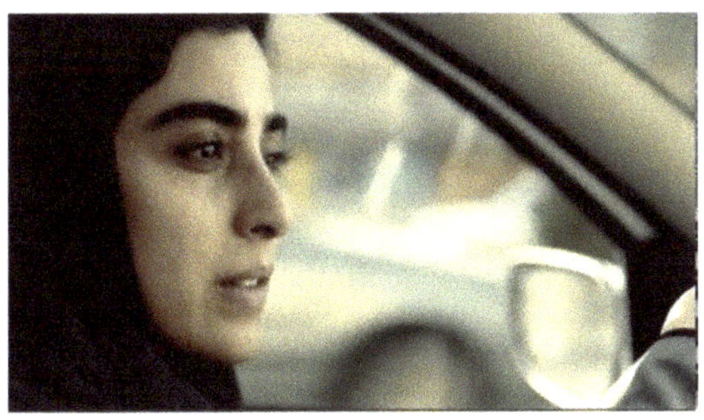

Director	Ali Asgari
Writers	Ali Asgari, Farnoosh Samadi
Producers	François Morisset, Laura Jumel, Khorshid Alami
Director of photography	Hamed Hosseini
Editor	Ehsan Vaseghi
Music	Ali Birang
Sound operator	Amir Partozadeh, Mohammad Reza Hosseini
Sound editing and mixing	Saman Shahamat
Executive producer	Reza Gamini
The Mother	Anahita Afshar
Elderly Woman	Nasrin Kourdi
The Little Girl	Selena Moradi

Link to the film on demand for a modest fee:
https://vimeo.com/ondemand/witnessbyaliasgari

Special Prize, International Competition, Minimalen Short Film Festival (Norway), 2022

Special Jury Mention, International Competition, Akbank Short Film Festival (Turkey), 2021

Synopsis

Seated alone in her parked car, a mother ends a telephone conversation and her young daughter enters the car. The mother has bought her daughter a white dress to wear at a party that evening but the daughter insists on having a red one instead. Now driving, the mother tries to change her daughter's mind, but gives in and agrees to exchange the dress. She drives to the shopping mall and parks just before its entrance, though a security guard tells her she may not park there. She insists, arguing she will be back in five minutes and agrees to leave her child in the car. On her way to the store where she had bought the dress, the mother is asked by an elderly woman if she knows where the elevator is. The mother answers that she doesn't know but points to a nearby escalator and walks on. At the clothing store, the mother requests an exchange of the white dress for a red one, which the clerk will have to look for in the stock room; he should be back with it in a few minutes. Meanwhile, the daughter, tired of waiting, leaves the car and enters the shopping mall, scanning the area in search of her mother. The daughter can now see her mother, who has noticed the elderly woman standing near the escalator, reluctant to use it. The mother, unaware that her daughter can now see her, joins the elderly woman and aggressively persuades her to use the escalator, placing her hand on the elderly woman's shoulder as she steps onto the moving stairs. But immediately the woman tumbles down the escalator steps, falling head over heels. The mother hurries away as though she had had nothing to do with the accident and continues walking, not taking a call on her mobile phone during a brief pause. She then runs down a staircase to the floor below, joining a crowd that has formed at the scene of the accident, and sees the lifeless body of the elderly woman lying on the floor. On enquiring, she is told by a man standing in the crowd that an ambulance is on its way. The mother asks him: "Is she breathing" to which he replies: "I don't think so." The mother then returns to the shop to pick up the red dress. The clerk mentions the woman who had fallen down the escalator and asks "Did you see what happened?" to which the mother falsely replies: "No, I only heard the scream." The mother finally sees her daughter and realizes that she must have witnessed the accident. The daughter is now looking at something off-camera – presumably at the lifeless woman. The mother rejoins her daughter and they hurry to their car. Once they are seated, the mother says "Fasten your seatbelt" and "I changed your dress," but as they drive away, not a word is spoken by mother or daughter about the accident that had just occurred or the mother's role in it. As she drives, the mother continually glances at her daughter without saying a word.

Shot-by-shot breakdown of *Witness*

What follows is merely a schematic outline of the film, making it possible to refer to specific shots by number.

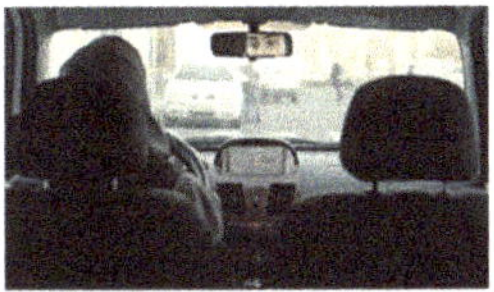

Shot 1a

MOTHER (*on phone*): No, I cannot be there in half an hour. I'm dropping my child home and I'll come by straight away. No, just do what I say. That's it. No more discussion. Bye.

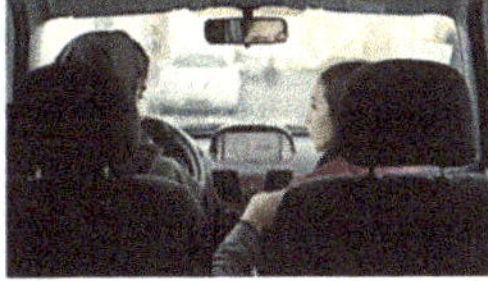

Shot 1b

MOTHER (*to daughter*): Hi, baby!
DAUGHTER: Hi Mommy!
MOTHER: Put it in the back seat.
DAUGHTER: I can leave it at my feet.
MOTHER: No, put it in the back seat. Leave your bag there too.

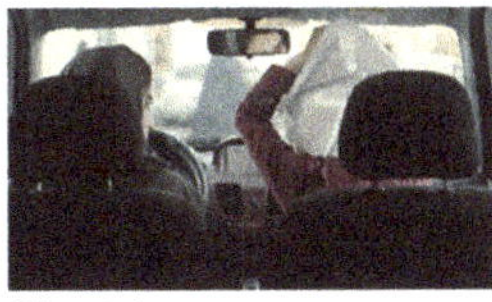

Shot 1c

MOTHER: Why didn't you give your handicraft to the teacher?
DAUGHTER: She said I hadn't done it by myself. I have to bring a new one.
MOTHER: Did you tell her that I had made it?
DAUGHTER: No, but she asked some questions about the making that I couldn't answer, so she found out.

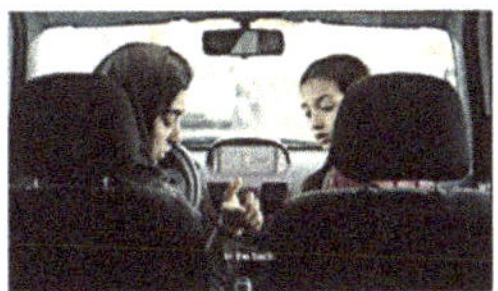

Shot 1d

MOTHER: I bought your dress.
DAUGHTER: Where is it?
MOTHER: In the back.

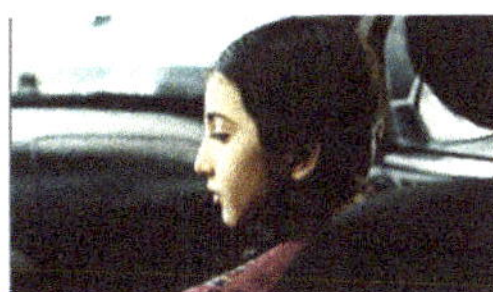

Shot 2

MOTHER: Why does it have to be red?
DAUGHTER: Mom, I love red.

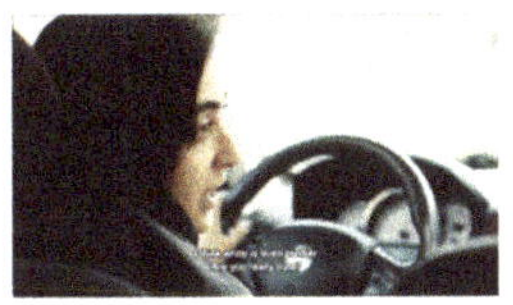

Shot 3

MOTHER: I think white is even prettier. Are you really sure?

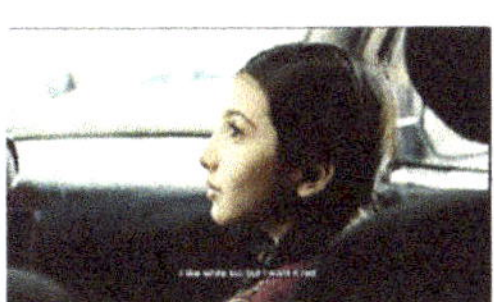

Shot 4

DAUGHTER: I like white too but I want it red.

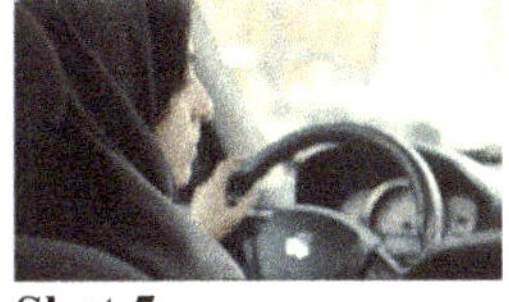

Shot 5

MOTHER: We have to go all this way through traffic jam just because you like red? Try it on at least.

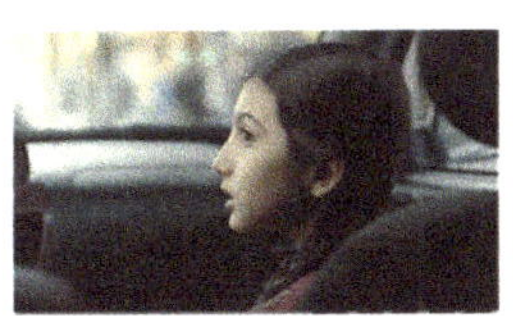

Shot 6

DAUGHTER: Everyone is going to wear red at the birthday party tonight

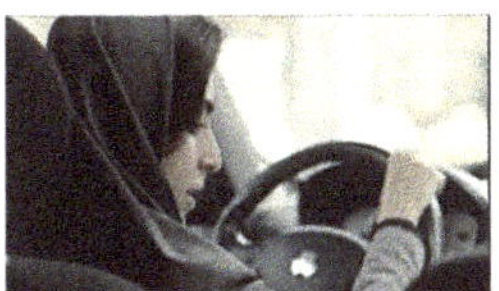

Shot 7

MOTHER: I see. It was all planned!

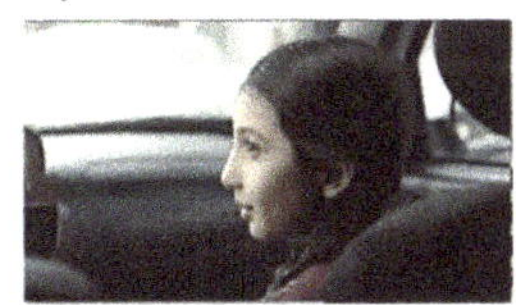

Shot 8

DAUGHTER: Please, shall we go?
MOTHER (*off*): Do we have another option?

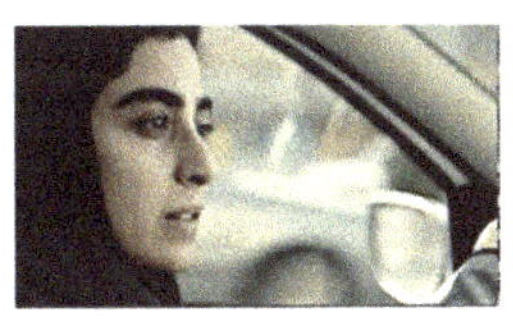

Shot 9

MOTHER (*to another driver*): Sir, are you leaving?
DRIVER (*off*): What?
MOTHER: Are you leaving?
DRIVER (*off*): No, I'm staying.

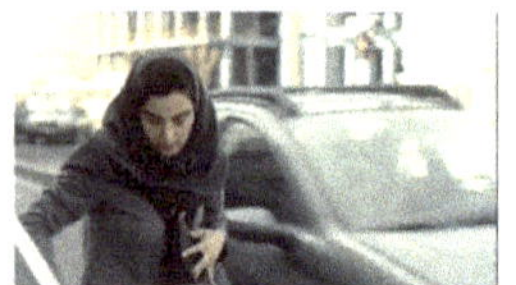

Shot 10a
MOTHER: I'll be right back!
GUARD: You cannot park here.
MOTHER: I'm just exchanging a dress.
GUARD: Parking is not allowed here.
MOTHER: I will be back shortly.

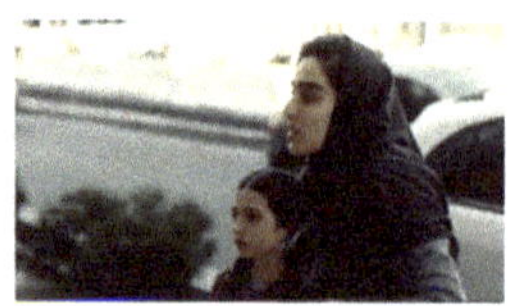

Shot 10b
GUARD: Your car will be impounded.
MOTHER: Will you tell them not to?
GUARD: They won't listen to me, they will just seize your car.
MOTHER: I will be back in 5 minutes.

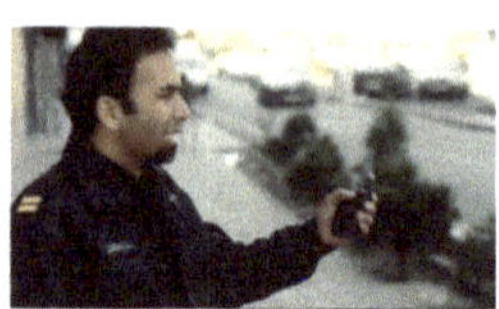

Shot 10c
GUARD: If you are back in 5 minutes then leave your child in the car. If they see her, they won't seize it.
MOTHER (*to daughter*): Honey, stay in the car until I'm back.

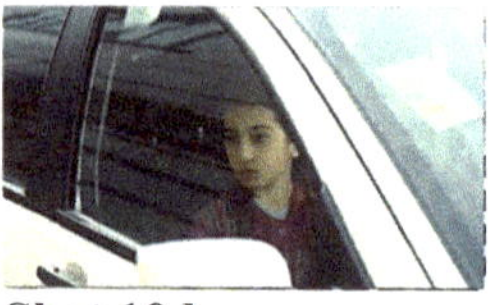

Shot 10d
DAUGHTER: Mom, I want to come with you.
MOTHER: Did you hear what he said?
DAUGHTER: Pfff. Please come back shortly and don't put me in trouble.
MOTHER: OK I will.

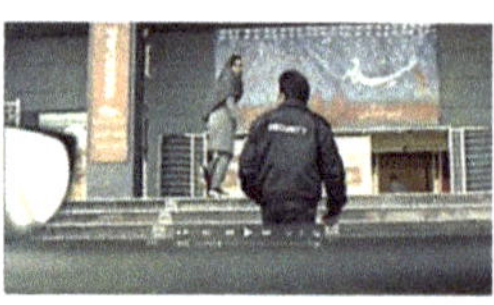

Shot 11

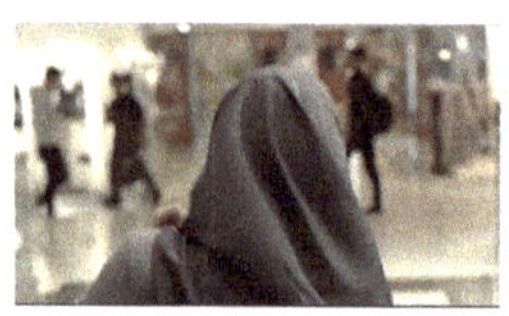

Shot 12

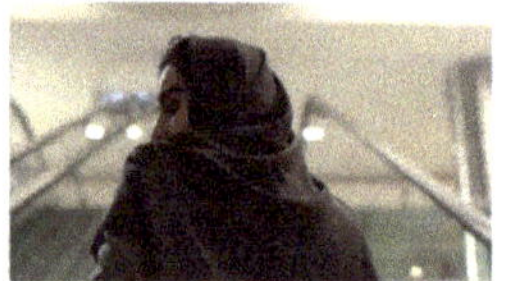

Shot 13

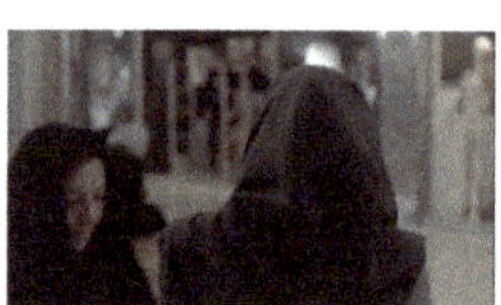

Shot 14a
ELDERLY WOMAN: Ma'am, do you know where the elevator is?

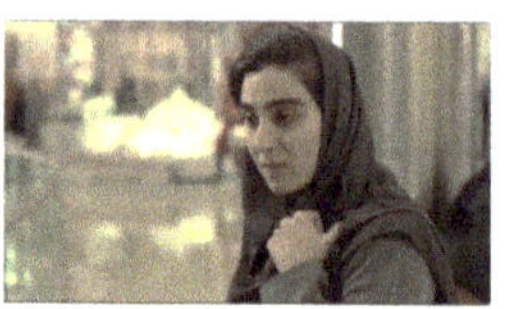

Shot 14b
MOTHER: Sorry, no, but there is an escalator there.
ELDERLY WOMAN: Thanks.

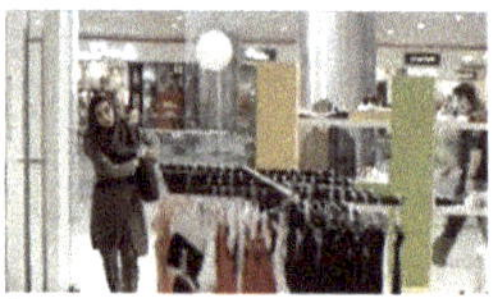

Shot 1

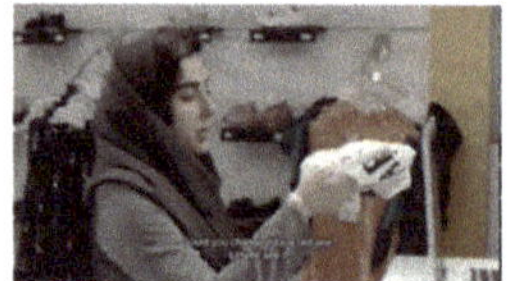

Shot 15b

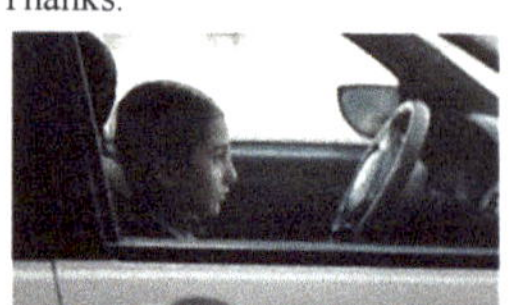

Shot 16a

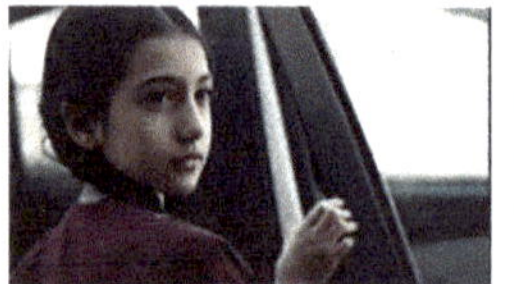

Shot 16b

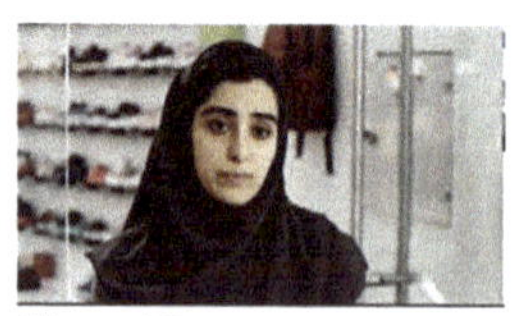

Shot 17

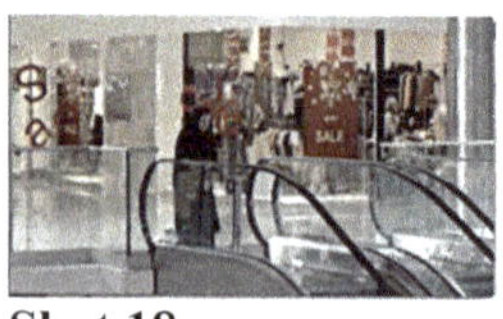

Shot 18

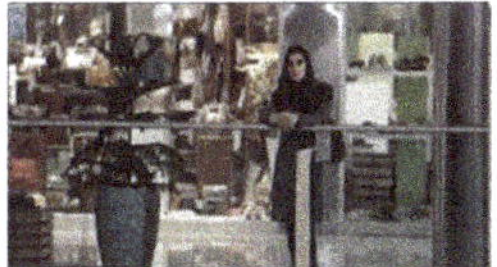
Shot 19

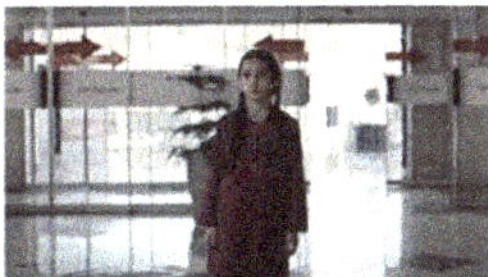
Shot 20

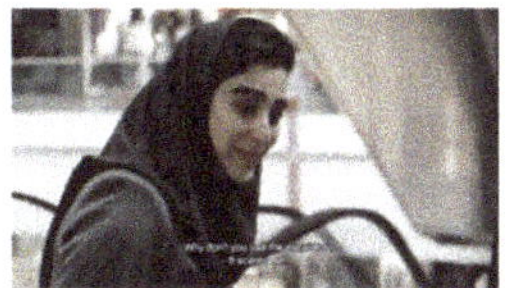
Shot 21a
MOTHER: Have you not found the elevator?
ELDERLY WOMAN: It's out of order.
MOTHER: What about the stairs?
ELDERLY WOMAN: I have a foot ache and cannot use them.

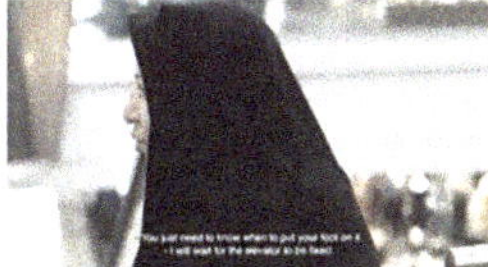
Shot 21b
MOTHER: Why don't you use the escalator?
ELDERLY WOMAN: It scares me.

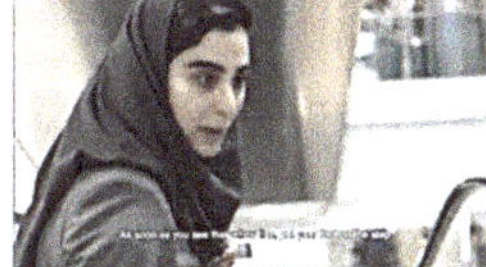
Shot 21c
MOTHER: Come on, there is nothing to be afraid of. You just need to know when to put your foot on it.
ELDERLY WOMAN: I will wait for the elevator to be fixed.

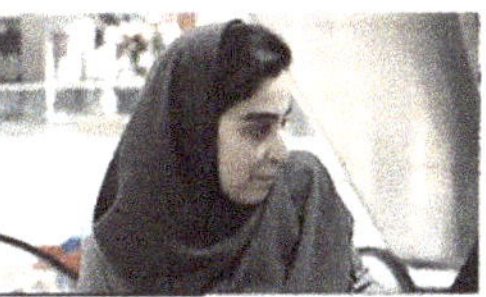
Shot 21d
MOTHER: Do you want to try?
ELDERLY WOMAN: No, no, thanks.

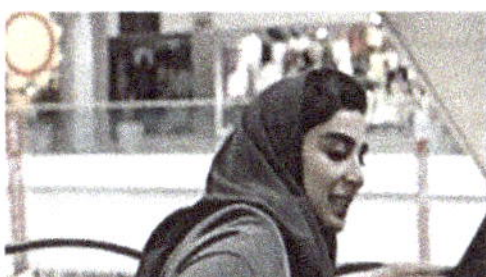
Shot 21e

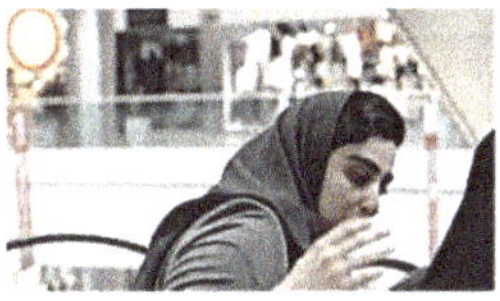
Shot 21f

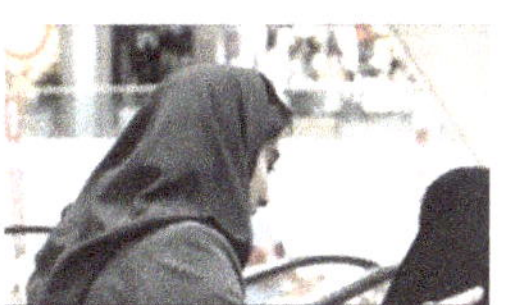
Shot 21g

MOTHER: As soon as you see the yellow line, put your foot on the step. Just look at me carefully! [*She demonstrates.*] See? That's easy!... Now your turn. I am looking after you.
ELDERLY WOMAN: Ok.

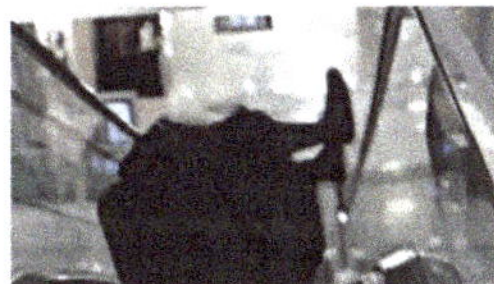
Shot 21h

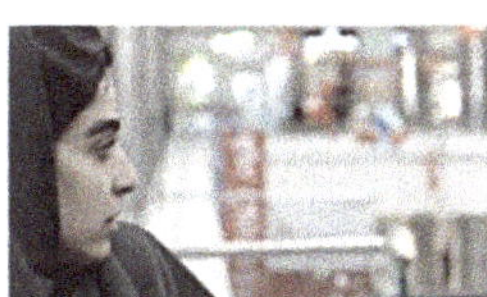
Shot 21i

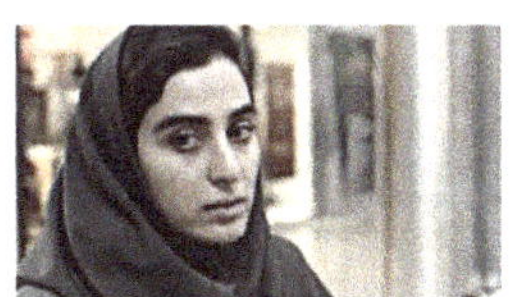
Shot 21j

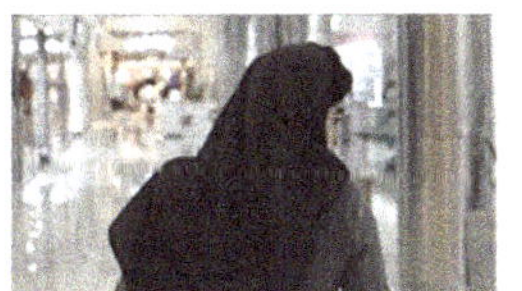
Shot 21k

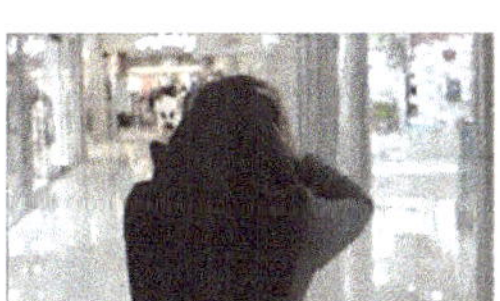
Shot 22

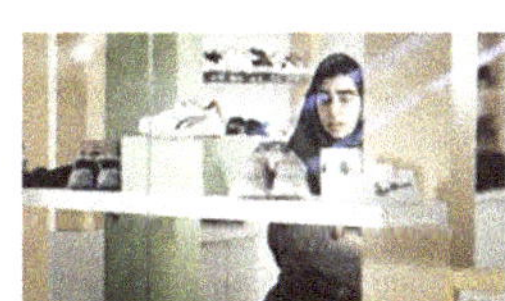
Shot 23

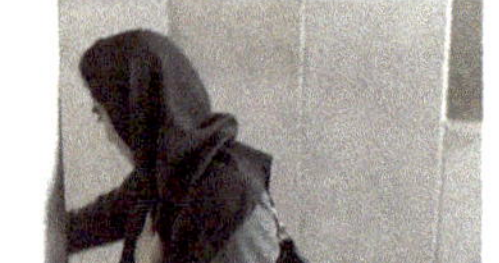
Shot 24

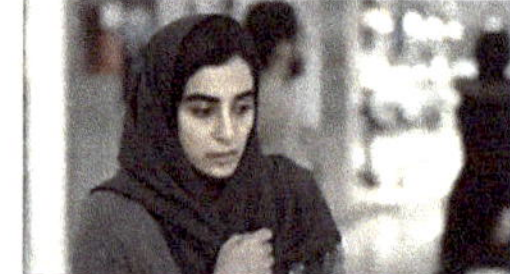
Shot 25

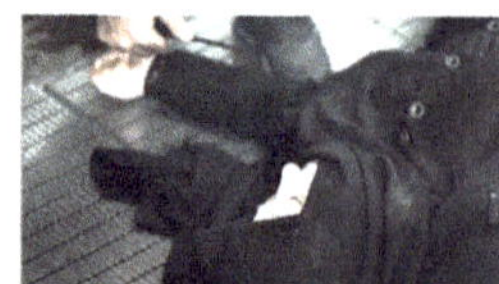
Shot 26

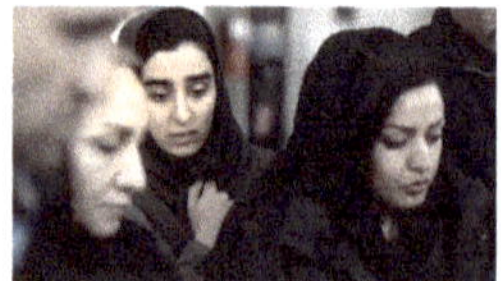
Shot 27
MOTHER: Is the ambulance coming?
MAN IN CROWD: Yes, it's on its way.

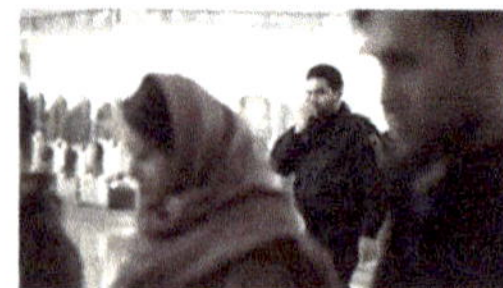
Shot 28

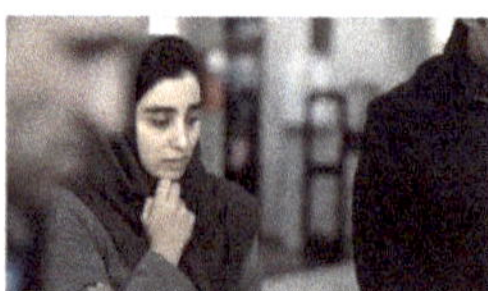
Shot 29

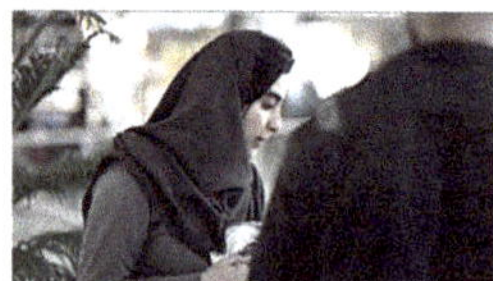
Shot 30
MOTHER: Did you find it?
CLERK: Yes, here it is. (*Looking down at floor below.*) It seems she fell down the escalator. Did you see what happened?
MOTHER (*also looking down*): No, I just heard the scream.

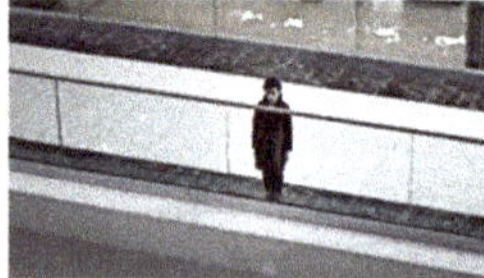
Shot 31

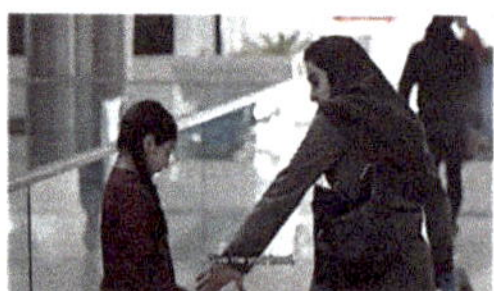
Shot 32a
MOTHER: Why did you get out of the car? Give me your hand.

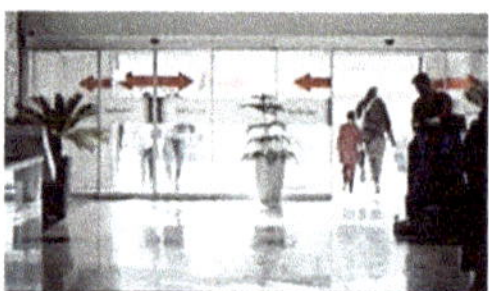
Shot 32b

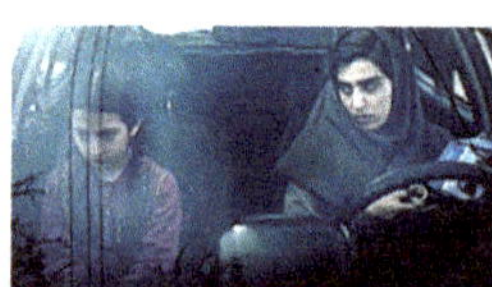
Shot 33a
MOTHER: Fasten your seat belt.

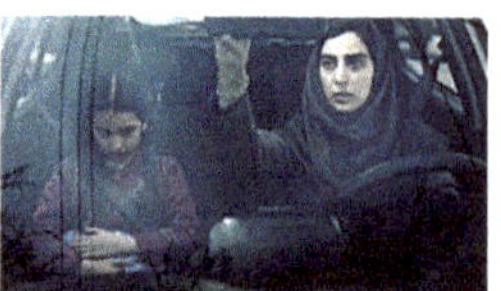
Shot 33b
MOTHER: I changed your dress.

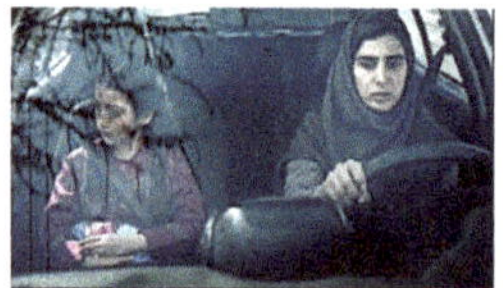
Shot 33c

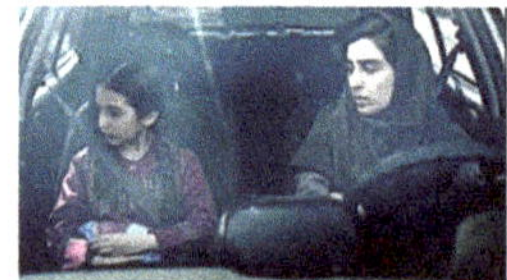
Shot 33d

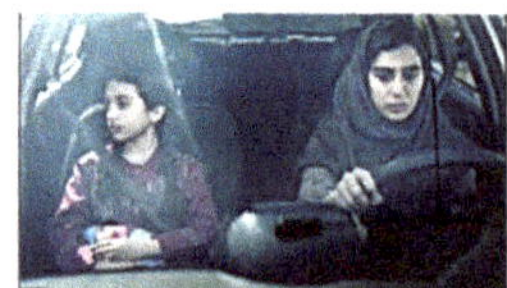
Shot 33e

From one mode of the *yin yang* complementarity to the other

At the start of the film, the mother is established as a *yang* person. Already in Shot 1, she ends a phone call by saying: "just do what I say." Nor does she take 'no' for an answer from the security guard who warns her against parking illegally (Shot 10). It is therefore consistent for her to be bossy when persuading the elderly woman to use the escalator she fears. What we have then are three moments, each of which is *yang* in itself, as well as additionally so in its *seriality* with the other two. There is also a *symmetry* of opposites in that the film begins and ends with a car scene, the first of which is talkative while the final one is painfully silent.

As this film comes to its conclusion, the main character and her daughter – who have taken on the roles of perpetrator and witness – say nothing to one another… perfectly exemplifying the *yin of non-doing* (Shot 22c-d-e). We know what event they are replaying in their minds as they sit together in their car, making their getaway from the shopping mall and the lifeless body of an elderly woman who had been afraid to use an escalator. Repeatedly looking at her daughter, the mother must wonder what her daughter is thinking of her; but the mother holds back, afraid or ashamed to ask. The daughter also holds back from speaking, doubtlessly not knowing what to say.

I stand by the view expressed earlier in this book that there is no character arc in short film storytelling. However, a character's situation and *yin yang* status can still change as a result of choices made at character moments. And that's what happens in *Witness,* where having caused the death of the elderly woman by overdoing, by going too far, the mother suddenly reins herself in, accompanying her shift from the *yang of being in charge* to the *yin of vulnerability* with an additional transition from the *yang of doing* to the *yin of non-doing.* This rare double shift is a most interesting aspect of *Witness* when seen in a *yin yang* perspective.

But also interesting is the embodiment of mechanical power – the escalator – that plays a *yang* role in the storytelling, perfectly meshing with the *yang* excesses of the main character as she was at the start, almost as though she were inadvertently feeding the machine its next prey.

Chapter Four

SUPPLEMENTARY EXAMPLES FROM OTHER ART FORMS

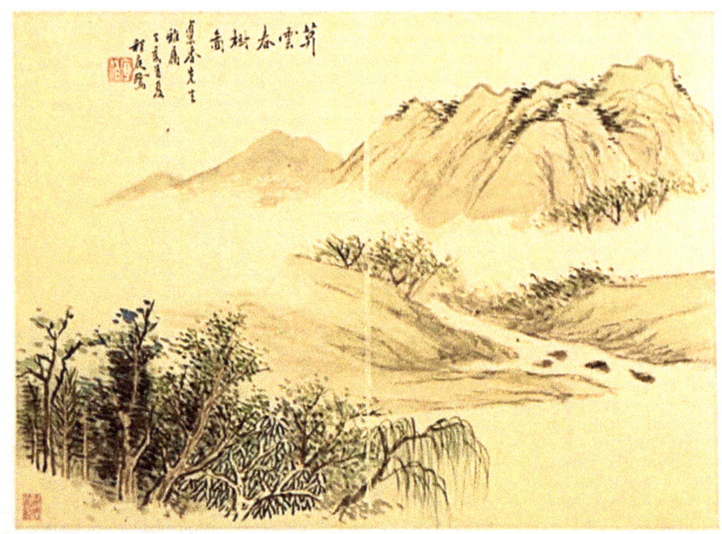

Figure 2. Chen Tinglu, *Landscape.* 1827. Qing dynasty. Album leaf: ink and colour on paper. Metropolitan Museum of Art. Public domain.

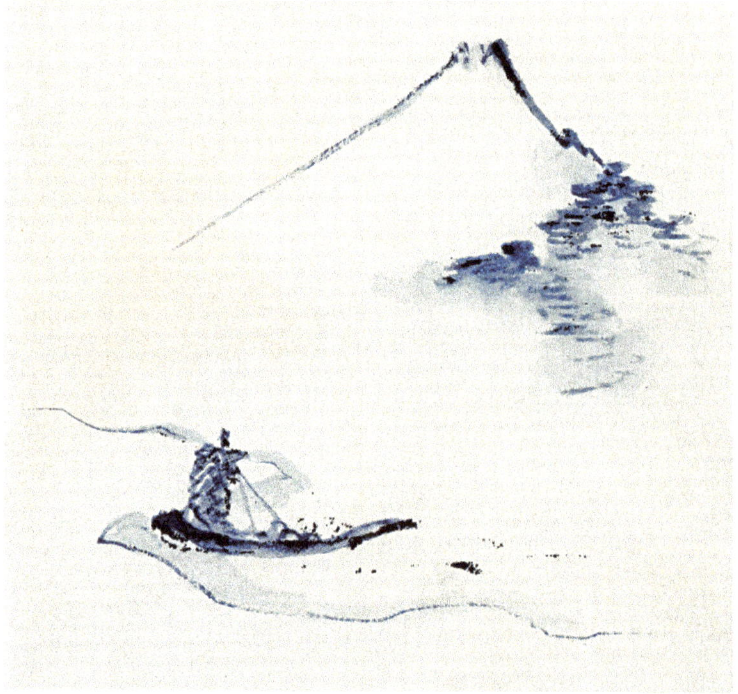

Figure 3. Katsushika Hokusai. *A Person on a Small Boat on a River with Mount Fuji in the Background.* Japan. 1830-1850. Ink wash and colour on thin handmade paper. Rawpixel.com

YIN OF INNER SPACE

PAUL AUSTER

The novelist Paul Auster once stated in an interview:

> The one thing I try to do in all my books is to leave enough room in the prose for the reader to inhabit it. Because I finally believe that it's the reader who writes the book and not the writer... There's a way in which a writer can do too much, overwhelming the reader with so many details that he no longer has any air to breathe (1997: 282-3).

Note that the habitable space inside the writing is the reader's breathing room. In his earliest poems, Auster had failed to leave that breathing room within. As he put it: "I started out by writing poems that resembled clenched fists" (McCaffery et al. 1992: 12). Later on, he learned to leave the openness inside that would enable readers to enter and breathe within the work.

Since the habitable space depends on omitting unnecessary details, there is a considerable overlap of the *yin of inner space* with the *yin of omission.* This becomes clear as the Auster quote continues:

> When I write, the story is always uppermost in my mind, and I feel that everything must be sacrificed to it. All the elegant passages, all the curious details, all the so-called beautiful writing—if they are not truly relevant to what I am trying to say, then they have to go (1997: 283).

YIN OF OMISSION

THREE FORMS OF OMISSION IN PAINTINGS

1. Empty spaces

For many centuries, leaving empty spaces – unpainted areas – within the image has been a widespread practice in the making of Asian landscapes, as illustrated by the paintings from China and Japan, in Figs. 2 and 3. Sometimes as much as two-thirds of the surface – whether canvas, silk or paper – is left bare (Cheng 1994: 37). Those untouched areas, with their own unaltered color plainly visible, function as parts of the picture. And as Cummins has pointed out: "Within a painting there are areas of yin and yang. The defined areas are yang and the implied areas are yin" (2021: 333). Or in another passage: "In the painting itself, strong bold areas are yang, while subtle and hidden or implied areas are yin" (275).

In his commentary on Chapter 11 of the *Daodejing*, Wing-tsit Chan identified the empty spaces in Chinese landscapes with the non-being of for example the hole at the hub of a wheel:

> ...it was because of the Taoist insistence on the positive value of non-being that empty space has been utilized as a constructive factor in Chinese landscape painting. In this greatest art of China, space is used to combine the various elements into an organic whole and to provide a setting in which the onlooker's imagination can work (1963: 119).

2. Hidden from view

In Henri Sørensen's sketch, *A Spring Day*, a woman has her head turned away from the viewer, with the curled fingers of her left hand resting on a chin we cannot see. The artist has withheld from us a view of the woman's face – the major *yin of omission* in this masterful sketch. Based on what can be seen of her arms and legs, her choice of clothing and shoes, her hair and posture, we can try to imagine what her face might look like. The woman is actually the artist's wife and one of the thoughts he had in painting this sketch was the challenge of making her recognizable, without showing her face (Sørensen 2022).

Other forms of *yin* in play concern the picture's 'sketchiness' – for example, the use of a few quick brushstrokes to denote the woman's inner left forearm and the palm and fingers of her left hand.

The *yang* resides in the painter's crafting of the sketch, including a concern for the interplay of colours, and for the challenge he had set for himself.

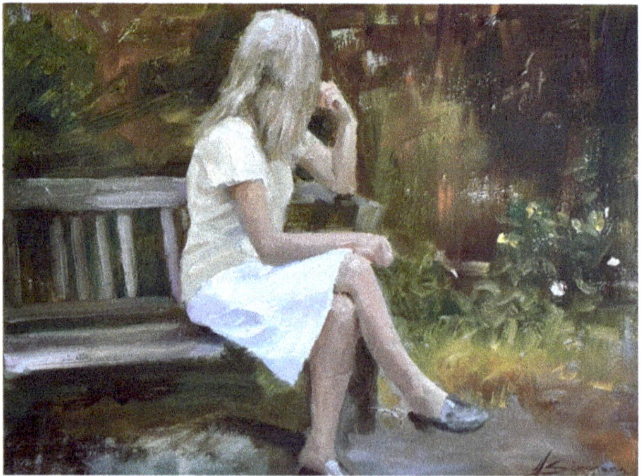

Figure 4. Henri Sørensen. *Forårsdag/A Spring Day*. Sketch. 2011. Denmark

3. Omitting materiality

Claude Monet's impressionism, as exemplified by his Rouen Cathedral series (1894), illustrates a third form of omission which may seem more abstract than the other two but which is just as important. This series consists of more than 30 views of the cathedral, painted at different times of day and from varying points of view.

What Monet rapidly painted with his visible brushstrokes was not a surface per se but rather the momentary play of light upon that surface. According to some, the vibrancy of colour impressionism achieved involved a "dematerialization" of the world. Impressionism "dissolved all solids in the vapor of light color" (Rothschild 1934:80).

For Oswald Spengler, impressionism

> tries to get as far as possible from the language of plastic and as near as possible to that of music. The effect that is made upon us by the things that receive and reflect light is made not because the things *are* there but as though they "in themselves" *are not* there. Things are not even bodies but light resistances in space, and their illusive density is to be unmasked by the brush-stroke (1962: 152).

This dissolution of materiality, in which forms "tended to vanish in a chromatic exhalation, in an amorphous, flowing mass of light and colored air" (Hunter1956: 70), also resulted in the disappearance of "the outlines and modeling of volumes" (Reutersvärd 1952: 27).

The discipline, control and sharp observation involved in the crafting of these paintings, which had to be executed quickly and with rapid brushstrokes in brief sessions before the light changed, might be seen as the *yang* in play, in these works that are predominantly *yin* in appearance.

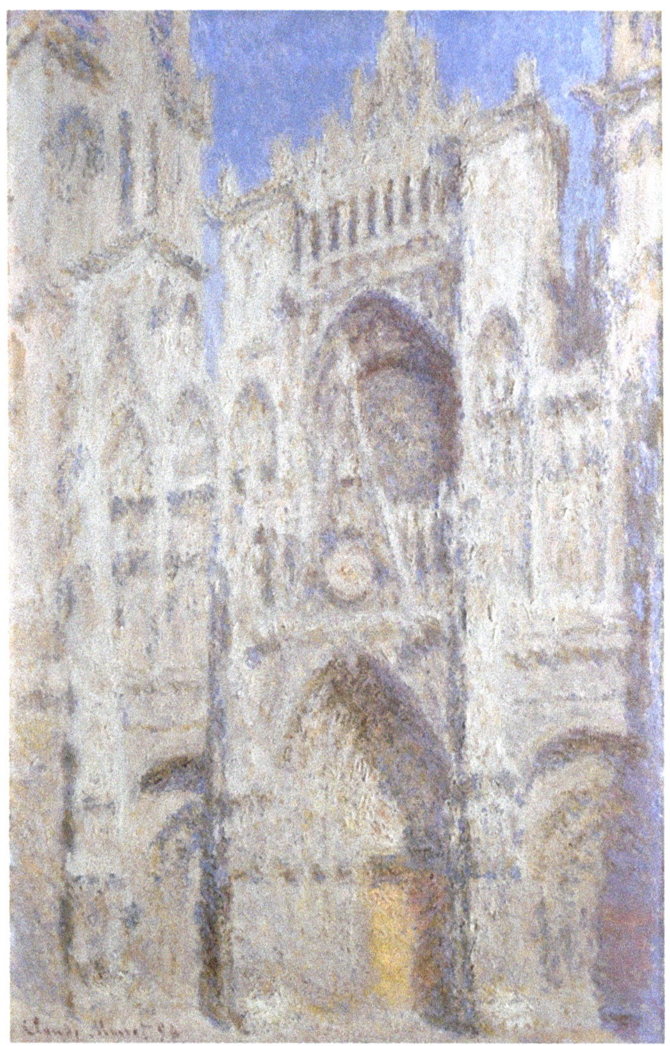

Figure 5 Claude Monet, "Portal of Rouen Cathedral in Morning Light" (1894). National Gallery of Art, Washington, D.C. Public domain. Rawpixel.com

Hemingway's *Theory of Omission*

Ernest Hemingway believed that omitting something from a piece of writing not only improves the quality of the writing but also gives readers something unexpected. He never quite explained how this alchemy happens and formulations of his *Theory of Omission*, sometimes called the *Iceberg Principle*, vary somewhat in what they promise.

For example, in his book on bullfighting, *Death in the Afternoon* (first published in 1932), Hemingway wrote:

> If a writer of prose knows enough about what he is writing about he may omit things that he knows and the reader, if the writer is writing truly enough, will have a feeling of those things as strongly as though the writer had stated them (2000: 169).

This is the version that appeared in "The Art of the Short Story" (written in 1959 but first published in 1981), intended as a preface to a collection of older stories:

> A few things I have found to be true. If you leave out important things or events that you know about, the story is strengthened…
>
> In a story called 'A Sea Change' everything is left out. I had seen the couple in the Bar Basque in St. Jean-de-Luz and I knew the story too, too well, which is the squared root of well, and use any well you like except mine. So I left the story out. But it is all there. It is not visible but it is there (1981).

And in his 1964 memoir, *A Moveable Feast*, Hemingway offered yet another version of his theory:

> It was a very simple story called 'Out of Season' and I had omitted the real end of it which was that the old man hanged himself. This was omitted on my new theory that you could omit anything if you knew that you omitted and the omitted part would strengthen the story and make people feel something more than they understood (1994: 63).

In all cases the story is strengthened by the *omission*, but what readers get of the missing things varies: a feeling of them (1932), everything that is left out is still there but just not visible (1959) or "feeling something more than they understood" (1964). The final formulation may be the one that best captures the mystery involved.

A soundless scream

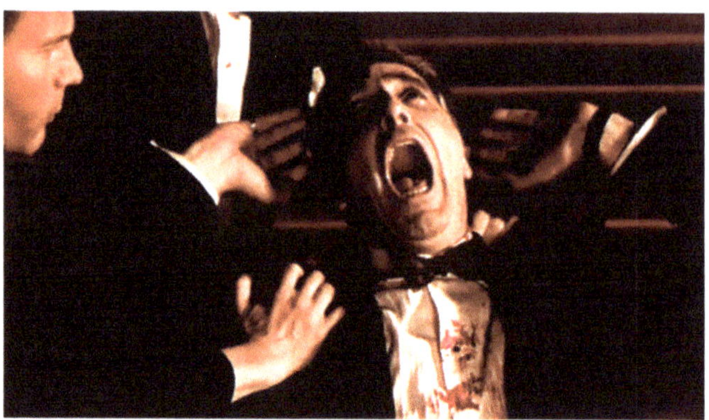

Figure 6. Still from *Godfather III*.
Copyright © 1990 Paramount Pictures

A striking auditory example of omission can be found near the end of *Godfather III* (Coppola 1990), when Michael Corleone (Al Pacino) cradles his lifeless daughter's body in his arms on the steps of the opera house in Palermo, and screams. There are four shots of Michael screaming, interspersed with shots of his son-in-law, sister and wife. During the first three shots of Michael screaming, along with the intercuts, no sound of screaming is heard. All we hear is background music. This absence of diegetic audio continues through the middle of the 4th shot of Michael screaming, for a total of 23 seconds. Finally, for the last five seconds of the scream, in the second half of the 4th shot of Michael, its sound is heard.

It was sound designer Walter Murch's idea to withhold the audio of the scream until it had nearly ended. He suggests that the absence of audio is designed to make us and other characters wonder "Is he having a heart attack? What's happening?" (Halskov 2018). My own view is that the audio is withheld as if to suggest that the anguish Michael feels over his daughter's death is too powerful for any finite amount of sound to carry. And the unexpectedness of its *omission* makes us all the more sensitive to the limitlessness of what it expresses.

YIN OF NON-DOING

No applause

On May 31, 1940, just weeks after the German occupation of Denmark had begun, a revue comedy called *Dyveke* had its premiere at a Copenhagen theater. It starred an immensely popular singer named Liva Weel, for whom lyricist Poul Henningsen and composer Kai Norman Andersen had written a ballad which every Dane knows today as a song of protest against the Nazis. Rewritten after an initial, overtly political version didn't make it through censorship, and retitled *Man binder os på mund og hånd* (literally: "Our mouths and hands are tied"), its new version was intended to fool the censor into thinking that the yearning for freedom it expressed concerned only liberation from the bonds of marriage. As it turned out, the censor was not fooled but pretended to be, and in giving his approval to the song, he "sanctioned one of the first and greatest acts of sabotage against the occupying power" (Hammerich 1986: 306). When the final verses were sung, the audience was in no doubt as to what the song meant. Here are those verses, in a literal translation:

> *Our mouths and hands are tied,*
> *but spirit cannot be bound,*
> *and no one is captive when thoughts are free.*
> *We have an inner stronghold here,*
> *Strengthened in its own worth,*
> *when we just fight for what we hold dear.*
> *Those who keep their soul upright can never be enslaved*
> *No one can rule what we ourselves decide.*
> *We promise this with hand and mouth,*
> *in the dark before the morning comes,*
> *that the dream of freedom will never end.*

When the final line had been sung, this is how Arne Weel, the manager of the theatre and former husband of Liva, described what happened:

> after a few moments of icy silence, not a hand moved, but as though by a shared impulse, everyone stood up and in silence celebrated Liva. Rarely have people – audience – artist – poet – bonded so strongly with one another as at that moment (Weel 1972: 217, my trans.).

The audience's holding back by not applauding was a *yin of non-doing*, while rising from their seats and bonding with the singer was a *yang of doing.*

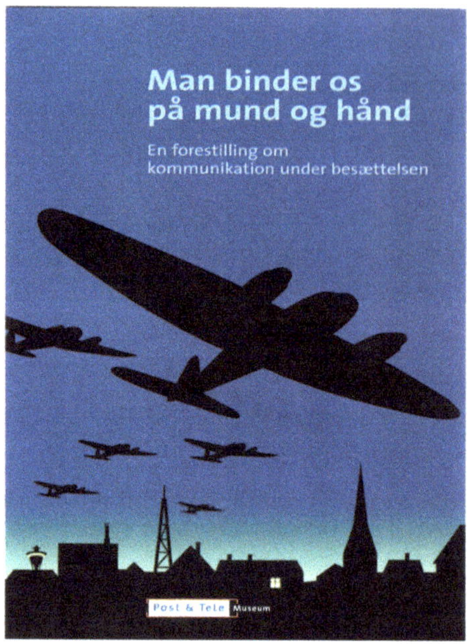

Figure 7. Poster designed by Anna Falcon for a 2005 exhibition about communication during the occupation.

Less is more

Another form of *non-doing* can be found in a scene near the end of *Schindler's List* (Steven Spielberg 1993). Here it is a matter of doing less, as in the story of the butcher whose knife never got dull because he knew how to cut along the natural lines of the meat (p. 13). Here we can see how the properties ascribed in that story to *wu-wei* (*non-doing*) might look cinematically.

The scene takes place in the Brinnlits factory, where Schindler's Jewish workers are all assembled on the ground floor while the German guards and their officers are standing for the most part on an upper landing or on a staircase. From a platform, Oskar Schindler (Liam Neeson) first addresses his

Jewish workers, denying that he deserves their thanks and describing himself in an unflattering light:

The unconditional surrender of Germany has just been announced. At midnight tonight the war is over. Tomorrow you'll begin the process of looking for survivors of your families. In most cases, you won't find them. After six long years of murder, victims are being mourned throughout the world. We've survived. Many of you have come up to me and thanked *me*. Thank yourselves. Thank your fearless Stern and others among you who worried about you and faced death at every moment. I am a member of the Nazi party. I'm a munitions manufacturer. I'm a profiteer of slave labour. I am a criminal. At midnight you'll be free and I'll be hunted. I shall remain with you until five minutes after midnight after which time, and I hope you'll forgive me, I have to flee.

Schindler then addresses the German guards and officers:

I know you have received orders from our commandant which he has received from his superiors, to dispose of the population of this camp. They're all here. This is your opportunity. Now would be the time to do it. Here they are. Or, you could leave and return to your families as men instead of murderers.

The young guards turn and leave. An officer continues thinking for a moment and then leaves as well. The workers turn to watch this miraculous departure of their designated executioners. Finally the commander of the guards, *Untersturmführer* Liepold, after prolonged eye-contact with Schindler, eventually leaves as well. Having observed this exit of the guards and officers, Stern (Ben Kingsley) looks up at Schindler and swallows hard in awe of what Schindler has just accomplished.

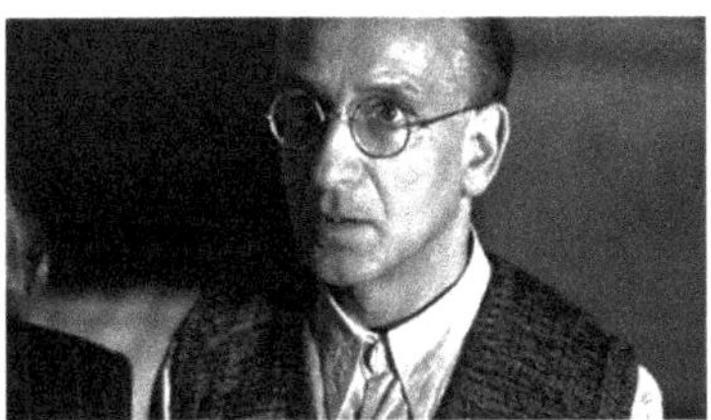

Figure 8. Still from *Schindler's List*
Copyright © Steven Spielberg 1993

Noticing that Stern is awestruck, and understanding his amazement that hundreds of lives have just been saved with so little effort, Schindler makes eye-contact with him and almost imperceptibly winks in order to share this moment with Stern – pure *yin of non-doing,* in the sense that it involved **holding back, doing less, not overdoing, knowing when to stop.** And it was because Schindler had understood the mindset of the German guards and officers so well that addressing them calmly, without having to resort dramatically to imperatives or threats or pleading as might have been expected, that he was able to prevent so effortlessly the imminent slaughter of the Jewish workers. Another marvel of *non-doing*, in the sense described above.

YANG OF DOING

Sunflowers

Just as Monet's impressionism is predominantly *yin*, Van Gogh's *Sunflowers* (1888-1889) are mainly *yang*, in at least three ways.

First and most obviously, they radiate their energy outward, toward the viewer. In describing the paintings he was planning, Vincent wrote that "raw or broken chrome yellows will blaze forth," and that his sunflowers will invite "us crazy ones" to "take delight in our eyesight" (Letter B15 to Emile Bernard in Van Gogh 1978: Vol. III, p. 511).

Secondly, the act of painting the *Sunflowers* was Vincent's way of combatting depression by tapping the regenerative power of nature (Letter W 1: III, 444). He could renew his spirit with the energy bursting forth from the sunflowers, and each time he captured that energy on a canvas, he conquered once again – if only while painting – his ability to affirm life in the face of everything that conspired to break his spirit, including setbacks in his relationships with women, family, fellow painters, authorities, dealers.

And thirdly, the paintings were designed to serve specific purposes in relation to fellow painter Gauguin, who had been invited to live in the Yellow House in Arles and to share Vincent's studio. There were to be 12 to 14 paintings of *Sunflowers* decorating Gauguin's bedroom alone (Letter 534: III, 30), providing such a massive source of intense visual pleasure that Gauguin would wish to stay on indefinitely, thereby helping Vincent to turn the Yellow House into a painters' collective – "a refuge and place of shelter for comrades at moments when they are encountering a setback in their struggle" (Letter 544a to Theo: III, 63).

What we find then in all three perspectives is the opposite of holding back or less-is-more, though I would also suggest that a seed of *yin,* consisting of Vincent's extreme vulnerability, keeps the *yang* forms from appearing unpleasantly excessive. (For further details, see Raskin 1983: 214-223).

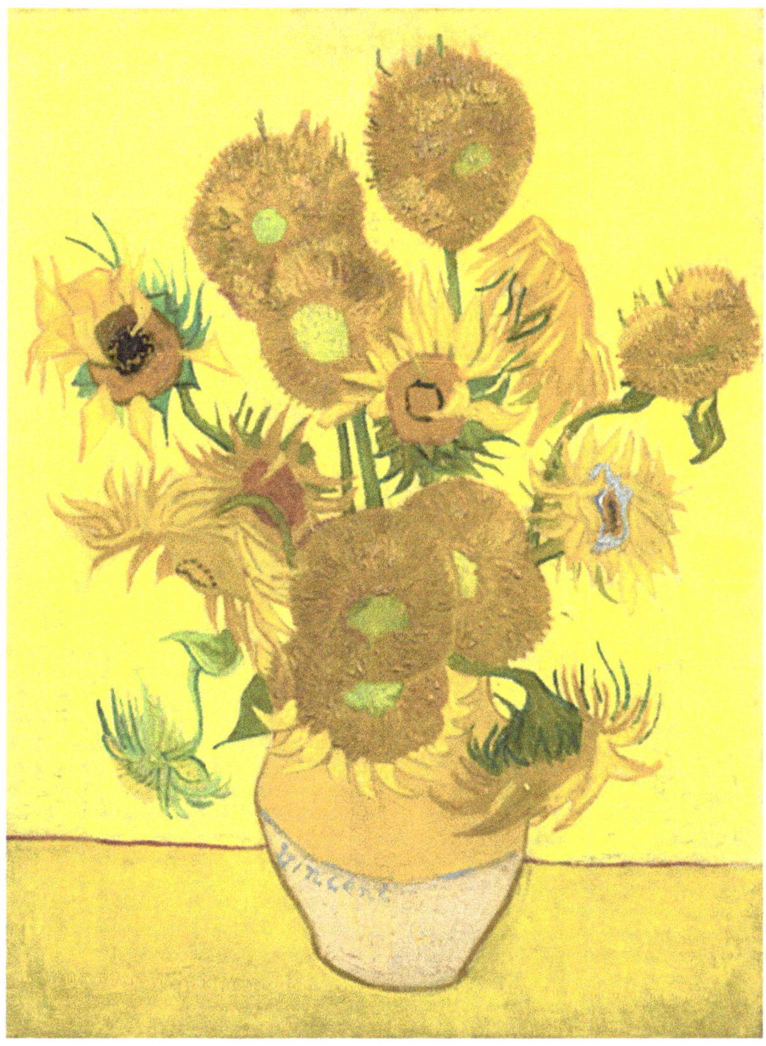

Figure 9. *Sunflowers*. Vincent Van Gogh. 1889. rawpixel.com

YIN OF NOT BEING THERE

An invisible angel

There is a memorable scene at a hotdog stand in *Wings of Desire / Der Himmel über Berlin* (Wim Wenders, 1987), in which Peter Falk, playing himself, senses the presence of the invisible angel Damiel, played by Bruno Ganz. Falk says to him: "I can't see you but I know you're there." In this as in many other scenes in the film, Ganz's angel is both there and yet not there, seen by us and a presence Falk can sense but at the same time, a purely spiritual being, longing for a material existence, and visible only to children within the story space.

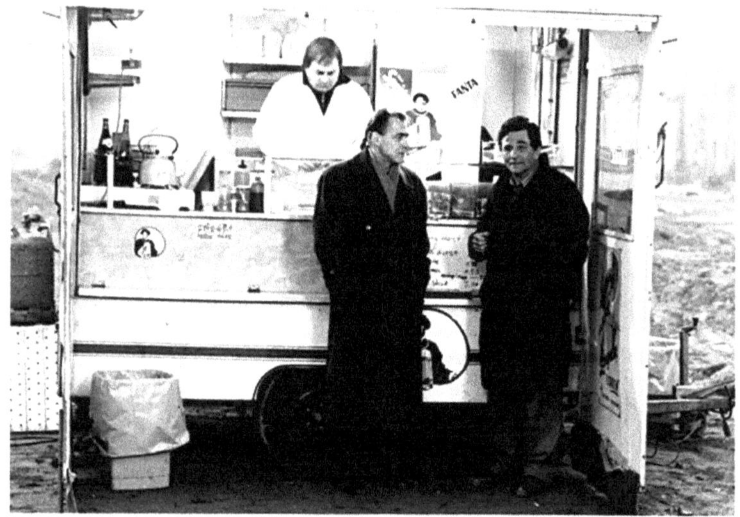

Figure 10. Bruno Ganz and Peter Falk in *Wings of Desire.* Copyright © 1987 Road Movies

There are similar situations in *Ghost* (Jerry Zucker, 1990) in which the murdered character Sam (Patrick Swayze), lingering in Limbo, is both there and not there – visible to us but not to his grieving widow, Molly (Demi Moore). It is also true of the British political thriller *Edge of Darkness* (Martin Campbell, 1985), in which a grieving father (Bob Peck) imagines the presence of and interacts with his deceased daughter (Joanne Whalley), who for us as for him is both there and not there.

An elusive hero

Yet another variant of that interplay, which makes the ending of Leslie Howard's *Pimpernel Smith* (1941) unforgettable, concerns a character who is neither of some other realm nor merely imagined. In this film, Leslie Howard plays Horatio Smith, a seemingly absent-minded professor, who during an archeological expedition in Germany, manages to smuggle scientists, artists, journalists, etc., to freedom from under the noses of their Nazi captors. A bulky Gøring-like character named General von Graum, played by Francis L. Sullivan, is determined to capture and execute the mysterious rescuer.

When Smith is finally in the General's hands, Von Graum has him placed at a flimsy wooden gate marking the frontier between Germany and France where the prisoner could be "shot while trying to escape." But once again, Smith slips through the general's fingers, disappearing behind the barrier when the general turns away for a moment. Von Graum fires his pistol in the direction of the puff of cigarette smoke Smith has left behind, and when von Graum shouts "Come back," Smith – no longer visible and safely on the other side of the wooden gate – calmly replies: "Don't worry, I'll be back. We shall all be back." Smith is invisible and out of reach, yet present and threatening – as he speaks his final words to the Nazi general. And even the final words, spoken when no longer there, are about being there again.

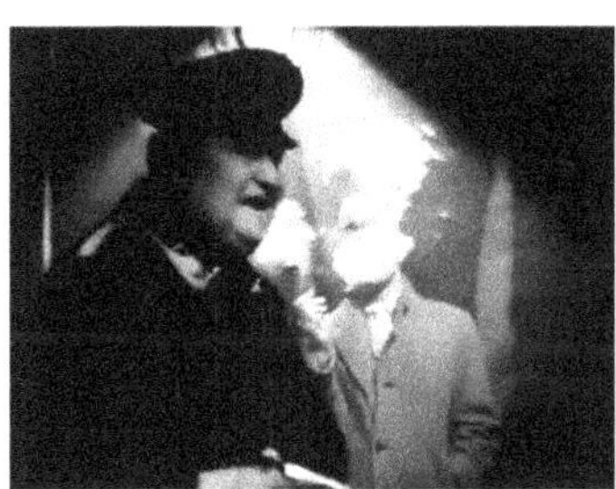

Figure 11. ***Pimpernel Smith.***
Copyright © 1941 British National Film

YIN OF WELCOMING THE GIFTS OF CHANCE

A moth

In the final shot of David Bowie as Major Jack Celliers in Nagisa Oshima's *Merry Christmas, Mr. Lawrence* (1982), Bowie's character has finally expired, having been buried up to his neck in sand and helplessly baking in the sun for several days. A moth has now alighted on the deceased character's golden hair and has been interpreted in a number of ways (Raskin 2007). For the co-author of the screenplay, the moth might symbolize Cellier's soul. For others, it might suggest a pollination/ germination process consistent with the title of the book on which the film is based – *The Seed and the Sower*. And one major commentator sees it as reflecting the desire of the Japanese commandant Yonoi who was irresistibly attracted to Cellier like a moth to a flame, and who had just moments before cut off a lock of Cellier's hair as a keepsake. However in the pre-production screenplay, there is no mention of a moth in that shot. And it turns out that the moth had unexpectedly landed on Bowie's hair during one of the takes, that Bowie liked it, and considering it a "welcome accident," Oshima chose to use that take in the film.

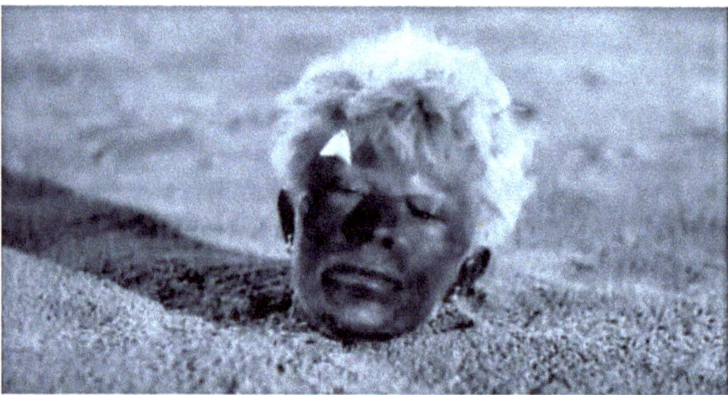

Figure 12. David Bowie in *Merry Christmas Mr. Lawrence.*
Copyright © 1982 Recorded Picture Company

YANG OF SEIZED OPPORTUNITY

I am Spartacus

A decisive moment in the film *Spartacus* (Stanley Kubrick, 1960) occurs when a Roman spokesman announces that any prisoner who identifies Spartacus as the leader will be spared crucifixion. Not wanting his fellow prisoners to be punished for shielding him, Spartacus (Kirk Douglas) stands up to reveal his identity, but before he can do so, Antoninus (Tony Curtis) jumps up with his arms waving, saying "I am Spartacus." Then David does the same, and soon hundreds of slaves are happily shouting "I am Spartacus!" turning a threatening moment for them into one that gives them the upper hand. It was Kirk Douglas who thought up this brilliant scene (Douglas 2012: 120-21), at the start of which the prisoners are dejected and which ends with them exultant. That trajectory can aptly be described as a shift from the *yin of vulnerability* to the *yang of seized opportunity*. And the scene refers indirectly to the pressuring of witnesses to name names when appearing before the House Committee on Un-American Activities. It was also this film – along with *Exodus* (Otto Preminger 1960) – that broke the Hollywood Black List by openly crediting Dalton Trumbo as screenwriter.

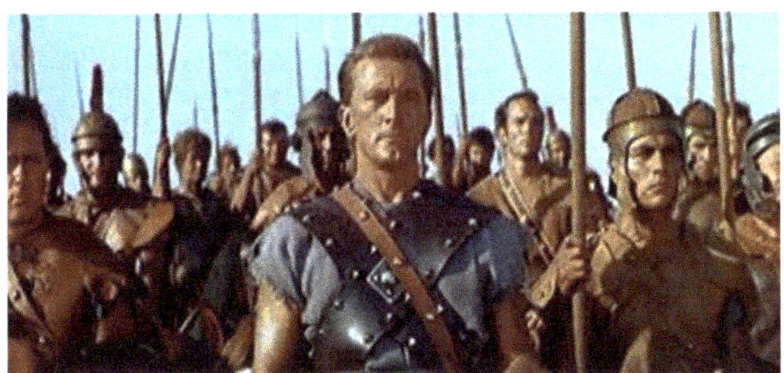

Figure 13. Still from *Spartacus*.
Copyright © 1960 Bryna Productions

IN A NUTSHELL

When short film storytelling is at its best, essentials are held back, left for the viewer to work out. The filmmakers' self-restraint is part of the film's *yin* which also includes whatever draws viewers into a welcoming inner space and enables them to construct meanings.

Though there may of course be exceptions, the story is generally simple, uncluttered, not overtold. The characters are not caricatures or mere plot devices; the actors underplay their roles with subtlety and suggestion. No production process, such as editing, calls attention to itself. The less-is-more principle governs every aspect of the storytelling and uncertainty often prevails as to what the story or any part of it means. All of this is *yin.*

The film is driven forward by causality and such other *yang* elements as serialities and symmetries, that also serve as counterweights to the relative formlessness and uncertainties of *yin* by helping to structure the story world.

The conception of *yin* proposed here combines the properties of non-doing and non-being. Non-doing can mean not performing a specific, expected behaviour; or holding back by doing less; or letting things take their own course. Non-being can mean an absence; an openness to interpretation; leaving things hidden or excluded; a habitable space and breathing room within the work. Within the story's design there may be *yang* loci – accessible realms of appearances, and *yin* loci – domains of hidden realities; *yang* characters *in charge* and *vulnerable yin* characters, subject to the will of those *in charge*.

A *yin* character may unexpectedly do an extravagant *yang* thing that stands out, or may seize an opportunity to take control of his or her own story.

The filmmaker carefully *crafts the production to the finest detail* (*yang*) yet remains open to the *gifts of chance* that may arise unexpectedly during the shoot (*yin*).

Openness and holding back are *yin*; structure, causality and control are *yang*, as is the energy propelling a story forward.

TOO LITTLE YIN can result in a film that could have told its story beautifully in 6 minutes but runs 15 minutes instead. It may be filled with unnecessary detail, with detours that add nothing to the story, with distracting darlings. The characters may be over the top, 'in your face.' There is a general lack of finesse, subtlety, nuance, depth. Everything is explicit, overtold. Nothing is left for viewers to work out by using their interpretive skills.

TOO LITTLE YANG can result in an assembly of mere narrative fragments rather than a story, because of a lack of causality. The viewer has nothing to hold on to, no 'scaffolding' of any kind, no sense of any power residing in the film, which lacks direction and ends abruptly, since no closural strategies prepare the viewer for letting go. The film may also lack vitality due to too little interaction between characters.

A short film with **YIN AND YANG IN BALANCE** is the true poetry of cinema. And the balance may be there even if *yin* for example is the dominant note. This is the case with *Derailment*, where omissions and interpretability have as their counterweight the power of the trains, which are not mere background for the story but very much a part of it. Balance doesn't necessarily mean that *yin* and *yang* are equally evident to the viewer as attention-worthy in the same number of shots, but rather that both are genuinely in play in the underlying dynamics of the film.

And the definition of poetry that I would use is the metaphorical one proposed by the Chinese master Wu Qiao (early Qing dynasty), and cited in this way by Barnstone and Ping (90):

> The [writer's] message is like rice. When you write in prose, you cook the rice. When you write poetry, you turn rice into rice wine.

AFTERWORD

This book is the result of two love affairs: one with the *Daodejing*, which started in 1959 in an undergraduate course at Dartmouth College with Wing-tsit Chan on Asian religion and philosophy; and the other with the short film as an art form, that for 30 years has been at the heart of my work. I hope the reader has sensed that underlying affection throughout, despite whatever limitations may have marred the present study.

I'm happy to have drawn on Asian thought in what would otherwise have been for me a purely Western perspective. This has enabled me to learn and accept more about the value of uncertainty in storytelling – not mystification but leaving things open for the viewer to work out. I still think beginners should aim for maximum clarity in their short films. But I can now appreciate more fully in the work of accomplished filmmakers the art of holding back and leaving the dots for the viewer to connect.

BIBLIOGRAPHY

Allen, Howard (2020). "What does it mean when someone puts their hands behind their head?" *Owlcation*, 23 February. https://owlcation.com/social-sciences/What-Does-It-Mean-When-Someone-Puts-Their-Hands-Behind-Their-Head. Accessed 9 June 2022.

Auster, Paul (1997). *The Art of Hunger*. Interview with Joseph Mallia (1988), pp. 282-283. New York: Penguin.

Barnstone, Tony and Chou Ping (1996). *The Art of Writing. Teachings of the Chinese Masters*. Boston and London: Shambhala.

Belmans, Jacques (1971). *Roman Polanski*. Paris: Seghers.

Ben Yosef, I. A. (1984) "Action and Non-action in Judaism and Taoism." *Religion in Southern Africa,* Vol. 5, No. 1 (January), pp. 63-74.

Berger, John (1992). *Keeping a Rendezvous*. New York: Vintage.

Bindeman, Steven (2017). *Silence in Philosophy, Literature and Art*. Boston: Brill-Rodolpi.

Bondebjerg, Ib (2002). "A Visual Kafka in Poland." *P.O.V. – A Danish Journal of Film Studies*, No. 13 (March), pp. 75-83.

Buber, Martin (1957). "The Teaching of the Tao" (1910), in *Pointing the Way,* ed. Maurice S. Friedman. New York: Harper, pp. 31-58.

Buchbinder, Amnon (2005). *The Way of the Screenwriter.* Toronto: House of Aransi Press.

Budriunaitė, Agnė (2004). "The Art of Stopping When It's Time to Stop: A Philosophical Approach to the Daoist Notion of *Wú wéi*." *International Journal of Area Studies*, Vol. 9, No. 1, pp. 5-18.

Cantell, Saara (2012). *Cinematic Diamonds. Narrative Storytelling Strategies in Short Fiction Film.* Helsinki: Aalto.

Carbonetti, Jeanne (1998). *The Tao of Watercolor. A Revolutionary Approach to the Practice of Painting*. New York: Watson-Guptill Publications.

Chan, Wing-tsit (trans.) (1963). *The Way of Lao Tzu*. Indianapolis and New York: BobbsMerrill.

Chase, David (2003). *The Tao of Bada Bing. Words of Wisdom from The Sopranos.* Home Box Office.

Cheng, François (1994). *Empty and Full. The Language of Chinese Painting*. Boston and London: Shambhala.

Costes, Claude (1960). "Entretien avec Raymond [sic] Polanski." *Positif,* No. 33 (April), pp. 12-15.

Cummins, Antony (2021). *Ultimate Guide to Yin Yang*. London: Watkins Media.

Di, Sun (2015). "Taijitu and Sequence of Baguas." *Shanghai Daily*, 22 November, p. A16.

Douglas, Kirk (2012). *I Am Spartacus! Making a Film and Breaking the Blacklist*. New York: Open Road.
Dunnigan, Brian (2003). "Derailment." *P.O.V. – A Danish Journal of Film Studies,* No. 15 (March), pp. 62-66.
Dunnigan, Brian (2019). *Screenwriting Is Filmmaking. The Theory and Practice of Writing for the Screen.* Wiltshire: Crowood.
Ebiri, Bilge (2021). "The Art of Ending Things: The Greatest *Godfather* Ending of Them All." *Vulture* (25 February), https://www.vulture.com/2021/02/the-godfather-part-iii-ending-explained.html Accessed 9 June 2022.
Einzelgänger (2019). "The Deep Meaning of Yin Yang." https://einzelganger.co/the-deep-meaning-of-yin-yang/ Accessed 9 June 2022.
Fetcher, Alan (2001). *The Art of Looking Sideways*. New York: Phaidon Press.
Felando, Cynthia (2015). *Discovering Short Films. The History and Style of Live-Action Fiction Shorts.* London: Palgrave Macmillan.
Forster, E. M. (2005). *Aspects of the Novel.* London: Penguin. Orig. pub. 1927.
Frandsen, Pia Strandbygaard (2003). "Cinematic Dreaming." *P.O.V. – A Danish Journal of Film Studies*, No. 15 (March), pp. 73-79.
Fung, Yu-Lan (1976). *A Short History of Chinese Philosophy*. Edited by Derk Bodde. New York: The Free Press.
Gelmis, Joseph (1971). *The Film Director as Superstar*. London: Secker & Warburg.
Gregory, Jason (2018). *Effortless Living. Wu-Wei and the Spontaneous State of Natural Harmony.* Rochester, Vermont: Inner Traditions.
Halligan, Benjamin (2003). "Modernism and Eroticism in *Derailment*." *P.O.V. – A Danish Journal of Film Studies*, No. 15 (March), pp. 67-72.
Halskov, Andreas (2018). "Unsung Heroes and Silent Pioneers: An Interview with Sound Designer Walter Murch." *16:9* (12 September). http://www.16-9.dk/2018/09/interview-with-walter-murch/ Accessed 9 June 2022.
Hammerich, Paul (1986). *Lysmageren. En krønike om Poul Henningsen.* Copenhagen: Gyldendal.
Hanich, Julian (2018). "Omission, Suggestion, Completion: Film and the Imagination of the Spectator." *Screening the Past*, Iss. 43 (April).
Harker, Jonathan (1959). Review in *Film Quarterly*. Vol. 12, No. 3 (Spring), pp. 53-55.
Haudiquet, Philippe (1963). "Nouveaux Cinéastes Polonais." *Premier Plan.* No. 27 special, p. 125.
Hemingway, Ernest (2000). *Death in the Afternoon*. New York: Vintage. First pub. 1932.
Hemingway, Ernest (1994). *A Moveable Feast*. London: Arrow. First pub. 1964.
Hemingway, Ernest (1981). "The Art of the Short Story" (1959). *The Paris Review*, Issue 79, Spring. https://www.theparisreview.org/letters-

essays/3267/the-art-of-the-short-story-ernest-hemingway Accessed 11 June 2022.
Hjort, Mette and Ib Bondebjerg (2000). *The Danish Directors. Dialogues on a Contemporary National Cinema*. Bristol: Intellect Books.
Hjorth, Rasmus Stampe (2003). "An Interview with Anne-Lise Berntsen on *Derailment*." *P.O.V. – A Danish Journal of Film Studies*, No. 15 (March), pp. 51-53.
Hoff, Benjamin (1996). *The Tao of Pooh* and *The Te of Piglet*. London: Methuen; works orig. pub. 1982 and 1992 respectively.
Howard, David and Mabley, Edward (1993). *The Tools of Screenwriting. A Writer's Guide to the Craft and Elements of a Screenplay*. New York: St. Martin's Press.
Hunter, Sam (1967). *Modern French Painting*. New York: Dell.
Idestam-Almqvist, Bengt (1964). *Polsk film och den nya ryska vågen*. Stockholm: Wahlström & Widerstrand.
J.-G. P. (1975). "Biofilmographie: Roman Polanski." *L'Avant-Scène*, No. 154 (January).
Johnson, Claudia Hunter (2000). *Crafting Short Screenplays that Connect*. Focal Press: Boston.
Kau, Edvin Vestergaard (2003). "Brief Encounters in Real Dreams? *Derailment* and Poetic Vision." *P.O.V. – A Danish Journal of Film Studies*, No. 15 (March), pp. 89-96.
Khan, Qiam-Ud-Din (2015). *Concept of Yin and Yang in Confucianism*. Islamabad: International Islamic University.
Knightly, Nickolas (2013). "The Paradox of *Wuwei*? Yes (and No)." *Asian Philosophy,* Vol. 23, No. 2, pp. 115-136.
Kyndrup, Morten (2011). "He, She, the Camera, the Movie: Chains of Enunciation and Spaces of Undecidability in *Derailment*." *Short Film Studies,* Vol. 1, No. 2, pp. 251-253.
Kølpin, Alexander (2008). Personal communication. 28 July.
Lawrence, Richard (2002). *Little Book of Yin & Yang*. Hammersmith: Thorsons.
Leung, Maggi W. H. (2014). "Unsettling the Yin-Yang Harmony: An Analysis of Gender Inequalities in Academic Mobility among Chinese Scholars." *Asian and Pacific Migration Journal,* Vol. 23, No. 2, pp. 155-182.
Liehm, Mira and Antonin (1977). *The Most Important Art – East European Film After 1945*. Berkeley and L.A.: University of California Press.
Liu, Jing (2017). "Being and Non-being in the *Dao De Jing*." *Asian Philosophy*, Vol. 27, No. 2 (3 April), pp. 85-99.
Lochmann, Erin M. (2018). "The Art of Nothingness: Dada, Taoism and Zen." *Journal of European Studies*, Vol. 48, No. 1, pp. 20-36.
Lyby, Troels (2021). Personal communication. 16 June.
Mai-Mai, Sze (1953). *The Tao of Painting. A Study of The Ritual Disposition of Chinese Painting*. New York: Pantheon Books.
Margulis, Elizabeth Hellmuth (2007). "Silences in Music are Musical not Silent: An Exploratory Study of Context Effects on the

Experience of Musical Pauses." *Music Perception,* Vol. 24, No. 5, pp. 485-506.

McCaffery, L., Gregory, S., & Auster, P. (1992). An Interview with Paul Auster. *Contemporary Literature,* 33 (1), pp. 1-23.

McKee, Robert (1997). *Story. Substance, Structure, Style and the Principles of Screenwriting.* New York: Regan Books.

Meadows, Kenneth. *Earth Medicine. A Shamanic Way to Self-Discovery* (1990). Longmead: Element Books.

Mitchell, Stephen (trans.) (1988). *The Tao Te Ching.* https://terebess.hu/english/tao/mitchell.html Accessed 9 June 2022.

Noguez, Dominique (1979). *Éloge du Cinema Expérimental*. Paris: Centre Georges Pompidou/Musée d'art moderne.

Palmer, Martin (1997). *Yin & Yang. Understanding the Chinese Philosophy of Opposites and How to Apply it to Your Everyday Life.* London: Piatkus.

Palmer, Martin (trans.) (2006). *The Book of Chuang Tzu*. London: Penguin Books.

Polanski, Roman (1982). *Roman*. London: Heinemann.

Prout, Ryan (2011). "Exploding Anonymity: The Romance and Risk of *Derailment.*" *Short Film Studies*, Vol. 1, No. 2, pp. 239-243.

Rabiger, Michael (2011). "Out of the Underworld." *Short Film Studies*, Vol. 1, No. 2, pp. 235-238.

Raskin, Richard (1983). *The Functional Analysis of Art*. Aarhus: Arkona.

Raskin, Richard (1998). "An Interview with Marcell Iványi on *Wind.*" *P.O.V. – A Danish Journal of Film Studies*, No. 5 (March), pp. 15-22.

Raskin, Richard (2001). *Kortfilmen som fortælling*. Aarhus: Systime.

Raskin, Richard (2002). *The Art of the Short Fiction Film. A Shot by Shot Study of Nine Modern Classics*. Jefferson, N.C.: McFarland.

Raskin, Richard (2003). "An Interview with Unni Straume on *Derailment*," *P.O.V. – A Danish Journal of Film Studies*, No. 15 (March), pp. 47-50.

Raskin, Richard (2004). *A Child at Gunpoint. A Case Study in the Life of a Photo*. Aarhus: Aarhus University Press.

Raskin, Richard (2006). "On Kieslowski's *Urzad*," *P.O.V. – A Danish Journal of Film Studies*, No. 22 (December), pp. 75-85.

Raskin, Richard (2007). "The Moth in *Merry Christmas, Mr. Lawrence.*" *Asian Cinema*, Vol. 18, No. 2 (September), pp. 281-287.

Raskin, Richard (2011). "An Interview with Nina Mimica on *The War Is Over*." *Short Film Studies*, Vol. 1, No. 1, pp. 21-25.

Raskin, Richard (2014). "On Short Film Storytelling." *Journal of Scandinavian Cinema*, Vol. 4, No. 1, pp. 29-34.

Raskin, Richard (2016a). "On Conflict in Short Film Storytelling." In *Compact Cinematic*s, ed. Pepita Hesselberth and Maria Poulaki. Bloomsbury Academic US, an imprint of Bloomsbury Publishing Plc, pp. 28-35. https://www.dropbox.com/s/3ab6b97v3xe340d/On%20conflict%20in%20short%20film%20storytelling%20%28rev%29.pdf?dl=0 Accessed 9 June 2022.

Raskin, Richard (2016b). "An Interview with Jenifer Malmqvist on *On Suffocation*." *Short Film Studies*, Vol. 6, No. 1, pp. 90-96.

Raskin, Richard (2021a). "The YIN and YANG of Teaching Short Film Production." *24 Frames*, 7 January.

Raskin, Richard (2021b). "The YIN and YANG of Short Film Storytelling." *24 Frames*, 6 March.

Rasmussen, Bjørn (1969). *Filmens Hvem Hvad Hvor.* Bind IV. København: Politikens Forlag.

Reutersvård, Oscar (1952). "The Accentuated Brush Stroke of the Impressionists." *Journal of Aesthetics and Art Criticism*, Vol. 10, No. 3 (March), pp. 273-278.

Rothschild, Edward (1934). *The Meaning of Unintelligibility in Modern Art*. Chicago: University of Chicago Press.

Sadoul, Georges (1972). *Dictionary of Film-Makers*. Berkeley and L.A.: Univesity of California Press.

Saint-Exupéry, Antoine de (1939). *Terre des hommes*. Paris: Gallimard.

Shaviro, Steven (2001). "The Cinema of Absence: How Film Achieves a Greater Reality by Showing Us What Isn't There." *The Stranger*, 5 July. https://www.thestranger.com/seattle/the-cinema-of-absence/Content?oid=7939

Slingerland, Edward (2000). "Effortless Action: The Chinese Spiritual Ideal of Wu-wei." *Journal of the American Academy of Religion*, Vol. 68, No. 2 (June), pp. 293-328.

Slingerland, Edward (2014). *Trying Not to Try. The Art of Effortlessness and the Power of Spontaneity*. Edinburgh: Canongate Books.

Smith, Julian (1970-71). "Hemingway and the Thing Left Out." *Journal of Modern Literature*, Vol. 1, No. 2, pp. 169-182.

Smith, Paul (1983). "Hemingway's Early Manuscripts: The Theory and Practice of Omission," *Journal of Modern Literature,* Vol. 10, No. 2 (1 June), pp. 268-288.

Spengler, Oswald (1962). *The Decline of the West*. New York: Knopf.

Straume, Unni (2021). Personal communication. 19 December.

Straume, Unni (2022). Personal communication. 6 March.

Sullivan, Mark (2007). "The Gift of Distance: Chinese Landscape Painting as a Source of Inspiration." *Southwest Review*, Vol. 92, No. 3, pp. 407-419.

Sørensen, Henri (2022). Personal communications. 20 April.

Taylor, Claire (2013). *The Tao of Storytelling. 30 Ways to Create Empowering Stories to Live By*. Croydon: Balloonview.

Thirifays, André (1958). "Un Film Experimental Polonais: Deux Hommes et une Armoire." *Le Soir* [Brussels], 2 May.

Van Gogh, Vincent (1978). *The Complete Letters of Vincent Van Gogh*. London: Thames & Hudson.

Walker, Brian Brown (trans. and discussion) (1995). *The Tao te Ching of Lao Tzu*. New York: St. Martin's Griffen.

Walker, Brian Brown (trans.) (1993). *The I Ching or Book of Changes*. London: Piatkus.

Walsh, Timothy (1992). "The Cognitive and Mimetic Function of Absence in Art, Music and Literature." *Mosaic: An Interdisciplinary Critical Journal*, Vol. 25, No. 2 (Spring), pp. 69-90.

Walton, Saige and Nadina Bolikovac (2018). "Introduction: Materialising Absence." *Screening the Past,* Iss. 43 (April).

Wang, Robin R. (2012). *Yinyang. The Way of Heaven and Earth in Chinese Thought and Culture*. Cambridge: Cambridge University Press.

Watts, Alan (2000). *What Is Tao*? Novato, CA: New World Library.

Watts, Alan (2018). *Tao. The Watercourse Way*. London: Souvenir Press; orig. pub. 1975.

Weel, Arne (1972). *Så festligt var det.* Copenhagen: Lindhardt & Ringhof.

Wexman, Viginia Wright (1985). *Roman Polanski*. Boston: Twayne Publishers.

Wong, Wucius (1990). *Tao of Chinese Landscape Painting. Principles and Methods*. New York: TAB Books.

Wong, Eva (trans. and discussion) (1995). *Lieh-Tzu. A Taoist Guide to Practical Living*. Boston and London: Shambhala.

Wong, Eva (trans. and discussion) (1997). *Harmonizing Yin and Yang. The Dragon Tiger Classic*. Boston and London: Shambhala.

Zhang, HongNian and Lois Woolley (2000). *The Yin/Yang of Painting. A Contemporary Master Reveals the Secrets of Painting Found in Ancient Chinese Philosophy*. New York: Watson-Guptill Publications.

Zhu, Rui (2002). "*Wu-Wei*: *Lao-zi*, *Zhuang-zi* and the Aesthetic Judgement." *Asian Philosophy,* Vol. 12, No. 1, pp. 53-63.

PICTURE CREDITS AND ACKNOWLEDGMENTS

Front Cover: Emperor Huizong, "Finches and Bamboo," Metropolitan Museum of Art, Public Domain.
Figure 1: SS Photo from *Stroop Report.*
Figure 2: Chen Tinglu, "Landscape." Metropolitan Museum of Art, Public Domain.
Figure 3: Katsushika Hokusai. "A Person on a Small Boat on a River with Mount Fuji in the Backgound." Rawpixel.com.
Figure 4: Henri Sørensen, "Forårsdag" ("A Spring Day"), 2011. The artist's collection.
Figure 5: Claude Monet, "Portal of Rouen Cathedral in Morning Light." Rawpixel.com.
Figure 6: Still from *Godfather III.* Copyright © 1990 Paramount Pictures.
Figure 7: Post & Tele poster designed by Anna Falcon. Copyright © 2005.
Figure 8: Still from *Schindler's List*. Copyright © 1993 Steven Spielberg.
Figure 9: Vincent Van Gogh. "Sunflowers." 1889. Rawpixel.com.
Figure 10: Still from *Wings of Desire*. Copyright ©1987 Road Movies.
Figure 11: Still from *Pimpernel Smith.* Copyright ©1941 British National Film.
Figure 12: Still from *Merry Christmas, Mr. Lawrence.* Copyright © 1982 Recorded Pictures.
Figure 13: Still from *Spartacus*. Copyright © 1960. Bryna Productions.

I am grateful to the following people for their kind permission to use images and dialog from these short films:

Film 1 Krzysztov Brzezowski at The Polish National Film, Television and Theatre School in Lodz for *Two Men and a Wardrobe*
Film 2 Krzysztov Brzezowski The Polish National Film, Television and Theatre School in Lodz for *Urzad*
Film 3 Jørgen Leth for *Andy Warhol Eating a Hamburge*r
Film 4 Mitko Panov for *With Raised Hands*
Film 5 Unni Straume for *Derailment*
Film 6 Marcell Ivanyi for *Wind*
Film 7 Nina Mimica for *The War Is Over*
Film 8 Alexander Kølpin and Ronnie Fridthjof for *Below the Belt*
Film 9 Jenifer Malmqvst and China Åhlander for *On Suffocation*
Film 10 Ali Asgari and Lea Triboulet for *Witness*

I also wish to thank Henri Sørensen for permission to use his sketch, "A Spring Day"; Toke Rude Trangbæk, Ine Urheim, Emilie Brandt, Lars Andeas Pedersen and Troels Lyby for their help; Martin Johansen and Anna Falcon for permission to use the Post & Tele poster; Claire Weatherhead at Bloomsbury for permission to provide a link to a published essay; and Aage Jørgensen for immensely appreciated help with proofreading.

And for their support and encouragement, I am grateful to Cynthia Felando, Per Fikse, Raha Amirfazli, Nastaran Dorgaraei, Adina Raskin Teplin and Melanie Raskin Nielsen.

ABOUT THE AUTHOR

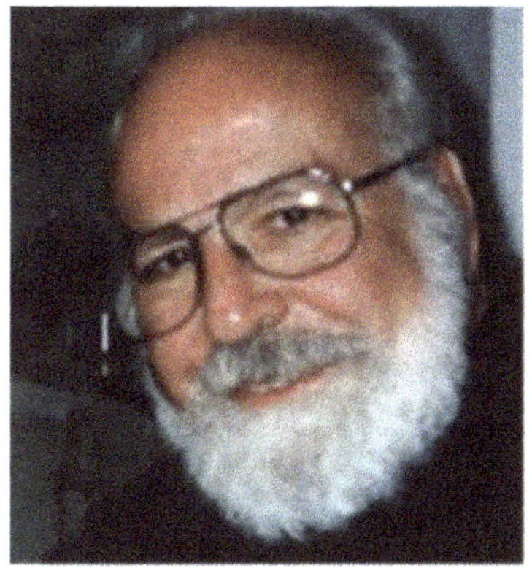

Born in Brooklyn in 1941 and educated in the U.S., Richard Raskin taught at Columbia University before emigrating to Denmark with his family in 1972. Now a Danish citizen, he holds both American and Danish doctoral degrees, and for many years taught hands-on production courses at Aarhus University in which students made short films and public service TV spots.

He has served on the juries of international short film festivals in many West European countries as well as India and Iran. He was the founding editor of *Short Film Studies,* a peer-reviewed journal published by Intellect in the U.K.; has given master classes on short film storytelling at film schools and festivals; wrote the script for a short film called "Seven Minutes in the Warsaw Ghetto," that won a number of international awards; and co-founded a highly successful film education in Denmark called Multiplatform Storytelling and Production. His books on film include *Alain Resnais's Nuit et Brouillard (1987), Kortfilmen som fortælling* (2001), *The Art of the Short Fiction Film* (2002), *Seven Minutes in the Warsaw Ghetto* and *With Raised Hands* (2013), and *Making Things Happen: On 'Casablanca' and Other World War II Icons* (2017).

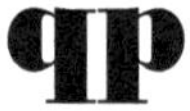

www.ingramcontent.com/pod-product-compliance
Lightning Source LLC
LaVergne TN
LVHW052345100826
845147LV00012B/759

* 9 7 8 1 6 1 0 2 7 4 6 1 6 *